A NEW INTRODUCTION TO MORAL EDUCATION

A New Introduction to Moral Education

John Wilson

CASSELL

Cassell Educational Limited
Villiers House,
41/47 Strand,
London WC2N 5JE, England

First published 1990

British Library Cataloguing in Publication Data
Wilson, John, *1928-*
   A new introduction to moral education. — (Education).
   1. Moral education
   I. Title   II. Series
   370.114

ISBN 0-304-31950-3 (hardback)
      0-304-31957-0 (paperback)

Typeset by Fakenham Photosetting Limited, Fakenham, Norfolk
Printed and bound in Great Britain by Biddles Ltd, Guildford and King's Lynn

Contents

Acknowledgements

I should like here to make acknowledgements and express my gratitude in two respects. First, I have drawn freely on my own earlier writings: in particular *The Assessment of Morality* (National Foundation for Educational Research, 1973), *Practical Methods of Moral Education* (Heinemann, 1972), *A Teacher's Guide to Moral Education* (Chapman, 1973) and *A Preface to Morality* (Macmillan, 1987), and articles published in the *Journal of Moral Education* and the *Journal of Philosophy of Education*. I acknowledge this with gratitude to the publishers and editors. Secondly, I am grateful to many critics who have given me the benefit of their advice in respect of this present work. They are too numerous to mention individually, but I should express a particular debt of gratitude to Richard Hare, whose work in moral philosophy has been a constant source of inspiration, and to Nancy Swift, whose personal friendship and wisdom has, I hope, enabled me to develop more psychological insight and understanding than I would otherwise have been able to deploy. Most of what I say, in so far as it is worth saying at all, derives from them.

Preface

It is now over twenty years since the publication of *Introduction to Moral Education* (Wilson *et al.*, 1967), a book which I put together with the help of Norman Williams and Barry Sugarman, my colleagues in psychology and sociology. Much has changed since then in the outside world, which in itself might justify this new introduction to the subject. More importantly, however, I have come to appreciate at least some of the defects of that book, and of my general approach. It is a privilege to have the opportunity of another and, I hope, more satisfactory attempt, the general nature of which may become clearer in what follows.

1. One major defect was that I naively and grossly underestimated the psychological difficulties of getting this new form of education properly off the ground. Of course there are many intellectual and practical difficulties also; but the really important problems, as I ought to have appreciated earlier, are not intellectual but emotional. Long experience in many parts of the globe has shown me that what stands in the way of moral education, both in its theoretical aspects and in putting it into practice, is our own personal prejudices, fantasies and other irrational but very deep-rooted feelings: one might say, our own moral failings (in a broad sense of 'moral', roughly equivalent to the modern 'psychological': see Chapter 5). These internal enemies have their social counterparts in contemporary climates of opinion; particularly those of relativism and its corresponding backlash of hard-line authoritarianism and fundamentalism. Unless we can free ourselves from these enemies, there is in my judgement not much hope that moral

education will make any real progress. A good deal of this book will be devoted to that aim, particularly in Part One.

2. Another defect, or at least a limitation, of the book was that I did not go thoroughly enough into the philosophical foundations of morality, and in particular into the question of what ground 'moral' ought to cover. Clearly without some kind of public working agreement about these points the subject cannot proceed in any honest or respectable way. Of course they are the subject of apparently endless philosophical discussion, and I am sure that not all philosophers will agree with what I shall say; but I have tried in Parts Two and Three of the book to do a somewhat better and more thorough job, at least to have faced the basic questions more squarely and to have made the importance of these questions more clear. In particular, in Part Three I hope to have elucidated and sophisticated the 'moral components' which, as I see it, must form the basis both of empirical research and of the development of practical methods of moral education.

3. A third defect raises one important point which may help to explain why I have not included much by way of empirical psychology, sociology and other empirical disciplines in the present work. I and my colleagues in sociology and psychology at the Farmington Trust, which I began to direct in 1965, found that it took us a good many years even to begin to understand the nature of each other's disciplines and to put them together in a coherent way, and in the original *Introduction* there was not, in fact, any really adequate cohesion. We had expected more time to do this, but unfortunately the structure, aims and staffing of the Trust were radically altered by its founder and financial sponsor before we were able to do so. The hard fact is that it takes a good many years for serious and coherent interdisciplinary work to bear proper fruit, and it necessitates a particular context of close understanding and communication of a kind which, so far as I know, exists nowhere in the world, at least for this topic (on this see Note A in the original *Introduction*, pp. 441ff.) It would be absurd for me to pretend either to adequate knowledge of these empirical disciplines or to being able to fix them together coherently in the absence of such a context. I have hence restricted myself to my own expertise in the fields of analytic philosophy and psychology, not wishing to repeat in a worse form the incoherence of the original earlier publication.

Fortunately, it is true, and importantly true as I see it, that these latter expertises are in fact those required for an introduction to the subject: the way in which the empirical disciplines may fit into it must be left for the future, if ever an interdisciplinary team is set up in the right way (on this see the Practical Postscript to this book). The basic point here is that empirical studies in moral education have not been geared normatively to a proper *concept* of moral education, and, lacking this necessary conceptual or philosophical foundation, much of their importance and interest is uncertain and at best indirect. Certainly the work of, for instance, Piaget, Kohlberg and Wright in psychology, Durkheim, Weber and Sugarman in sociology, and of course many other scholars, is demonstrably interesting and relevant; but how far and in what ways it is relevant to the proper goals of moral education are open questions. (On this see Wilson, 1972.)

4. The last defect I want to mention concerns practical methods. Originally we suggested a great many of these and the effectiveness or ineffectiveness of most of them should await empirical research. There are some, however, which can be properly advocated in advance of such research because they are conceptually connected with the basic aims. I hope now to have become clearer about which these are, and in particular about where our basic practical failures lie. Hence, rather than make a (virtually endless) list of possible methods, techniques and materials, I have concentrated in Part Four on two methods which seem to me (1) of central importance, (2) demonstrably lacking in most schools and (3) justified or seen to be necessary by the general nature of the enterprise.

Many other defects in the original work spring to mind, but this is not the place for an extended piece of self-criticism. I want finally to stress again my conviction that the lack of progress in moral education is not primarily due to lack of money or of empirical research, to an insufficiently 'caring' attitude, to government policy, to the incompetence of teachers, to the structure of 'society', or to anything else but our own failure to confront the problems with sufficient rationality and sanity. The tools relevant to such problems can be described, if we need academic terms, as analytic philosophy and analytic psychology or psychotherapy; but these, it might be said, are not much more than grand names for the application and sophistication of common sense. That does not make the task easier: common sense and its cognate virtues – honesty, patience, attention to concepts, freedom from fantasy and others – are rare and difficult to hold steady in the mind. But until we can do this, there is little point, and much danger, in pretending that the subject can be turned happily over either to the academic research psychologists and sociologists, or to those who try to put it into practice in schools and society. We have to face the fact that *we do not know how to do* this subject, how to set up the basis of this form of thought and life. As in all such cases, and there are many, the first steps are crucial: hence the term 'Introduction' in the title. I shall be content if what I say helps both researchers and practitioners to see the subject for what it is.

J.B.W.
Oxford, 1989

Introduction: First Steps

GENERAL APPROACH

I want to address the reader, right at the start, as one person to another: talking not to an academic (a philosopher or psychologist or sociologist), nor to a practitioner (a teacher or parent or social worker), but just to a person. This is not so much from a desire to be friendly or egalitarian or 'democratic', but because our approach to 'moral education' – whatever we are going to make that mean – is something which depends almost entirely on our personal feelings and reactions. It is not so much something we need to be clever or 'academic' or 'practical' about; it is something we need to be sane, unprejudiced, sensible and clear-headed about.

A great deal of what is said and written and done about moral education is not much more that the 'acting out', as psychotherapists put it, of our own emotions and internal pressures. Sometimes we are fairly sane about it, secure, not frightened or trying to prop up our own identities; and then it goes well – a good deal of excellent moral education goes on in families run by secure, loving and sensible parents, for instance. But very often (more often than we like to think), even with the best intentions, we off-load our own hang-ups and fears on to our children or our friends. This happens and has always happened all over the world, not just in very obvious cases of insanity like Nazi Germany. This is the enemy we have to guard against.

What weapons do we have to defeat this enemy? Again, we do not have so much to be clever or hard-working or paragons of moral virtue. We have first to be humble, and recognize that these enemies are within ourselves and have a great deal of power over us. Then we have to use some kind of mental discipline in order to help ourselves become less prejudiced, less a prey to fantasy, more understanding, more reasonable. In particular we have (1) to look very hard and very patiently at the *concepts and ideas* which we use, and see if we can at least get these free from our internal hang-ups; and (2) to look as bravely and calmly as we can at the hang-ups themselves, at the postures we almost instinctively adopt in order to feel safe, at the kinds of things we are frightened of, in the hope of achieving some sort of liberation from them. (1) and (2) might be called 'philosophy' and 'psychology', if we want pompous names for them, but what matters is that we subject ourselves to the discipline.

It is difficult to do this via the printed word, but fortunately (or unfortunately) there are some fairly widespread or common fears, mistakes, hang-ups, fantasies and prejudices to which we are all more or less subject. I shall try to take the reader through some of these. Inevitably this will look somewhat impersonal; sometimes even rather 'abstract' or 'academic'; sometimes perhaps arrogant or paternalistic. I shall have to talk generally about relativism, authority, reason, ideology and other things, in the hope that the reader will apply the talk to his or her own thinking and feeling. Inevitably, again, we shall encounter an immense amount of (often unconscious) resistance to such talk – even if the talk is right, which may not always be the case since I have my own hang-ups just like everyone else. But it is possible that, with patience and goodwill, we may be able to see more clearly together in the course of the journey.

Those are the first, and by far the most important, steps in the subject. Having taken these in Part One, I shall make the (optimistic) assumption that we are sufficiently in agreement, sufficiently in control of our internal pressures, to approach moral education in a less personal way. Then in Part Two we can look at the basis of moral education, its definition and aims; in Part Three we can consider some problems about how to assess a 'morally educated person', and other fundamental questions; and in Part Four we can go on to look at some more practical suggestions for schools and other communities.

TITLES

It is a symptom of our basic uncertainty about the subject that, in various parts of the world and at various times, we use (or have used) a great many different titles which – more or less vaguely – cover some or all of what I am calling 'moral education'. Thus, currently in many maintained secondary schools in the UK, the title 'PSE' – 'personal and social education' – is used to cover some of the ground. Some of it, again, is covered by 'value education' (particularly in the USA), or 'values clarification'. Earlier, such terms as 'character building' were widely used; more recently terms like 'life skills', 'learning to live', 'moral decision making' and others have been favoured. Often the titles have been overtly ideological: 'Christian upbringing', 'socialist values' and others. The list is virtually endless, and the titles often more quaint than helpful ('juvenile decency', from one set of local educationalists, is only one example).

The fact is that such titles already have built into them most of the features, values, concepts and assumptions that themselves need to be looked at. Some take a fairly hard and overt ideological line, assuming that the 'answer' to whatever problems we have must be 'Christian' ('socialist', 'Islamic' or whatever): indeed many countries make moral education subordinate to some kind of religious education (or indoctrination). Others are determinedly liberal or 'open': in 'values clarification' there is not much idea that one can have right or wrong values – they are just to be 'clarified', not criticized. Or people may be struck by one or another aspect of contemporary behaviour: for instance, by the undoubted fact that young people often behave in a vulgar and improper fashion (hence 'juvenile decency'). Or, again, people sometimes think that some particular institution or method is the right one to use ('counselling', for instance).

I have stuck to the title 'moral education' in the hope that this might be taken as parallel to such terms as 'scientific education' or 'classical education': that is, as *education in a particular form of thought or department of life*. 'Education in morality' might perhaps be even more explicit, parallel to 'education in science' (mathematics, history, modern languages, etc.). I shall try to show that this parallel is a useful and fruitful one: basically, that *there is such a thing* as 'being educated in morality' or 'being morally educated', just as there is such a thing as being educated in science (history, religion, personal relationships, etc.). The key question is what exactly that thing is: *what is it* to be 'educated in morality'? What does the phrase *mean*? What *constitutes* moral education? What is the form of thought, or department of life, and what is it for a person to be 'educated' in it? We can then go on to consider its aims in more detail, how to assess progress in it, and what methods we should use to make it effective in practice.

I want to stress, again, that we are likely to feel considerable resistance to this approach. We like to think of 'morals', as perhaps we also feel about religion, politics, personal relationships and other areas in which our own emotions are deeply invested, as somehow immune from the approach: something sacrosanct, not to be analysed, to be defended against any possible attack. This is, naturally, because our own particular moral ideas and feelings (like our religious, political and other ideas and feelings) are very dear to us: we want to preserve them intact. But we cannot retain this feeling without some modification if we are genuinely interested in *education*, for that idea necessarily involves submitting our own ideas and feelings to criticism, in order to achieve some sort of rational consensus about how to proceed in moral education.

A CULTURE-FREE FORM OF THOUGHT

If this approach can be made to stick, as it must if we are to believe in 'education in morality' at all, then we can already see that moral education will not be the private possession of any one culture, creed, country, ideology, political party or anything else. Just as forms of thought which we call 'science', 'history', 'mathematics', etc. may be more or less effectively practised in different cultures, but are nevertheless not logically dependent on them – just as these subjects transcend or stand above any particular practice in space or time – so also 'education in morality' will be an attempt to enable ourselves and our pupils to stand (so far as possible) outside our own and other people's cultures, creeds and ideologies, and become initiated into a form of thought which will allow us to accept or reject, endorse or criticize, this or that element in any culture. It will be international and time-free, not based on the particular views or values of any one social group.

This idea too meets with resistance because we are frightened of standing outside our own social group or gang: we gain security by belonging to a Christian or socialist or Islamic or some other ideological group. At the same time we are, at least, ambivalent about it: we have also the conflicting idea that we – perhaps even more, our pupils – should be more than just blind recipients of the ideology: we want us and them also to be able to criticize the ideology and if necessary to change it. Hence we are apt to dither: on the one hand, we do not want to lose the security of a partisan line; on the other, we want to be free to criticize and reject. The same would be true if, for instance, we were worried about whether 'history' should be taken as a culture-free form of thought. We might want to preserve a picture of, say, British history according to which the British were always the good guys, or of Islamic history according to which Islam was always in the right. That would lead us to be ambivalent about accepting a picture of 'history' *as a subject in its own right*, tied indeed to historical method and the procedures needed to find out what happened in the past, but not tied to any particular concepts or values which reflected our own desires and fears. So, too, with 'science': think of the opposition to Galileo.

These and other resistances are, I say again, very deeply rooted, and naturally express themselves in various rationalizations, sometimes of a highly sophisticated kind. It is extremely important to do these rationalizations some kind of justice, as I shall try to do in what follows. On the one hand, it is no good just dismissing them, or trying to bully people into something more sensible; on the other, they are after all rationalizations and not rational views, so that we have at the end of the day to see them for what they are. We must try to imagine ourselves as under some kind of psychotherapy. A good therapist will naturally attend to, and not be dismissive about, the various feelings and fantasies that a client may have: the client cannot be browbeaten or bullied out of them. But the therapist has to avoid conspiring with the fantasies: he has to show, ultimately, that they *are* fantasies, and that the client need not (as he thinks) hang on to them so tightly. Abandoning fantasy is painful, but necessary.

Part One

The Background of Moral Education

I have made the claim that moral education is or can be – putting it briefly – a subject, or form of thought, or department of education, in its own right. In the present climate of opinion, at least in many circles, that will appear as a bold claim, and certainly it needs to be substantiated. Even if it is true, it is a claim that meets with wide resistance, and it is important to be clear about the nature of that resistance. In the first part of this book, then, I shall try to say something useful about these matters. It may help to begin by means of an indirect approach. For moral education is only one instance of our difficulties here. These difficulties arise in all areas which are – to use an obscure but perhaps helpful term – controversial: in politics, religion, personal relationships and other fields which are disputed more passionately, and perhaps more profoundly, than education in, say, French or mathematics or geography. We all, or nearly all, feel that *something* should be done by way of education in these controversial areas; but we are not all clear, or all agreed, how to approach them. Let us see if we can shed some light on this.

Chapter 1

Education in Controversial Areas

Let me first try to sharpen up the rather vague title above. In certain areas or departments of life, not only do people vary dramatically in respect of their *particular* beliefs or values, but also there is no general agreement on *procedure* – on *how to handle* whole departments – and people are apt to invest in them a good deal of emotion. I shall call these 'ideological' or 'controversial' areas. Examples might include morality, politics and religion. Now, let us try to lay down principles that have to be followed if we are to speak seriously of 'education' in these areas and if we are actually to educate people in them. That seems like a rather 'abstract' or 'philosophical' approach, as people sometimes say, to a notorious practical problem, but this appearance is misleading: the main practical obstacles consist, as I see it, precisely in the fact that we either do not want to educate people in these areas or despair of being able to do so. Once we get a clear grasp of what such education would look like in principle, the difficulties of putting it into practice may be less than we suppose.

It is worth noticing, as preliminary encouragement, that there are several areas that might well be regarded as 'ideological' but in general are not, simply because educators have retained sufficient nerve and common sense to keep satisfactory educational practices going. Generally speaking, teachers of science have not, and long may this continue, been so unnerved as to have serious doubts about the educational validity of their subject. One may think that is so because the central features of scientific methodology – what counts as 'doing science well' – are, in fact, tolerably clear. But it is also true that teachers of English literature, art and other subjects continue to teach despite the fact that these areas, perhaps more than any others, present great difficulty. Just what does count as 'being good' at literary criticism or musical appreciation? By what criteria do we – if indeed we do – judge some works of art better than others? What principles of reason or standards of success do, in fact, govern aesthetic matters? It is very hard to spell out, or even to be clear about, the answers to such questions, but it is possible to be fairly confident, nevertheless, that in making certain practical moves in education – getting pupils to note the development of character in a novel, or pick out the voices of a Bach fugue, or whatever – we have a kind of tacit knowledge of the area.

I am not saying here that the mere existence of practical consensus guarantees the right educational moves in these areas. I am saying, rather, that our tacit understanding of an area, when suitably clarified, may be quite sufficient to give us a satisfactory start, provided – and with 'ideological' areas it is a big proviso – we are content to stay within the area and treat it for what it is. We get on fairly well with literature and music (generally speaking: I do not deny there are disputes) because we recognize tacitly what sort of business we are in. If somebody starts objecting to the literary merits of P.G. Wodehouse because he broadcast on behalf of the Nazis, or the musical merits of Beethoven because he was a bourgeois, we recognize that he is in a different business, the business of politics. This understanding protects us, though in these ideological days not infallibly, against this kind of category confusion.

By 'educating pupils in X', where X is some department of life or form of thought, we should normally be taken to mean at least three things. First, that we show the pupils the appropriate criteria for success in thinking and acting in this department or form of thought, the way in which X comes within the scope of reason – in particular, what counts as *relevant evidence* for opinions and beliefs. In a word, we encourage them to be reasonable (perceptive, sane, knowledgeable, well-informed, etc.) in X. Not just about X: it is one thing to know a lot (as a historian or a sociologist or whatever) *about* mathematics and religion, another thing to have learned to perform well *in* those departments. Secondly, that we can justify our title 'education in X' (rather than Y) only if we pay particular attention to what is *peculiar* to X as a department or form. Thus 'education in religion' would be at best a misleading title if all we did was to educate children in respect of certain historical or scientific facts that happened, as it were accidentally, to be connected with certain religions, or of the literary merits of certain religious writings. Thirdly, that we should encourage the pupils to make up their own minds in X, by using the methodology or principles of reason appropriate to it, rather than (or anyway as well as) encouraging them to believe certain conclusions or 'right answers'.

These, it might be argued, follow from what we mean by 'educate', via the connection of that term with what we mean by 'learn'. (The notion of learning marks not just any change but a change in the direction of truth by the application of reason and the use of evidence: see Wilson, 1979.) In any case, it seems that we are here talking about a coherent and worthwhile enterprise, whether or not it is the only enterprise meriting the title 'education'. Of course, there may be those who do not wish to engage in this enterprise at all, perhaps because they are frightened of the possible outcome, but the chances are that in a pluralistic and shrinking world such people will be driven willy-nilly to pay some attention to it – for instance, to allow some time for 'education in religion', in the above sense, even if they insist on using other time to inculcate certain specific religious beliefs and practices. Our worry is, rather, about educators who would like to engage in this enterprise but are unclear about how it can get off the ground.

The main difficulty, I suspect, is that many people only half-believe (at best) that the various titles – 'politics', 'morals', 'religion' and so on – can stand, or be made to stand, for distinguishable enterprises that are *about* something distinguishable and have some sort of distinguishable *point*. We see them rather as arenas in which various combatants do battle, providing material for debate and amusement for commentators but not otherwise engaging in any co-operative or constructive endeavour. That is certainly not an inevitable view: not only Plato and Aristotle but many of their successors saw at least some of these fields as enterprises with their own peculiar goods and virtues, somewhat by analogy with the arts and crafts. Less apt to take anything as given, or influenced more by the variety both of particular ideologies and of conceptual systems that the study of history and sociology has displayed to us, we feel much more insecure: some philosophers going so far as to claim that the very concepts marked by 'politics', 'morality', etc. are 'contestable', thus putting everything to the service of ideology. I shall clarify this more fully in later chapters.

A different approach, however, may make us recover our senses. Thus it is not difficult to see that there is, or might be, a sense of 'politics' such that it is inevitably an important human concern, whatever one's preferences or 'values', and, properly understood, contains within itself a number of non-disputable goods and virtues. Politics, we shall say, is an enterprise concerned with the good of associations or communities (*poleis* in Greek) as such. Not only the need for child rearing but many other needs (the development of language, for instance, which cannot happen in isolation) make this enterprise inevitable for human beings; and, since human beings are always potentially vulnerable to each other, everyone must necessarily be concerned with politics – how much is another matter. At the same time, there will be certain necessarily desirable features in any community: justice, individual freedom, security and good communications are among these. Anyone who rejected these as goods would have failed to understand what it is to be a human being or what it is to be a member of a community: they are not ideological but logical goods, and the virtues that go with them are also logically required by the nature of the enterprise.

To make this sort of approach conceptually watertight would require much more philosophical argument than is appropriate here. But at least we can see that there are some logical necessities and some concepts that are inherent in politics, around which the pupils' understanding can legitimately be built, and that these have a very different status from those of particular ideologies, current practices or 'values' that happen to be flying around. Thus the ideas marked by 'rules', 'sanctions', 'authority', 'contract' and many other terms are inalienable, and pupils need to get a firm grasp on them – not only a conceptual grasp, but the kind of grasp best given by practical participation and the assumption of political responsibility (in particular, perhaps, taking the rap for bad decisions or arrangements). If we also give those pupils the attitudes, abilities and skills that are logically required for dealing appropriately with other people in any context – respect for other people's interests, emotional insight, determination and so forth – then they will be equipped to think and act rationally in political contexts, and it will eventually be up to them to decide what practical realizations of the inalienable concepts they think best in this or that situation.

Nor is it difficult to distinguish this approach from one that more or less overtly recommends a particular set of political values. In our own society the most tempting candidate is 'democracy', whatever this may mean, and it is moderately scandalous that most suggested programmes of political education incorporate 'democracy' in a way that takes its value for granted. Still more scandalous, if less naive, are attempts – usually tacit but sometimes overt – to define 'politics' in such a way that other sorts of government (oligarchy, for instance) do not count as political at all. Such moves make it more difficult for pupils and teachers to raise the very important political question of whether 'democracy', in some or all of its senses, is actually a good thing; they are illegitimate from a strictly educational viewpoint, and ultimately impractical because sooner or later pupils will raise the question anyway.

In this and some other cases we see a way forward. But some areas, or at least their titles, present greater difficulty – a difficulty that relates to the second of the three principles mentioned above. In order to establish a viable and specific area of education, we need to be sure that our titles stand for something tolerably distinctive. We have to be able to distinguish – even though there may be overlaps – between matters of politics and matters of mental health, between politics and morality, and between morality and religion. Most educators abandon this struggle and are content to teach very general courses under some extremely vague headings – 'Learning to Live', 'Growing Up' or whatever. Even when the titles in themselves are not as vague as these, the practice itself may be: under 'religious education' all sorts of things may go on that have no distinctive connection with religion.

We may now be tempted to go back on our second principle, for why should this distinctiveness matter? If we can cover all the relevant ground under the broad title of 'Learning to Live', what is the point of these philosophical or classificatory exercises? The trouble is that, without an effective set of categories, we cannot be sure that we are covering all the ground. These 'ideological areas' do exist, though we may be unclear about them; there are important differences, though they do not always appear in the titles. In a similar way we could abolish the distinctions between school subjects or forms of thought and run a succession of classroom periods all entitled 'Life' or 'The Environment', but pretty soon we should have to think about just what the differences were between the various kinds of teaching and learning that we might put under this heading.

In much the same way we need to know what may be distinctively put under the title of 'religion': what kind of truth, if any, religious truth is, as against the truths of history, morality and other enterprises. Having determined this, it is then indeed a tactical question how best to organize our time – to decide whether we should have separate periods specifically devoted to this distinctiveness, or whether we should allow it and other kinds of distinctiveness to emerge in the study of some general topic or field. But we have to distinguish it in the first place if we are to have anything worth calling 'education in religion' at all. Simply to avoid the charge of indoctrination or to tell the pupils something about religion (or, more commonly, about various particular creeds) is not good enough.

Educators in most liberal societies, at least recently, have been so anxious to avoid the charge of indoctrination that they have, generally speaking, failed even to confront these problems, let alone make a serious effort to solve them. Their continual and, as far as it goes, justifiable concern for 'neutrality', particularly if they are directly susceptible to the political pressures of a pluralist society with many articulate interest groups (pressures that may deter them from even attempting certain 'hot' areas, such as sex or race), has encouraged them to duck the task. In this way they have received much support from a relativistic climate of opinion which would deny any sense to the idea of a pupil's becoming more reasonable, or perceptive, or well-educated in X, as those terms are normally used. ('Reasonable' for relativists presumably means 'what this or that society takes to be reasonable'. I say 'presumably' because the translation is obviously an inaccurate one, and it is hard to see how any English-speaker with his wits about him could offer it.)

It is very remarkable that, at a time when there is more discussion of the curriculum than perhaps ever before, educators are more than ever unwilling to ask the right questions – questions in the form 'Just what is X?' (where X is the title or potential title of some subject, area or department), 'How is X different from Y and Z?', 'What is the point of X?' or 'What is it to do X well?'. It is one thing to compile a general, heterogeneous and impressive list of 'aims and objectives' and to attach them (tenuously) to a title; quite another to make the kinds of distinction we need in order to make sense not only of these 'ideological areas' but of the curriculum generally. Where there is already a satisfactory set of practices attached to a title, and provided (another big proviso) that educators are not swayed to change them by mere fashion, this may not matter too much; but where we have only a set of possible titles, as with the 'ideological areas', the way forward is to try to make the right distinctions.

I am inclined to suspect, though this is no more than a guess, that the causes lie deeper than the desire to cling to one's own values or ideology on the one hand, or despair of any non-relativistic application of reason on the other. These symptoms themselves perhaps indicate a more basic dislike (amounting, when philosophers press the point, to hatred and alarm) of making distinctions and categories in general. It is certainly no accident that many educators in our society put a lot of money on the notion of 'integration', almost as if the mere existence of different categories or the mere fact of separateness and difference were threatening or otherwise intolerable. For consider what we should have to face if and when we got the categories sorted out and properly understood. It would then appear, first, that there were specific standards and criteria that we had to meet in politics, morality, religion and the rest if we wanted to be taken seriously, just as we have to meet standards when doing mathematics or science. Secondly, it would be evident that some of us were *very bad at* politics, morality, etc., and others of us much more expert – so much more, perhaps, that the idea of entrusting political, moral and other decisions to experts would no longer seem ridiculous. Above all, it would be clear that we could no longer amuse and comfort ourselves by clinging to a set of 'values' or an 'ideology' in a highly general sort of way, because we should be under pressure to assign different 'values' to different categories, where they would fall within the scope of rigorous discipline – just as we cannot now respectably claim to have identified the 'truth' across the board of all the empirical disciplines, for we recognize that 'truth' in mathematics, science, history and other disciplines is different.

There is also, of course, a natural resistance to the whole idea of authority. Thus if one tries to persuade or prove to educators that there is a set of attributes, demanded by pure reason, that anyone seriously concerned with 'morality' (in at least one sense of the term) ought to have and ought to encourage pupils to have, one rapidly comes to appreciate the strength and nature of resistance to any such idea. Very often, if one simply lists these attributes, explains each and shows why each is demanded by reason, such resistance will be very strong. But if one adopts the strategy of asking educators to make their own list of attributes – to write down what, if anything, they honestly believe is required by reason of any serious moral thinker and agent – it nearly always turns out that the lists they make are more or less identical, give or take a bit of terminology, both with the one originally put forward and with each other's. That is hardly surprising when the items on such a list are often obvious and require no immense intellectual talent to discern. What is more surprising is the intense dislike of being *told*, or any suggestion of 'authority', even if the authority has got it right. That may be a powerful argument for giving teachers and other educators much more autonomy, for putting them on the spot and getting them to face the right questions themselves rather than reacting to the pressures of others.

In the above I have been deliberately brief and have deliberately avoided any direct or sophisticated attack upon those philosophers who, in a way rightly, would challenge me on a good many points. I say 'in a way' because, while it is very important that the classifying and working out of these areas should be carefully inspected and criticized, it is equally important that all those concerned should want to find the best answers they can; and this desire is often absent. Yet until we have all equipped ourselves with at least a plausible set of views about what a sensible classification would look like and what the criteria of reason or success actually are for each X in each category, it seems largely a waste of time to study the curriculum from the viewpoint of sociology or any other empirical discipline. If we have no clear grasp of what we are trying to do or where we are trying to move towards, we cannot even know *what* empirical facts are relevant. Does not much – perhaps almost all – of the study of 'curriculum innovation' depend on just *what* 'innovations' one should be trying to introduce? Social science may not help us much even to identify the opposition unless we know what it is opposition to. The only way forward, as I have tried to show, is to be clear about the basic concepts and criteria.

Chapter 2

Authority and Paranoia

I want now to look further at what I take to be the main difficulties in undertaking the programme mentioned in Chapter 1: that is, briefly, in establishing moral education as a subject or field in its own right, as a discipline governed ultimately by pure reason. Here, too, it will be best to proceed somewhat indirectly, and look at the kinds of general ideas and feelings that stand in our way.

Perhaps the first reaction to the idea of moral education – first both in the history of most societies and in the minds of most individuals even today – is to seek for a 'basis of morality' by accepting some unquestioned *authority*: not the authority of pure reason, which must be the only ultimate authority for anyone interested in educating, but an authority of some more simple and compelling kind – really, an authority of a more *familiar* kind, like the authority of our parents when we were very young. In fact, education in morality is like education in other areas of human thought and action in that there are right and wrong answers to moral questions, and a set of abilities, rules, procedures and qualities which enable us to obtain right answers and act on them – in brief, a *methodology*. In this way, morality has a 'basis' just as other subjects or forms of thought or departments of life have a basis. But, for important psychological reasons, this leaves many of us unsatisfied.

Imagine that in a pre-scientific culture – perhaps in the Middle Ages or in some primitive tribe – different groups and individuals deal with disease and ill-health in different ways. There are witch-doctors who cut holes in people's heads to let out the evil spirits, those who advocate 'herbal cures', those who pray to some god, those who prescribe leeches and so on. Most of these methods will derive from the particular fantasies, fears, desires and prejudices of the group, often as expressed in some quasi-religion or metaphysics – gods, devils, ju-jus etc. Now along comes somebody who says words to the effect of 'Look, there is actually a subject which we call "medicine", which has its own methodology; we have done research and experiments on it in our country', and then he begins to explain about anatomy and chemistry and all the abilities and procedures which go to make up medicine. How is such a person received?

He may of course be received with shock and horror by the old witch-doctors and those who fear any change, or with jubilation by the younger members of the tribe who are fed up with the witch-doctors and welcome any change. But even those who are less prejudiced are likely to say, 'This is all very interesting, but what is the *basis* for this anatomy and chemistry and things you talk about? Are you really trying to introduce a new god called Medicine or Scientific Method, and if so how powerful is he, and how do we pray to him, and what good will he do us?' And the person would have to reply, 'No, it's not exactly a new god. And though medicine will eventually do you a lot of good, it takes time to learn – perhaps in a few years, if you work at it, you will begin to see the point', and so on. And then it would not be surprising if they said, 'Well, this is all very difficult, and too much like hard work: a simple chap like me had better stick to the old gods. And anyway I don't see what the *basis* is, if you haven't a new god to sell us: what's the *authority* behind what you say, what is there we can cling on to?' And the person could not find any reply – or any brief reply – which would satisfy them.

Of course, not only with morality and religion but with other areas of thought also – history, science, etc. – we need to make sure that we have the right 'basis' in the sense of the right methodology, the right way of thinking about moral (historical, scientific) questions. This is a reasonable demand, and is for philosophers to answer. But it is not, or not only, the demand which people actually make. When they ask for a 'basis', they want some *object*, or some *person*, or some simple *picture*, to hang on to. Most people live, as Plato said, in the world of sights and sounds: they find abstractions difficult – just as, to very simple people, God may virtually *be* the statue of Jesus in the church. People look to these for many purposes, of which reassurance that their moral behaviour is correct is only one. They look to them, above all, for strength and psychological security: they see in them a *solid authority*, a *source of power*. This saves them not only from the dangers and difficulties of thinking for themselves, but also from feeling lost in an unstructured, empty world, and from feeling that there is no solid 'goodness' inside or outside of them – a feeling that makes them very anxious, as if their personalities were splitting up, fragmenting or disintegrating. This is the sort of anxiety that we see, for instance, when we argue with somebody who is desperately concerned to preserve his own views intact. Often this anxiety will turn to anger and hate, directed at those who seem to be conspiring to cast doubt on this 'solid goodness' in which he believes – or is trying as hard as he can to believe.

It is in this sense that people seek and cling to a 'basis'. This may take the form of a particular person (Christ, Mao Tse-tung), a scripture (the Koran, *Das Kapital*), a picture of a 'new world' (the Age of Science, the Revolution), their own inner 'consciences', what their friends do, what the fashion is, and so on – the list is endless. Even if they appear to accept, in theory, obviously reasonable principles such as concern for other people, honesty and sincerity, nevertheless when they feel that these principles threaten their 'basis' they backslide. The areas of feeling threatened also vary: they may be prejudiced against a particular race or colour, or in the areas of sex, dress, hair or various food taboos, or in political areas, or many others. Most civilized people will acknowledge, again in theory, the existence of prejudice in at least some of these areas. But few people are free from it. The principles of love and concern and understanding go by the board as soon as the threatened areas are reached, and at this stage there is little that argument can do. They do not want to argue; they just want to cling to their feelings.

There have, of course, been similar cases in the history of thought, like our semi-historical picture of the introduction of medicine. Notoriously the introduction of the beginnings of science and scientific method in the time of Galileo caused great anxiety to many people: it took a long time before people realized that, when trying to explain and control the natural world, this method was appropriate – so that they had to lay aside their natural feelings and desires, and get down to the very hard task of scientific research, of *learning* rather than just *feeling*. Even today the old attitudes are likely to erupt under pressure: to take a trivial example, I tend to kick my car when it will not start, instead of remembering what in theory I know well enough, that the real world will only yield to intelligent behaviour.

But to introduce a sane and sensible set of procedures for morality and religion is far more difficult. Even under the threat of global war and self-extermination, to say nothing of crime, delinquency, mental illness, anarchy and other such, people will still cling to their objects and simple pictures. The most we can hope for, short of very radical methods of changing human psychology, is that people will learn to *recognize* when they are doing this. There is all the difference in the world between someone who says, 'Bloody Jews, kill the ——s!' and someone who says, 'Yes, well, honestly I do hate the Jews, I feel very violent towards them, but I suppose I mustn't just follow my feelings: we'd better try and discuss what to do sensibly and calmly, and perhaps do some research on it, whatever I feel.' The second is the remark of one who, although he cannot stop himself having these feelings, is at least not prepared, so to speak, to *vote* or *act* on them – at any rate, not in public and after reflection.

It seems therefore that there are certain crucial types of learning which anyone seriously concerned with moral education, whether as teacher or pupil, must master. They involve, above all, learning to keep clearly in mind the distinction between (1) what one *feels* and (2) what, on reflection and after consideration of evidence, discussion, reading, etc., one would *think*. To many people this distinction, even if comprehensible, is not psychologically real at all: they take their feelings (hunches, 'revelations', wishes, 'intuitions', desires, fears) as somehow self-validating. To them, they must be all right because they are *theirs*: there is no question of submitting them to public criticism or to reason in general.

How, in somewhat more practical terms, is this to be learned? It has much to do with the general notion of being *initiated into public communication*, involving criticism and discussion: as, for instance, in a seminar or group discussion. This very basic type of education underlies all the others, and is the only alternative to allowing ourselves and others to relapse into autism – that is, into a posture where we are cut off from the world, alone with ourselves, hugging our own particular fantasies, fears, desires and ideals, without trying to relate them to the real world at all. We need, by hook or by crook, to initiate ourselves and our pupils into situations where this public communication is required of them.

When people react casually to words like 'moral' and 'morality', their reactions can be roughly categorized under two headings. (1) Some people, perhaps particularly older people, are emotionally attached to a very clear picture of a definite morality with a definite content. 'Morality' for them *means*, say, obeying the law, being sexually pure, loyal to one's country, respectful towards religion, and so on; 'moral education' for them will mean persuading or indoctrinating pupils into sharing these values. (2) Other people, perhaps particularly some young people nowadays, react sharply against this picture. 'Morality' for them means something like 'what other people tell you to do', 'what adults want to foist on you', 'what's conventional'. These people would be against 'moral education' because they suppose that 'moral education' means foisting a particular set of values on to pupils.

Notice that both (1) and (2) share this common picture of 'morality' as having a particular *content* (the content may differ from one society to another). It is as if they both believed that morality consisted of *given rules*, perhaps laid down by some authority, but anyway somehow *theirs* and not of our own choosing. The people in (1) accept this and wish to promote it; those in (2) resent it and oppose it. Neither seems very interested in such notions as what it means to be *reasonable* or *sane* about morality, or what moral judgements really are, or what sort of evidence we ought to use in making them. We have to improve on the reactions in (1) and (2) if we are to make any progress.

These two reactions both go back to a common fantasy, which has its roots in childhood, and which I shall try to describe briefly. Consider first this common picture: 'Moral education must be about making people good. To do this, we must put people in a position where they can receive goodness from what is around them. Their surroundings must consist of good men, good literature, good works of art, good natural conditions (perhaps the unspoiled country). They will then imitate, or be infected by, this surrounding goodness. Virtue and goodness will enter their hearts (minds, souls), radiating from these sources or by imitation of them.'

This model is deeply embedded in the language and moral judgements of our own society, and of almost all other societies. We talk naturally of 'corruption' and 'filth', call people 'swine' to express moral disapproval, and, if we are religious, employ the concepts of grace, sin, devils, angels, holiness, etc. which bear witness to the model. Not so long ago the notion of 'bad blood in the family' would not have been entirely metaphorical, and words like 'defilement' and 'dishonour', particularly with reference to feminine sexuality, tell the same story. It is hence not surprising that the mere *association* of A with B, if B is 'bad', is thought to 'corrupt'. The badness or guilt is thought to *rub off*, as it were, like ordinary dirt. To tolerate the presence of 'bad' people in one's country – racialists if you are a liberal, communist leaders if you are a hater of communism – is thought to degrade one's own moral purity. Jesus was criticized for associating with 'publicans and sinners'. Often 'bad' people are the aliens, the foreigners; they are seen, as the Nazis saw the Jews, essentially as poisoning the 'good', infecting the bloodstream – hence to be cast out or exorcised, like devils in a pre-scientific era.

The model accounts also for an inveterate human tendency to regard 'moral authorities', or those who are 'great' in the moral sphere, essentially as *sources of good power*. These 'authorities', whose particular beliefs may vary very greatly (Jesus, the Buddha, Savonarola, Mohammed, Hitler, Lenin and Mao Tse-tung are only a few in a very mixed bag), are seen as radiating virtue and strength, inspiring and exalting their followers, filling them full of goodness. If such people act in a way apparently contrary to this picture, their *mana* is diminished (as when, even today, the notion of a *clergyman* swearing, or engaging in sexual activities of any but the purest kind, is regarded as somehow contradicting his 'moral authority'; contrast this with the acceptability of a doctor suffering from ill-health). A 'moral authority', according to the model, is not supposed to be one who *knows about* something, or has the wisdom and understanding to guide others, but one who *is* something – 'a shining example', 'an inspiration', 'a saint', etc.

In discussions of morality and moral education, many people never get far beyond this picture. They feel empty, hungry, impotent, in need of 'the good'; for them it is a question of identifying a source of good power and sucking the goodness from it, somewhat as the infant sucks at its mother's breast. At the same time they will feel anger, disgust, fear and hatred of 'bad' or 'corrupting' sources. Unfortunately different people choose different sources – they follow different gods, different heroes, different scriptures – and these differences, being violently and non-rationally maintained, can only be settled by war or by the total isolation of one part from another. The hunger for 'the good' is so strong as to preclude any possibility of serious thought, or communication with those of other persuasions: they are immediately identified as 'bad', in order to sustain the person's picture of his own 'good' source. This is a very common fantasy and needs to be thoroughly understood. As children, our desires are inevitably (and rightly) repressed. For this we pay a price: the price of feeling that our 'good' selves are in constant danger from our 'bad' selves. Unconsciously, or semi-consciously, there are all sorts of things we would like to do, all sorts of pleasures in which we would like to indulge, which are not allowed: things usually, at least in our society, connected with sex and aggression, with physical pleasure and physical violence.

Consequently, any impulse or temptation to do these things strikes us in two ways: on the one hand, a part of ourselves (conscious or unconscious) wants to do them, but on the other hand we are frightened or feel guilty about doing them. The idea of abandoning ourselves to the pleasurable rhythms of music, of indulging in 'animal' pleasures, of 'letting ourselves go', fills us at once with secret delight and with alarm. This mixed feeling becomes transferred to *second-hand* representations of these unconscious desires. Not only doing these things in real life but doing them in imitation or pretence also involves guilt and fear. Even by *acting* them, we feel that our security is threatened.

The whole trend of thought which we describe as 'puritan' illustrates this fantasy. Any form of imitation, pretending, acting, 'dressing up', etc., is regarded as dangerous in principle, because it may open the door to the unconscious desires of which we are afraid. The fear is naturally associated with authority, in our culture perhaps particularly with the father who punishes or disapproves. (Thus in *Mansfield Park*, Jane Austen's characters rehearse a play, *Lovers' Vows*: the sense of what Austen calls 'undefined alarm' which some of them feel is associated with Sir Thomas Bertram, master of the house, who in fact returns after a long absence and castigates them. They are naughty children who have been caught indulging in a sort of sexual game.)

Even if we ourselves do not act them, the representation of the feared behaviour and motives is dreaded. Most of the debate, from Plato to modern times, about problems of censorship, pornography, obscenity and so on is governed by this fantasy: it becomes a battle between those in whom this fear is uppermost and those who wish to rebel and assert themselves against it by deliberate 'naughtiness'. Both the teacher who is shocked by obscene scrawls on the lavatory wall and the boy who finds secret delight in scrawling share a common picture; both the censorious critics of sexual representations in literature, television, etc. and those who delight in such representations as gestures of defiance are fighting the same battle. Little room is left for any serious thinking on the subject.

I have sketched this model far too briefly and superficially, but perhaps sufficiently to enable us to recognize its hold on us. For it is not to be denied that it *has* a hold on *all* of us. Not only is it deeply rooted in our own and all other languages, but it is difficult to see how any human being could grow up without some concept of 'good' and 'bad' objects, without reacting to some things as 'nasty', 'disgusting' or 'obscene', as 'infecting', 'polluting' or 'corrupting', or on the other hand as 'pure', 'virtuous' or 'holy'. There is indeed much psychological evidence about the development of this picture in terms of 'good' and 'bad' objects in very young children. It is impossible, for conceptual and/or empirical reasons, for any of us to escape the picture completely.

What we can do, however, is to recognize the picture and thereby enable ourselves to control it. The essential move consists in the perception that our own reactions are not, as it were, God-given or immediately authoritative. We cannot hope to free ourselves from the immediacy of the reactions themselves: each of us is bound to see certain objects as 'good' or 'bad', bound to find some things 'disgusting', bound to feel threatened or anxious at certain types of behaviour or representation. This is inevitable and – unless it cripples our personal lives, as an extreme fear of sex or art might do – in itself harmless, provided we do not take these reactions as part of the laws of the universe. There is all the difference in the world between saying 'It disgusts me' and 'It is disgusting', between saying 'I don't like using bad language' and 'Bad language corrupts'.

We can now see how the two reactions with which we began this chapter can easily arise. The people (1) who wish to sell some set of partisan values, to indoctrinate a particular 'morality', are those who remain wholly attached to this picture of 'goodness'. The 'goodness' exists in God, or 'conscience', or some external authority, or sacred scripture, or a set of rules; it has to be preserved and inculcated into pupils. Those (2) who react against the people in (1) have, at least consciously, disowned the picture. They are just not going to be 'moral' or 'good' any more; they are going to enjoy themselves and do what they like.

It is important to see that those in (2) are just as wholesale and unreasonable as those in (1). Both picture morality as a sort of *thing* or *force* or *power*: one wants to suck it in and transmit it to others, the other turns away from it. But in turning away, those in (2) turn away also from the whole business of rules, reasons, principles, plans, standards, values, criteria – in a word from the whole business of moral *thinking*. According to them, there is nothing to think about, since 'morality' is something they entirely reject. They turn instead to what their impulses or tastes or desires direct them to do, to feeling and behaviour which is not governed by reason at all. To put this another way: those in (1) believe in certain things being really right and wrong; they accept that there are some rules or principles or signs which make one thing right and another thing wrong. Their mistake is to talk as if you could tell what was right and wrong very easily, as it were by touching or smelling or tasting it – by some sort of immediate experience of 'goodness', or by just accepting some authority. Those in (2) talk as if they did not believe anything was right or wrong at all, as if 'This is right' meant only 'I like this'.

Both reactions share this same fantasy, and both are clearly mistaken. Most people tend towards either (1) or (2), and it is well worth while to observe one's own leanings towards one or the other. Do we detect in ourselves a longing for security, for a solid 'goodness' that nothing can take from us, a 'goodness' we invest in some authority, or hero, or our own consciences? Or do we detect a cynical, despairing, rebellious or simply lazy rejection of the whole notion of right and wrong, a refusal even to ask serious questions about what we ought to do and why? Or do we detect both elements in ourselves? Whatever may be true in the case of each of us, we need to be aware of it, and we need then not so much to steer a middle course or effect some compromise between (1) and (2), but rather to try to suppress the basic fantasy underlying both and turn our minds to a rational consideration of the matter.

The only kind of 'basis' for morality of which most of us have had any experience has been an authoritarian basis. We have accepted, if only half-heartedly, some particular creed or set of values without asking too many questions; or, if we have asked questions, we have not been clear about how they should be answered. Now that the old basis has let us down, we naturally look for a new basis *of the same logical type*. An extreme form of this is the type of person who starts by accepting some very clearly defined authority (perhaps the Roman Catholic Church), finds it unsatisfactory and then switches to another authority (perhaps the Communist Party). He has acquired a 'new basis' for his morality, but it is not *really* new: he has just changed one authority for another. The new authority may *happen* to be a better one (or a worse), but unless he is in some position to judge whether it is better, unless he knows *how* to make this sort of judgement, he cannot know whether he is any better off.

Moreover, unless we are able to judge intelligently between one basis and another, we cannot know whether this change of authority will be more than a short-term solution to the practical problem. If one basis or authority can be rejected and hence result in break-down, chaos, uncertainty, etc., then so can another. We may give our children a 'new basis' by devising a new moral code, drawn from whatever source, but will this do the job better than the old one? Is it likely to last? *Ought* it to last? It may seem immediately attractive, and be easily available, but what are its real merits? If the next generation of adolescents is going to challenge it, have we an answer? If we just want *any* 'new basis' to adopt, any authority to follow, then we can find one for ourselves tomorrow without any trouble at all. But if we want to find the right basis, or at least a more reasonable basis, then we shall have to think about it: we shall have to try to answer the general question 'How are we to judge between one basis and another?'

Now as soon as we take this question seriously, we begin to see that it is not the 'new basis' itself which is going to be ultimately authoritative, but the *criteria by which we judge*. As soon as we get into the position of questioning authorities, of asking for a 'new basis' – and as soon as we begin questioning we cannot get out of this position, whether we like it or not – then in a sense these authorities are no longer ultimate. We are no longer searching only for a leader, a hero, a clear and simple moral code to put all our trust in; we are searching for general principles which will enable us to assess and perhaps choose between leaders and codes. Hence it is really *these principles*, whatever they may be, which we are going to put our money on. It will be these principles which, if we can be clear about them, may form a genuinely 'new basis'. But it is now fairly obvious that these principles will not themselves be moral principles or codes; they will be principles *by which one judges between* various moral codes or authorities.

Our concern with moral *education*, rather than just with our own morality, reinforces this point. For if we are educating our children, we are setting out to give them some idea about *how to do* morality, to put it crudely, and obviously we shall not succeed until we ourselves are clear about this. We may feel, perhaps quite wrongly, that we know 'the right answers' for ourselves, but there is more to education than just handing out right answers. It is one thing to work out our own moral values, for ourselves and perhaps for our society as well; it is quite another to say that these alone will form an acceptable basis for moral *education*. Of course the two interconnect. But the view which may be expressed as 'First we find out the right answers, and then we tell them to children, and that's moral education' is plainly inadequate.

Suppose we were in the Middle Ages and tried to find a 'basis for scientific education' by combining those beliefs which were generally accepted. We might say, 'Well, at least we all agree that the sun goes round the earth, etc., so let's call that science and teach people to believe it, and then they'll be educated in science.' The point here is not (or not only) that some of these beliefs are mistaken. It is rather that 'educating people scientifically' is not simply to make them repeat certain scientific truths, but to be clear about what scientific method is and to *teach them how to do science well*. It is to be clear about what counts as success in science, and to give them the skills to be successful: to show them that it involves, for instance, close and patient observation, accuracy, testing by experiment and so forth. So too with history, literary criticism and any other field of human activity. Educating people in these activities is not to extract 'right answers' from them, but to teach them what counts as 'a good reason' in history, literary criticism, etc., and how to think and act in accordance with these reasons. Hence any 'basis for moral education' should consist of imparting those skills which are necessary to make good or reasonable moral decisions and to act on them. We are not primarily out to impart any specific *content*, but to give other people facility in a *method*. This is what eventually happened with science, this is why science and education in science eventually prospered, and this is what must happen to morality. Such an approach does not deny that we have moral knowledge now, any more than we would deny that the Middle Ages had scientific knowledge; but it does involve trying first to reach agreement about the second-order principles governing morality, rather than about what should be the (first-order) content of particular moral beliefs.

Now of course this is very difficult, but I think that the study of the principles governing morality (which we can call 'moral philosophy' if we like) is sufficiently far advanced to make it worth while trying to bring it to bear on education. Indeed, whilst of course there are many important disputes amongst moral philosophers and many objections that might be made to any statement of such principles, I do not think that the main difficulties in forming a reasonable conceptual framework for moral education are primarily intellectual or academic at all. To put it in a grotesquely extreme way, we all really know how to do morals – if we think about it, are prepared to be honest and are willing not to 'run wild' or play some other game instead. It is not that the rules of the game are wholly obscure; it is mostly that we just do not attend to them.

If we are to approach moral education properly, therefore, we must not remain too firmly wedded to our own particular moral codes and beliefs; initially, at least, we must be willing to start from scratch. It is very tempting to say things like 'Well, everyone agrees about so-and-so at least' or 'There isn't much dispute about such-and-such, anyway', and of course nobody would want to throw away commonly held beliefs without the most careful and painstaking examination. But we have to remember that this *may* be like saying 'Everybody accepts X and Y as scientifically true', in a society whose 'science' was merely astrology and superstition. And we cannot tell without going into the whole question of what the subject – be it morality or science or anything else – actually *is*.

I have suggested that our first reaction is to seek for some kind of simple authority in morals, and that this reaction is misguided. But there is also another kind of reaction, to which many of us (particularly in liberal and pluralistic societies) are liable, which is likely to afflict us if and when we turn away from seeking for authority. This reaction often occurs at a time when challenging and large-scale questions are raised about education: about its nature and purposes, about who is to control it, about the training, powers and conditions of work for teachers, about the relations between education and the demands of society, about discipline in schools, about particularly controversial aspects of the curriculum (moral, religious and political education) and so on. Such questions are especially prominent at times of actual or perceived crisis, whether such crises are to do with financial shortage, dissatisfaction on the part of governments or of educators themselves, or – as I hope to show – major if largely unconscious shifts in the conceptual and emotional states of societies and individuals within them. This is, I believe, true at the present time: not only in many western societies, where the general euphoria and expansive spirit of the 1960s is now called into question, but throughout the world. Many societies are facing these problems for the first time: increased pressure from various social groups, and increased awareness of what other societies are doing resulting from improved communications, make it difficult or impossible for even the most remote countries to proceed along traditional lines.

The requirements and limits of education are constantly in danger of being forgotten, chiefly because it is something very close to our hearts and passions, so that we tend to import our personal values – political, moral, religious, even aesthetic – into education without regard to its essential nature. In order to avoid, or recover from, this danger we have to adopt a methodology which is, most regrettably, not widely used in educational discussion or practised in those institutions which study and control educational systems (if it were, it would have acted as a self-adjusting mechanism and we should not now be in a state of crisis). We have to do two things which go together: first, to grasp the nature of the enterprise more firmly, to understand its internal logic and the practical demands which flow from the concept itself; and secondly, to understand the kinds of pressure which distract us and tempt us to corrupt the enterprise. To take a parallel, suppose that medicine or astronomy were in the uncertain and controversial state that general enterprises like education are now in, so that people went in for witch-doctoring and astrology as well as sometimes doing some genuine science. Then we should need (1) to be clearer about the nature of medical and astronomical science, its logic and principles, and (2) to be aware and fight off the temptations to do something else instead – to get quick answers, or more certainty about the future than we can reasonably claim, or miracle cures, or whatever the temptations are. We should need to marry up (1) and (2): that is, to see just how the temptations distracted us from certain key features of the enterprise.

There are of course strong and predictable resistances to this approach. Usually – and here educators behave in much the same way as patients undergoing psychotherapy – the practical problems which educators cannot help but bump into are not seen as in any sense neurotic or concerned with their own fantasies, but are simply projected on to some feature of the external world. In most liberal societies, where it is not fashionable to off-load problems on to God, or the Devil, or Nature, or specific scapegoats (the Jews, for instance), the villain is commonly 'society': a type of projection accompanied if not encouraged by the spread of social science. The main points to remember here are tolerably obvious. First, whilst of course it is true that social institutions have a profound effect on individual thinking and feeling, such institutions are the creations of individuals and take their tone in large part from the way in which individuals handle their unconscious emotions (the Nazi regime is an obvious example). Secondly, the major problems and temptations to which individuals are liable in this context arise from certain non-negotiable features of early childhood, features which would exist even in the best possible form of society. Thirdly, the only permanently secure way of improving social institutions is by educating individuals. Attempts to avoid the force of these points inevitably end up in a kind of conspiracy theory, 'If only we can get rid of certain tyrants or alter certain power structures, our problems will be solved'; a view which the history of social revolutions alone (the French and Russian revolutions, for instance) shows to be naive.

I omit further discussion of this point because, in many practical cases, nothing much may turn upon it. Thus, to take an example which is fairly typical of my main thesis, it is currently the case in many maintained schools in liberal societies that teachers do not exercise enough disciplinary powers to maintain a sufficiently high degree of order and obedience (not a popular word amongst liberals) for their pupils to learn efficiently. It may be said, with truth, that they often do not in fact have such powers, that 'the system' fails them, that they are trained not to exact obedience but rather to behave as advisers and helpers, even perhaps that they are selected for having a 'caring' rather than an authoritative attitude to the young. In these ways, it may be said, 'society' and particular social institutions (schools) are to blame. Nevertheless, it remains true both (1) that many individual teachers side with the institutions, rejecting the idea of power and authority in favour of a more tender-minded attitude, and (2) that these institutional and social climates have been generated or at least accompanied by changes in individual attitudes and feelings. Roughly, the 'authoritarian' attitudes of the last century have been replaced by more 'democratic' attitudes, both institutionally and individually. So the problem remains to identify the particular unconscious elements which constitute this change, elements which, if you like, have both personal and social dimensions.

Much has been written on the necessary features and limits of the enterprise of education from a strictly logical or philosophical viewpoint (see Hirst and Peters, 1970; Peters, 1966; Wilson, 1977 and 1979, with references), and perhaps the first and most important thing to be said is, bluntly, that we have little hope of extricating education from a state of crisis unless the basic philosophical points are understood – as, currently, they are not understood by many people, including most of the influential educational politicians and administrators. For our purposes here, however, it may be sufficient to mention two basic ways in which we are tempted to go wrong. Both ways stem ultimately, or at least at a fairly basic level of the psyche (see below), from two different postures or attitudes to authority; at least they can be usefully so described.

1. The first involves *identification* with authority. Here the individual sees himself as the unquestionable representative of a corpus of truths and values. He has the 'right answers' and his job is to pass these on to his pupils so that they end up believing them and acting in accordance with them. Confident in this assumption, he welcomes the power, authority, sanctions and disciplinary measures deemed necessary to put it into practice. The authority may be described or rationalized in different ways: 'Marxist ideology', 'a Christian way of life', 'British (French, etc.) culture and traditions', 'middle-class values' or whatever. This posture is visible, in extreme forms, in totalitarian and authoritarian societies, though of course not confined to them.

2. The second involves *rejection* of authority. Here the individual is in a state of reaction against whatever he takes to be current authorities ('the establishment'). He does not regard his own beliefs and values as having priority over others, or as forming a firm and secure basis for education; he may indeed adopt some kind of relativist position in which the objectivity of truth and value is itself called into question or even denied. He is likely to favour a non-hierarchical ideology and some kind of egalitarianism (as it were, dismantling existing authority and dissipating it throughout society), along with certain interpretations of 'democracy' or 'participation', and he is likely to favour 'integration' and object to some practices as 'divisive' or 'élitist'. This posture is visible more often in liberal societies (the UK is a fair example).

It is easy to see how each of these strays from the concept of education. On the one hand, (1) the notion of education – indeed of learning itself – is connected with the logically basic notion of a *rational stance* towards the world. It is this stance that is primary: items claimed as truth or knowledge or worthwhile values derive their validity from that stance, from the primary concept of reasonable procedures, rather than vice versa. 'Right answers' cannot be the starting point of education, since their rightness (if they are indeed right) can only be a function of the criteria of reason which justify them as right. This is perhaps most obvious in the case of moral education, where it is clear that no first-order set of values - no specific moral *content* – can be taken for granted; for such education, we have to rely on initiating pupils into a grasp of the rational procedures which they can use to generate their own values. Objections to indoctrination, or the socialization of pupils into norms and practices that may well be questioned, rest ultimately on this point, as do the legitimate demands under such headings as 'autonomy' and 'critical thinking'. In a word, the only authority an educator can ultimately recognize is the authority of reason itself, not of any particular or partisan ideology. On the other hand, (2) to dismantle or reject authority in general, to fall into any kind of relativism, to react against the whole concept of 'right answers', is equally to stray from education, for the notions of reason, learning, knowledge, truth and hence of education itself are connected to that concept. Rational procedures (if we can be clear about them) do have authority, and educators can and must have authority in so far as they act as representatives of these procedures – for instance, as representatives and teachers of how to think reasonably about the physical world (science), about the past (history) and so on. Further, educators need the practical or social authority necessary to transmit these procedures to their pupils: briefly, the *authority and power necessary to enforce whatever discipline is required for education*.

Of the two general temptations already mentioned in (1) and (2) above, there are good reasons for concentrating at the present time on (2). First, (1) is a much simpler reaction: the individual simply takes on the mantle of authority passed to him by his parents (or elders, or whoever represents 'the establishment'). Secondly, that reaction may be regarded as in some sense the natural state, and the reaction of rejection as more complex and sophisticated, at least at the public or social level (I do not deny that the psychic roots of rejection lie very deep, as the work of such post-Freudians as Melanie Klein shows). Thirdly, again at a public or social level, as I have hinted earlier, increased communications and a widespread surge in the desire for 'liberation' or 'autonomy' – one might say generally, for 'doing one's own thing' – make (1) much more difficult to sustain; to continue the traditions of an authoritarian folk society in the face of potential revolution and a desire for independence is extremely difficult in the modern world. Finally, there is some evidence (though I shall not discuss it here) that those who control and operate education in many societies, particularly in the western world, favour (2) rather than (1): for instance, in the UK many of the most articulate and influential teachers and educators have gone in for the rejection of authority in a fairly big way, favouring relativism, egalitarianism, 'integration' and other ideas that symptomatize that rejection. These points are of course very briefly stated, and much sociological and psychological enquiry needs to be devoted to them. Further, it is of course always true that reaction (1) is permanently available and will to some extent occur by a swing of the pendulum or even concurrently (for instance, that the dissatisfaction with 'liberal' or 'wishy-washy' religious and moral education will generate a desire to have one's children educated in much more authoritarian regimes, perhaps based on Christian fundamentalist principles or some other hard-line ideology; this seems to be occurring in some western democracies). The motives here are, again, not always complex: a desire for security at all costs, a clear and hard line, a fear of some sort of schizoid split, both in society and in the individual psyche, which can only be staved off by *simpliste*, uncritical acceptance of a straightforward ideology, a 'faith to live by', 'law and order', 'the preservation of standards and traditions'. All these are fairly familiar to us and have been tolerably well documented, sometimes under headings like 'the authoritarian personality'. Reaction (2) is more complex and deserves our more immediate attention.

Certain generalizations and diagnoses are possible, and have sometimes been usefully made in the past: the 'authoritarian personality' is a fair example of something that has been quite well explored. Indeed the much more tentative explorations I want to make may be seen as a sort of parallel to this, though it is difficult, and certainly premature, to pick the title. Terms such as 'liberal', 'relativistic' and 'egalitarian' come to mind, but these are loaded terms, and progress is more likely to be made by a detailed analysis that is not too strictly guided by any general thesis about personality type. The best methodology consists of observing a number of surface symptoms and trying to render these down, so to speak, into a succession of progressively fewer features. This is what I shall attempt here, but I need to make it quite clear in advance that even this brief attempt is fraught with doubt and difficulty. Much more work needs to be done, and even then – as commonly in clinical psychology – there is no absolute or clear-cut set of proofs.

I can begin fairly confidently, having been in the midst of the educational world for several decades, with some beliefs or feelings common to many inhabitants of that world, at least in the UK. Very briefly, they are apt to think or feel:

1.   That 'education' is a 'contestable concept', without any fixed definition or meaning and without specific values of its own.
2.   That one cannot or should not distinguish between educational goods and reasons on the one hand, and political (or other) kinds of goods and reasons on the other.
3.   That there are no innate, basic or non-negotiable differences between people of different sexes, races, cultures, colours, classes, etc., all such differences being due to 'society' or social conditioning.
4.   That integrating people is good, segregating (separating, selecting) bad.
5.   That equality is a good in itself, and that more equality means more justice.
6.   That 'democracy', 'autonomy', 'participation' and 'freedom' are good, 'authority', 'obedience' and 'conforming' bad and dangerous.
7.   That anger, aggression, violence and power are bad.
8.   That 'competition' is bad.
9.   That punishment is bad.
10. That rules are restrictive, rather than enabling, and should be reduced to a minimum.
11. That education does not require discipline and obedience to the *impersonal* authority of the teacher.
12. That schools are potent enough, and that teachers do not need more power.
13. That schools should not be isolated but 'integrated with the community'.
14. That schools should not be 'selective' but 'comprehensive'.

15. That examinations are bad because they brand pupils as 'failures'.
16. That we ought to 'break down subject barriers' and 'integrate' different subjects.
17. That there are no subjects, disciplines or forms of knowledge existing in their own right, with their own rules and standards, independently of 'society'.
18. That there are no demonstrably objective or correct or absolute values, and that teachers should not impose their own values on pupils.
19. That private (independent) schools are immoral and should not be supported by those concerned with the public educational system.
20. That children are naturally good, and that their apparent faults are wholly the product of bad education or of 'society'.

A few obvious points are worth making here. First, many of these thoughts/feelings overlap: items on the list are not discrete (some, for instance, are particular cases of others). Secondly, these brief descriptions do not do justice to more elaborate theses: (20), for instance, might be seen as a grotesque attempt to reduce Rousseau to a single sentence. Thirdly, and this accounts for my somewhat random selection of inverted commas, many of the terms that appear when people express such feelings are of course obscure in their meaning. However, I am not dealing with these views as rational or irrational in their logic; any reasonably sophisticated person would, naturally, neither agree nor disagree with any of them as stated – he would want to expand and analyse before doing either. It remains true, nevertheless, that a considerable number of people (a) say things for which the above twenty sentences are fair summaries, and (b) are willing to give a general assent, even without elaboration, to such brief sentences. It is the feelings behind the expressions that we want to look at.

The most useful reduction of these twenty items is perhaps achieved by trying to pin down what these people seem to be *frightened* of, what they hate or what, as it were, raises their hackles. Amongst these seem to be:

1. The idea of segregating or differentiating between people.
2. The exercise of any kind of judgement, punishment or domination.

3. Impersonal authority.
4. Objectivity (of values, knowledge, concepts).
5. Competition or conflict.

Some of these, again, are perhaps not discrete. Thus it seems likely that the fear of differentiation in (1) and perhaps also of objectivity in (4) are generated by the fear of domination in (2): the thought, conscious or unconscious, is perhaps something like 'We must not differentiate, otherwise we establish a hierarchy in which those at the bottom of the pile suffer.' (This thought seems to me very clearly to lie at the root of much thinking in the areas of race and gender.) Similarly, the idea of objectivity suggests potential domination by those who are the repositories of supposed objective values. (Perhaps the commonest speech form used by those alarmed by this is 'Who are *you* (we) to impose *your* (our) values on...?', followed by some supposedly underprivileged group.) It is less threatening to adopt some kind of relativism, so that at least the thoughts and feelings and practices of individuals are not challenged or crushed by any objective standards.

Further illustration of these items, though desirable in a fuller work, is not in place here. They lead us, pretty quickly and obviously, to the position of the young child. His position is essentially powerless: that is the inevitable price he pays for being raised from infancy, being looked after, fed, taught and, of course, told how to behave. He is in effect under a parental mandate, in which his freedom and power are abrogated. Of course he feels ambivalent about this: on the one hand, he wants the security which the mandate gives him (psychological as well as material security), but on the other he resents parental domination. Clearly, any development of a potentially rational creature from birth to adulthood faces this general problem, and would face it in any family or set of social conditions. Under normal conditions, the problem is solved (with more or less difficulty) by a mixture of affection, love, concern, sharing, tenderness and care on the one hand, and the application of concepts like discipline, rules, punishment, obedience and the reality pressures of other people's rights and the demands of the external world on the other.

All that is, I hope, common ground, constantly retrodden in almost all books on child rearing or child psychology. But because the child is constantly striving towards adulthood, that part of his mind and thought which fears, resents and hates adult power is apt to be uppermost, and hence to find more frequent expression than the need for security and limits which he also feels. He does not want (1) to be differentiated as a child, or (2) to be judged and dominated; he prefers to do what he is told only if and when he feels warm enough to adults as individual people, not impersonally (3). He rejects the alleged objectivity of adult values (4), but at the same time does not wish to be the loser, as he almost certainly will be, in any competition or conflict (5).

A good deal of this is to do with the fear of domination or aggression, but some of it also concerns separation anxiety. The child inevitably lives in a world which sometimes seems a world of isolation and slavery; he is alone, powerless, surrounded by adults larger and better equipped than he is, where his only allies as he gets older are other children, the peer group. (Hence, unsurprisingly, the immense power of the peer group – whether in the form of street-gangs or any other – in modern liberal society: they represent the only defence against the powerful adult.) Impersonal adult authority – the police, for instance – is particularly intolerable because the authority is here divorced from the idea of adults as also caring and sharing parents: the child is brought up sharply against impersonal notions like rules and their attached penalties.

This is essentially a paranoid position, and it has, I think, to be accepted that all children are inevitably paranoid. This is not, as some may take it, a cheap pseudo-psychiatric jibe, but a simple recognition of an inevitable psychological posture adopted by the small and weak in the face of what is, indeed, virtually total domination by the adult. The children, of course, are not able to appreciate the necessities of any form of child rearing, the necessity of adult power. Even when the adults use their mandated power for the child's benefit, which is by no means always and everywhere the case, the *feelings* of the child remain hostile, suspicious and fearful, even if he is capable of some intellectual grasp of the necessary mandate. As I have said, successful child rearing gradually weans the child from the paranoid position by sharing and discipline, but even the best upbringing leaves much of these feelings untouched in the unconscious mind.

It is easy to see how the business of being an educator – a parent or a teacher – regenerates one's own paranoid feelings by reactivating one's own childhood position. Interestingly, those who are most vehement in expressing the ideas and feelings listed above have not, in fact, grown up in families or schools where the mandate was much abused. They are not the offspring of some tyrannical Victorian paterfamilias, but have often grown up in extremely liberal circumstances. It is the *idea* (again, often unconscious) of the highly punitive adult rather than the real-life existence of such an adult that seems to count, and that idea becomes more ferocious and threatening when the adult resigns his authority and tries to behave more like a child himself. The child is fully aware, more aware than the adult, that there is virtually infinite power on the adult side, and if the adult seems to deny or conceal this by behaving with too much liberality and not enough authority, the child naturally supposes that there is, as it were, another much more powerful and threatening figure behind the real one. (There is a useful parallel here with what Tacitus says in his *Annals* about the Roman emperors: the bad ones were bad, and the apparently benevolent and good ones must somehow have been concealing their badness under a cloak of liberality, thus adding hypocrisy to their other vices – a very clear example of an unfalsifiable paranoid outlook.)

Adults who abdicate from their positions of authority, under the influence of the reactivated paranoid child within themselves, are of course particularly frightened by the use of what one may term *naked power*, because the possibility of deploying such power brings their problems to a head. It is here that the compulsive quality of their fears becomes most apparent. It is one thing to encourage, cajole, support or even bribe children into obedience; quite another to say something like 'Look, you have got to do this, and without caring whether you like or respect me as a person I am going to make life sufficiently unpleasant for you to make sure that you do actually do it.' Only an adult who feels himself metaphysically backed by God, or the Party, or some other legitimating agency who will give him the required nerve and self-confidence, can easily take such a line; in contemporary liberal and pluralist societies, not many such adults are left, at least not in the educational world. It is, of course, an unpleasant line to have to take, yet any parent who needs to stop his son bullying a little sister, or any honest teacher who needs to make absolutely sure that the weak pupils are not done down by the strong in school, knows perfectly well that such a line has sometimes to be taken. For many people, however, this is the sticking point: to apply straightforward fear as a motive, particularly fear of overt forms of power such as corporal punishment, seems to them morally intolerable and (for themselves) psychologically out of the question.

We may here usefully compare professional pacifists, and certainly it is not only with children that this compulsion is evident. In the politics of most liberal societies, certain kinds of action are, as they say, just 'not acceptable'. The kinds of force, for instance, that might be required to crush terrorism in Northern Ireland, or even football hooliganism, seem in themselves intolerable; we prefer, it seems, to allow the weak to be bullied and killed rather than use such ferocious methods. This is a kind of moral absolutism which, whatever may be said for it at the philosophical level, nevertheless clearly stems from a deep fear of power and violence. It is of course an empirical question what forms of power are necessary to deploy in order to get rid of what sorts of social disorder, but one has some sympathy with an old lady whose arm was broken by football hooligans: when told that much research was being done on the social causes of such hooliganism, she said, 'What they ought to do research on is why the authorities don't stop it.'

The deployment of violence, indeed of any form of power, is no doubt something which any civilized person must consider seriously; but it is a fantasy to suppose that we can shield children from it. Children experience, and have to come to terms with, much more profound and naked fear than anything which adults normally admit to the conscious mind. Their fear of actual, real-life adult power and punishment is by no means the worst of their fears; indeed the deployment of such power may come as a kind of relief. The super-ego, if I may use this terminology, is not and could not be built up in children by any amount of kindness, affection or rational explanation alone; it is inevitably based on the fear of some kind of retribution. We do children no kindness if we behave as if that were not so: what we can do is to give that retribution some sort of manageable shape and some connection with the real world, so that it can develop into a respectable adult conscience.

The paranoid fear of violence and domination would be less destructive in educational and social practice if it were confined merely to the compulsive taboo on overt or dramatic forms of force: for instance, on forms such as torture or hanging or severe corporal punishment. Unfortunately the fear lies so deep, and is so well defended in the conscious mind by various forms of rationalization ('violence breeds violence', 'a caring attitude' and so on), that it extends to the whole business of interaction between those in authority and their clients. It is now more or less standard practice in educational circles that teachers are encouraged not to confront disruptive or disobedient pupils, but rather to 'defuse' potential conflict by some form of evasive action – smoothing things over, cajolery, humour or whatever. The pupil challenges the teacher's authority, but the challenge is evaded rather than met head on. Given that teachers have in fact little real power to make their authority stick – since the paranoia is institutionalized in the educational system, which in liberal societies does not trust teachers with enough power – teachers can hardly be blamed for using such methods: they have often to act as advisers or missionaries rather than as authorities, and keep some semblance of order in any way they can. But the psychological results are clearly corrupting, for the pupil is treated not as a person in a world where there are rules and other people with their own interests, but rather as a 'case' who (one is tempted to say, which) has to be 'handled'. The effect is not to educate, but to avoid trouble at all costs: to keep the temperature down. Yet at some point, and backed by some clear deployment of authority together with whatever force, pressure or sanctions are needed to make the authority stick, any educator must bring it home to the pupil that there are certain limits beyond which he is not allowed to go – if necessary, is forcibly prevented from going. In this way an essential feature in the development towards adulthood is blurred or 'smudged': the child is not even allowed to face the necessary conflict and hence not allowed to make a psychological adjustment towards reality. The whole concept of authority, and also of discipline (which is essentially obedience to legitimate authority), is abandoned in favour of a desperate and doomed attempt to preserve some kind of order without infringing the taboos against fear and force.

If we now raise the question of how we may hope to cure or educate ourselves out of this paranoid position, it is above all important to avoid the equal and opposite error of identification with some (any) authority which seems to offer hope by 'taking a firm line', 'standing for solid values' or whatever. This move tends to occur in history with boring regularity. An authority exists and is respected; later it is undermined (often for good reasons, since many authorities are irrational and unjust); there follows a period of anomie, chaos or uncertainty; another authority is then produced, and the cycle starts again. (Many would say that something like this has been happening in British politics over the last decade or so.) It is as if the child within us were unable to grasp the concept of rational authority, being capable only either of swallowing some personal or charismatic authority hook, line and sinker, or else of retreating to some sort of egalitarian, relativistic and in general anti-authority position: either we must identify with some specific and substantive set of 'solid values', a partisan moral or political or religious line, or else each of us can do what he likes according to his fancy. That apparent dilemma, which has inhibited the advance of any serious moral (or political or religious) education, stays as powerful as it has always been, despite its intellectual absurdity; and it is, obviously enough, the direct result of retaining the ways in which the world appeared to us as young children – either we blindly obey the powerful adults, or we just do what we feel like.

We escape from this, of course, as with any other kind of mental illness, only by first of all recognizing it; but the chief difficulty that has to be faced is the almost total lack of any public context or arena which encourages such recognition. In educational circles much of what passes as 'theory', or is considered as supposedly rational and objective exploration of various educational issues and ideologies, tends to be not much more than the acting out of particular ideologies that merely echo either the paranoid position described earlier or the reactive identification with some (any) authority at all costs – perhaps some severe or fundamentalist kind of religion, for instance. As with arguments about religion, nearly all the crucial moves have already been made unconsciously before the arguments start, and often what is supposed to be free and frank rational discussion turns out to be a pietistic exercise in which the faithful reinforce their own fantasies.

On any account – and, as I need to stress here, quite independently of whether my own descriptions are at all accurate – education is an extremely difficult area: not merely 'controversial', but liable to the sort of unconscious pressures we have been talking about. The mere recognition of this in principle, without specific diagnoses, should lead to establishing contexts and methods in which we can hope to fight our way out of fantasy. It is in fact fairly plain what such contexts and methods would look like, and I have described them at some length elsewhere (Wilson, 1975); suffice it to say here that they must involve the close analysis of concepts and feelings in small-group discussion. Such a context is an attempt to introduce (or reintroduce) both staff and students to something that ought to have happened (or, rarely, has happened) to the young child in a well-ordered and loving family. In such a family, the children come to grasp the idea and practices of rational discussion –

a very sophisticated notion to which all educators need to pay far more attention than they usually do. The child learns to wean himself from the merely autistic expression of his own feelings, or the equally autistic fear of saying anything at all, and to take part in a kind of public game with rules and procedures of its own. He has to submit himself to criticism, not mind too much about making a fool of himself, attend to the meanings of the words he uses, make some respectable connection between what he *feels* and what can truthfully or sensibly be *said*, exercise tact and tolerance towards others, not become too angry, not take criticism personally, stick to the point, face the facts, keep the rules of logic and so forth. This rag-bag and fragmentary list of procedures and abilities carries one overall message with it: roughly, that when interacting with other people, not just in discussion but in life generally, *his own particular views, feelings and 'commitments' must take second place to the overall procedures of reason*, even when – *particularly* when – his feelings are especially passionate.

This is of course a very hard lesson to learn. Its importance is both obvious and wide ranging: for one thing, the whole business of interpersonal morality, of which interpersonal discussion is merely one context, rests on the acceptance of some principle of universalizability (see Hare, 1981) – roughly, that there is nothing special about one's own desires, including one's own ideals. We constantly try to evade it, at both the theoretical and the practical level: we want to be able to think that some views, those we particularly hate or are frightened of, are intolerable, beyond the pale, clearly absurd. At the same time we do not want to be the ones whose views are thus censored, so we pay some kind of lip-service to universalizability without always practising it. (The test of a genuine belief in various forms of universalizability – tolerance, for instance – is that it should sometimes cost us an effort, that it should sometimes hurt.)

The again obvious but commonly neglected psychological point is that we are unlikely to learn this lesson unless our learning is rewarded. In the family, the child learns to play the game with loving parents: the reward is not so much extrinsic, but comes from the child's pleasure in sharing something that the parents have to offer, wanting to imitate them and enjoy what they enjoy. There is a close parallel here with the sharing of food and drink, and of other mutual pleasures less sophisticated than discussion; indeed it is arguable that more primitive forms of sharing are a necessary step towards the more sophisticated. This must mean that those leading group discussion have much more psychological work to do than make an hour or two's space for seminars; they have somehow to interact and share with the group sufficiently to generate something like the trust and security of family discussion. That has obvious implications for the structure, timing and organization of such groups; implications that educational institutions need to take much more seriously.

Such genuine discussion (rather than internecine argument: Plato contrasts 'dialectic' with 'eristic') can be seen not so much as 'an alternative method of delivery' in respect of certain complex academic issues in education, to be preferred to mass lectures or deep reading at a theoretical level, as a microcosm of the general methods required to make progress in educational thought: that is, a microcosm of the sort of interaction, between individuals and various disciplines of thought, that educational problems require. It is not a way of keeping the consumers happy by freeing them from 'irrelevant' academic demands; on the contrary, anyone who has had experience of such a context, whether in psychotherapy, philosophy or any other serious enterprise, knows well enough that it is far more demanding, because more personally challenging, than most routine academic work. One has constantly to wrestle with what Iris Murdoch well describes as 'the fat, relentless ego', presented to oneself and criticized by other disputants. To make any serious progress, one has rapidly to abandon both the blind faith in institutionalized authority and the equally blind rejection of any authority at all, even the authority of rational procedures; and that can only be done if one's own hang-ups about authority in general – one's own paranoia or reactive identification with power – are constantly monitored.

Chapter 3

Relativism and Politics

I want now to make a further attempt to look at our basic difficulties, this time in a slightly more 'philosophical' and less 'psychological' way. Many people will, quite understandably, still feel that it is dismissive and arrogant to treat so much of our thinking and feeling as 'paranoid' or in some other way irrational. The difficulties are commonly met with under the heading of 'relativism', and more particularly in connection with the idea that educational issues are inextricably intertwined with political values and beliefs.

RELATIVISM AND TEACHING

I use 'relativism' to entitle a cluster of thoughts and feelings, often incoherent but immensely powerful in education (and elsewhere), which emerge in remarks like 'There's no such thing as objective truth', 'It's all a matter of belief', 'Values and knowledge are just social products', 'What right have we to impose our ideas on pupils?' and the like. There are of course a number of different ideas here; meanwhile perhaps this will suffice to identify a rough target area. I want to show why some of these ideas are false or illusory or incoherent.

There is a very considerable, and often unnoticed, difficulty in making any kind of start at all on these matters. Terms like 'false', 'illusory' and 'incoherent' are among the very many words we use to refer to certain general criteria of rationality. (Others are 'right' and 'wrong', 'mistake', 'evidence', 'a good reason', 'verify', 'sane', 'reasonable', 'improbable', 'know', 'certain', 'true'.) When we discuss or argue with other people, we commonly make use of these ideas. Indeed it might be said that their use is inevitable for anything we would normally call a *discussion* (argument), since discussions are about whether something is or ought to be the case, whether we could reasonably or truly say this or that about something. We could, though with difficulty, imagine people together simply expressing their feelings ('I like dry sherry.' 'Oh, really? I like sweet.' 'How do you react to genocide?' 'Oh, I don't care for it much.' 'The earth is flat for me, how about you?' 'No, I find it round.'), as if discussion could be no more than the exchange of ideas – mutual exchange, but no mutual criticism or evaluation. Even this is hard to make plausible, as phrases like 'I find it round' and 'flat for me' suggest, in many areas: there are not many, if any, matters about which we use absolutely no criteria of truth or evaluation. Further, one may of course be wrong about one's own feelings (reactions, ideas), not just in reporting them, but also in identifying them. One may deceive oneself, and deception implies the notion of truth, of getting things right. Now if somebody denies the whole possibility of this enterprise, strips all such terms as 'truth' and 'mistake' of their normal sense, and objects to the whole notion of applying general criteria of reason, how can discussion with such a person be possible?

Even that is not quite right: to *deny* a possibility is normally to say that those who think something possible are *wrong*. It is indeed hard to see how an out-and-out relativist can *assert* anything at all (or *believe* anything, or take up any kind of *position*), for these ideas too carry with them the idea of truth, of what is the case – whether this be a truth about things, or about concepts, or about the way words are used. Again, the notion of communicating with other people presupposes certain other notions – the law of non-contradiction, a norm of truth-telling and so on – and if the validity of these is denied, how can we proceed? Yet again, if the notion of having a good reason for action is denied, how can we really *act*, since action normally implies some kind of goal, purpose, reason or point? Not much is left of a normal human being if we strip these things away. Of course somebody can just *opt out of* being (in these ways) human, just *not be inclined* to use the usual criteria of rationality and communication; indeed we all of us do this sometimes.

All this is perhaps sufficiently obvious, but it is worth saying because it is these general criteria of reason that are logically prior to other notions that relativists may want to attack. I suspect that in practice many relativists think something like this: 'We are given various "answers", particular truths or values, in various areas of life (science, morality, art, etc.); but it is abundantly clear that these answers are not universally agreed – they vary from one society to another, and from one age to another. Indeed many of them are, very obviously, just the answers that happen to suit the interests of particular social groups. So what we call "truths" or "knowledge" or "right answers" are relative to the frameworks or rules of enquiry that happen to be favoured at particular times – most obviously, relative to the values that prevail in particular societies. So there is no such thing as certain knowledge or absolute truth: it's all relative, and we have no reason for imposing our frameworks and answers on other people (including our pupils, if we are educators).'

There is much that is right here, and relativism may be defused by agreement about the following:

1. No beliefs are beyond the reach of criticism: all can in principle be challenged, none is absolutely incorrigible, we may always be mistaken.
2. What counts as 'truth', 'a mistake', etc. is relative to particular frameworks of enquiry, the rules of a particular game, certain methods of verification, certain concepts of what counts as evidence or a good reason.
3. All beliefs, claims to truth, 'answers' etc. are, of course, produced by people in particular societies. These people have their own particular backgrounds and interests which affect these products.
4. The question whether we are entitled to impose our views on others is different from the question whether we are entitled to call our views (or anyone else's) 'right' or 'true'; we may answer 'no' to the first and 'yes' to the second.

The crucial mistake made by relativists is to suppose that all this makes our beliefs and values arbitrary, in the sense that the rules of games may be (though not always actually are) arbitrary. If we consider (2) above, we can see how the temptation arises. The relativist will say, 'Yes, of course *if* – but only if – you want to join in the game called "mathematics" ("science", "morality", etc.) as defined by certain paradigms or sets of rules or frameworks, then you will find yourself accepting certain things as true, or good reasons, or whatever. But why should you join in? There is no rational compulsion to do so, and in fact these paradigms have shifted, the rules have changed, during the history of these games, which doesn't exactly inspire confidence in absolute truth.'

The short answer to this is that deciding to join in enterprises like science or morality is not like deciding to join in a game of football or cricket. This is because these enterprises are too closely bound up with what it is to be a human being to allow much scope for opting out altogether. Here relativism is close to autism. One can say, '*If* one wants to discuss and communicate then no doubt one has to obey the law of non-contradiction (one won't succeed in *saying* anything, if one utters words like "I've read the book but not looked at it"); but why should anyone want to discuss or communicate?' But what is the force of saying this? One is merely saying that people are not always compelled to be rational language-users. Nor, similarly, are they compelled to make sense of the physical world (the enterprise for which 'science' is ultimately just a grand name), or to find out what happened in the past ('history'), or to live together in society according to certain norms ('morals' or perhaps 'politics'). Indeed they are not compelled to live at all – they can always commit suicide. But human beings do in fact find it worth while to engage in such enterprises and the rules that constitute them. More than that, certain inevitable pressures are exercised on them, sometimes tantamount to compulsion. How, after all, could a growing human being not have *some* interest in language, or in the physical world, or in the past, or in his relationships with other humans?

In engaging with the world, and different aspects of the world – physical, historical, moral and so on – human beings immediately bump up against an equally inevitable distinction, a distinction between how they see things (or how they feel things must be or how they would like things to be) and how things actually are. The notion of making a *mistake* is central here: of saying the right word to bring Mummy to one's side, of making the right moves to avoid being burned by the fire, of remembering rightly where one put one's money, etc. This is the foothold for the whole apparatus of reason, truth and knowledge; a foothold from which the apparatus falls down, if the individual has absolutely no desire to get anything right, or satisfy any of his needs, or avoid any kind of pain or disadvantage – in other words, if he resigns from being human.

Here the prime concern is that of *being reasonable*, which as it were stands above and inspires the particular frameworks and criteria and procedures that the individual may find useful. To be reasonable is not to claim the validity of particular frameworks, still less of particular answers; it is, rather, to adopt a certain *posture* – to acknowledge the possibility of error, to be eager to scrutinize evidence, engage in critical discussion and so forth. If modern science is to be preferred, as a way of sorting out the physical world, to witch-doctoring or blindly following Aristotle, this will be because a reasonable man who seriously asks the question 'What is the physical world like? (Does the earth move? Is it round or flat? How big is the sun?)' is logically driven to use certain procedures. It is *contradictory* to say, 'I want to know whether such-and-such is true of the physical world, but I do not want to use my senses or conduct experiments.' One is led by logic from an initial position of wanting to be reasonable, *via* the differentiation and understanding of certain questions (about the physical world, about the past or whatever), to the use of certain frameworks and procedures, and then ultimately to certain (of course always provisional) sets of 'answers'.

Some people – one might say, *semi*-relativists – adopt a half-way position. Thus it is commonly believed that truth, knowledge, etc. are possible in certain fields but not in others: in mathematics, science, perhaps history, just possibly psychology and sociology, not in morals, politics, art, literature, religion and personal relationships. Here it can justly be said that the general outlines, at least, of the frameworks which make truth possible are clear in the former cases but not in the latter. Briefly, we know (are agreed about) *how to do* mathematics, science, etc. but not how to do morals or politics or literary criticism. With the former, there is (rational) agreement about what counts as evidence, a good reason, a relevant consideration; with the latter, it is not so clear. Not only do people have different moral, political, aesthetic and religious beliefs but, worse, they reach their beliefs by different criteria: they play different games. To one man the starry heavens above constitute a reason for believing in God; to another they do not. This suggests that, in these fields, what counts as a good reason is arbitrary.

However, we should hesitate before swallowing this whole. First, it is not true that we have absolutely *no* idea about how to proceed in at least some of these disputed areas. There are criteria of relevance which we apply. To some extent we actually know these and can articulate them; to some extent they are latent, guiding our discussions unconsciously. For example, it is striking that, even though we may be at a loss to state precisely the rules and procedures for determining the aesthetic merits of a painting, we all recognize that its weight, size or price on the open market are irrelevant. Similarly, whether we are or are not at war with Germany has no bearing on the merits of German music. Again, even in the much-disputed area of morality we could hardly make sense of, let alone give weight to, just *anything* offered as a reason: 'I'm going to kill someone because it's Tuesday' makes no sense in the absence of an explanatory background.

Secondly, even if there were no kind of overt or tacit agreement about procedures, it would still be possible to *choose* one set of procedures as against another, on the grounds that it did certain jobs better. Often this choice depends on getting clear what the enterprise is *for*. Thus, to summarize a lot of history brutally, one can construe Galileo as saying something like 'If – only if – you want to know how objects in the phenomenal world behave, and want to predict things, then it's reasonable to use telescopes and so forth. There may be other procedures, involving obedience to the words of Aristotle and the sacred scriptures, which do other jobs.' Similarly, it is one thing to decide on the motives, actions and purposes of people in the past, according to the evidence; another thing (perhaps a kind of theology?) to consider how God is related to human history and destiny. 'It was the will of God' does not contribute to the former enquiry (what we now call 'history'). Again, there may be forms of life which we could call 'following the Führer' or 'doing what lies closest to one's heart', but these differ from a form which is concerned with satisfying human needs and interests, making up rules for our mutual benefit in society, etc.; and if 'morality' is defined along the latter lines, clearly something important follows about what counts as a good reason. Moreover, reasons may be advanced as to why this latter form of life is incumbent on any reasonable person.

The temptation to relativist despair in these fields arises, I suspect, partly from an undue concentration on 'right answers'. The reason why science and other clearer fields are respectable is not that we can feel incorrigibly certain of particular answers – on the contrary, we cannot – but that we can feel reasonably certain of the procedures. It is extremely hard to maintain that *nothing* can be said about the application of reason or about sensible procedures in more controversial areas. Getting to know the facts, becoming aware of one's own prejudices, immersing oneself in what is (on any account) relevant to making up one's mind about moral or political or aesthetic questions, talking things over with people of a different persuasion – all these, and many more, are ways in which reason gets brought to bear. And the more closely we look at, and agree upon, what is to count as a question of a particular type – moral, aesthetic or whatever – the more we come to see what criteria of relevance, what 'rules of the game', are actually applicable. Thus even in the extremely difficult case of mental health, we can see that it is one thing to determine whether a person fits well into a particular society, or is likely to be politically dissident, and another thing to determine whether he is flourishing well as an independent human being. But we cannot even begin to be clear about these differences if we make the too hasty (and, significantly, linguistically absurd) move of saying that 'sane' translates adequately into 'what such-and-such a society thinks is sane'.

The 'right answers' temptation may also lead us to expect answers of a kind that reasonable enquiry, appropriate to the field of thought, cannot give. No sensible person thinks, for instance, that the question 'Whom ought I to marry?' can be settled by the same methods, or even with the same degree of rigour, as we expect in trying to settle questions in natural science or mathematics. Yet equally we consider ourselves entitled to say, and with reason, things like 'I married the wrong person'. Again, there may be no unexceptional moral rules or principles; but that does not mean that we cannot get right answers to moral problems, any more than the fact that different medicines suit different people means that it does not matter which medicine we give to whom. Again, certain terms ('proof', for instance) may be inapplicable to, say, discussions of the merits of literature or art; but that does not mean that all changes of mind or perception are arbitrary – there is such a thing as coming to understand a work of art better, coming to see 'what's in it'. (One of the temptations here may be to suppose that *talk*, even a certain kind of talk, is the only way reason can operate; whereas, in many fields like art and personal relationships, certain kinds of experience may be much more important. The notion of reason extends far beyond the notion of applied logic.)

I incline to think that the way forward here is not to discuss matters at the highly general level in which we are accustomed to do so, with people taking up attitudes entitled 'relative', 'objective', 'absolute' and so on, but simply to *look* much harder at – in the first place, anyway – what actually goes on when we discuss matters of morals or aesthetics or whatever. What kinds of things are advanced as reasons, what things are ruled out, how do we actually proceed here? Failure to do this has, I believe, held up our thinking even in particular fields. What we may need is not so much more *theories* of 'how to do' morals, aesthetics and so on, but much more careful descriptions of what actually goes on, what games are actually played.

My own view, which I have defended elsewhere (Wilson, 1986), is that we are as human beings *landed with* certain concepts, certain interests, and therefore certain roughly demarcated fields of enquiry which necessitate certain rules of procedure, which in turn would, if we understood and applied them properly, yield provisional 'right answers'. Progress consists in understanding these and sorting them out into proper categories. It is, after all, only recently in human history that some fields – notably 'science' – have achieved respectability, emerging as a reasonably clear and differentiated form of thought which we can contrast with astrology, witchcraft and other activities. There is no good reason to suppose that we cannot do a similar job on morals, politics, aesthetics, religion and other fields where at present we are just confused. Relativists are right to point to the difficulties of this task, but wrong if they try to persuade us to throw in the towel and abandon the task as hopeless.

EDUCATION AND POLITICS

Most people believe that education and politics are inextricably intertwined. This is not a new phenomenon, and the belief has prevailed at even the loftiest arenas of discussion. Thus asked to reply to the question 'Is education necessarily political?' nearly all contributors to a special number of the *Oxford Review of Education* (vol. 2, no. 1, 1976) answered with a resounding affirmative. We need to do justice to this view before suggesting that a negative answer may be of greater importance, if only because less widely understood. An analysis of the remarks made by these contributors – and by those many other people who insist, sometimes with what seems to be a sort of ill-concealed Thrasymachean delight (Plato, *Republic*, Bks 1 and 2), that education is inevitably political –

suggests that they may want to make some or all of the following points:

1. One thing we may have in mind when we say 'yes' to the question is tolerably obvious. Educational systems throughout the world – what goes on in schools and universities and else-where under the heading of 'education' – is of course constantly subject to political pressures, in any plausible sense of 'political', from outside.
2. Further, politics is necessary to facilitate or make space for education: it has to be politically possible to educate, i.e. to enjoy a context in which education may be done. In this sense education depends on politics just as it depends on other things, like a sufficient degree of health and consciousness for people to learn.
3. Education may be influenced by the politics of the educators themselves. I can, as a teacher, bring my political opinions to bear on my pupils – it may even be argued, though somewhat less plausibly, that I cannot help doing this because my politics (or my 'ideology', another obscure term) in some sense con-ditions my whole being and makes me what I am.
4. Another equally obvious point is that it is hard to avoid all mention of political issues in education. Even if we do not engage in something specifically called 'political education', political issues will arise in the teaching of many subjects (some would say, in all subjects). In that sense, we cannot keep free of politics.
5. Slightly less obviously, schools and other educational institu-tions are themselves political entities, and a great deal of politics, if in a slightly extended sense of the term, will inevi-tably go on within them. There may be, perhaps will necessarily be, a 'hidden curriculum' which reflects the political values and practices of the institution.
6. Less obviously still, *any* act, practice, remark or piece of behav-iour *can* be viewed politically, in that it can have political consequences or fail to do so. Whether to wear green in modern Ireland or ancient Byzantium can be viewed aesthetically (does it suit my complexion?), but it can also have political signifi-cance and effects. This is perhaps what tempts people to say that 'everything is political'.

Powerful and unseen emotions fuel some at least of the above ideas, and the reader may be tempted during what follows to regress to, or reiterate, one or another of them; but let us now start from a different place. We have at least two *words*, 'education' and 'politics' (or 'ideology'; see below), and prima facie they stand for two different things or enterprises. This difference would be granted if we said things like 'Education overlaps with politics', or 'Education always has political aspects', or anything which suggested connections or relationships between the two: there would have to *be* two things for them to be connected or related. It is as if we said, 'Chess always depends on economics', meaning perhaps that we have to offer adequate economic rewards to chess-players in order to get tournaments of a high standard, but recognizing that chess is one thing and economics another. We recognize this because we can describe an enterprise, chess, which has its own rules, values, concepts, procedures and reasons for action, different from those which would be used by, say, a chess administrator who wanted to get a good tournament, and who would have to use reasons and concepts categorized under different headings – 'economics' or 'diplomacy' (if he wanted to persuade the Russians to enter a tournament in the western world, for instance). In the same way we distinguish the kind of concepts and reasons a child might use when moving chess-pieces around because they looked prettier or neater in certain positions from those used by chess-players, and perhaps categorize the former as 'aesthetic'.

Any well-developed or sophisticated form of human life makes use of these categories. We distinguish, say, the reasons a Communist commissar might have for insisting that environment is more important than heredity in biology from the reasons a biologist might have for claiming the opposite, perhaps calling one 'political' or 'ideological' and the other 'scientific'. We distinguish objections to Beethoven on the grounds that he was bourgeois from objections on the grounds that he was a bad composer musically. We distinguish reasons for choosing a car that are based on its appearance from reasons based on its performance. We distinguish the moral merits or demerits of a story from its literary merits. Words that label categories – 'political', 'moral', 'aesthetic', 'economic', 'scientific' and so on – classify, albeit roughly, a number of enterprises, types of goods, classes of reasons and sets of concepts that hang together. We may not always be clear about, or (a different matter) be able fully to articulate, the categories and their differences; but we do in fact use them, and it would be difficult if not impossible to conceive of any modern society that did not. Certainly there are takeover bids, as with the Russian commissars or the Nazi leaders who use political or ideological reasons to discredit enterprises that normally come under other headings ('because he's a Jew', 'because it's bourgeois'); but then we say, rightly, that these enterprises – science or music or whatever – have been invaded or taken over by politics or ideology.

Of course they *can* always be taken over in practice. But the only intellectually honest way of doing this is to say, 'We can't afford to bother about whether X is scientifically true or aesthetically meritorious; we have to maintain the state, and X is disruptive.' Mental health just *is different from* political dissidence: to say 'X is dissident, therefore he is mad, therefore we can lock him in an asylum' makes no sense, whereas to say 'X is dissident, therefore we can lock him away – never mind about whether he is mad or whether we're justified in calling the prison an "asylum"' is at least honest. In the same way it is honest, and may often be right, to say, 'We're fighting for our lives, so we haven't got time to worry about whether doing X is educational – we just have to do X for political reasons or reasons of survival.' But if someone were to say, 'It is politically important' (in time of war, for instance) 'that everyone should hate all Germans and believe them to be an inferior race that ought to be exterminated – and that's how we should educate our children, never mind about whether it's true or reasonable', we should wonder whether he was really interested in education at all. He would do better to say, 'Alas, we can't afford to educate our children, we just have to indoctrinate them in order to survive.'

I have suggested, by implication, that 'education' entitles an enterprise which incorporates its own concepts, values and reasons: that one can view situations and practices educationally, just as one can view them politically or economically or aesthetically or in lots of other ways. I find it hard to see how this can intelligibly be denied, since we very commonly say things which imply such contrasts: going on an expensive holiday to some disease-ridden part of the globe might be bad for one's pocket or one's health, but good for one's education. No doubt 'education' marks a pretty broad concept, hard (but not impossible: see Wilson, 1979) to define; but nobody seriously thinks that 'education' can mean just *anything*. Someone who said it was educational for children, or was part of their education, to be taught falsehoods, or to be consistently prevented from thinking, or to be given memory-destroying drugs, would not know how the term 'education' was normally used; yet all of these might, without logical absurdity, be seen as desirable in certain circumstances on various ideological or other grounds. Education at least seems to have close logical connections with learning, and that in itself is sufficient for it to stand as a broad enterprise with its own values and virtues.

This point does not depend on an analysis of normal usage. We could, for instance, try to make do with some more general term – 'upbringing' or 'what we do to children' – which would allow us to include the examples above (teaching falsehoods, etc.); but pretty soon we should want to make some distinctions between different aspects or goals of 'upbringing'. We should recognize the differences between a concern for a child's health (medicine), and his/her appearance (aesthetics), and his/her learning (education). Again, we should of course recognize the connections between these – medicine can make one's appearance improve, and one can learn to be healthy. But this would not destroy our awareness of the different enterprises and types of goods.

On what, then, do we rely if not on normal usage? One sort of answer might run as follows. We might say, 'Look, surely it is at least clear that these distinctions are *possible* both in theory and practice: that is, they are consistent and based on real rather than imaginary differences. It is one thing to regard a child as a physical object, and to be concerned with the proper functioning of his body or (a secondary distinction) its appearance; it is another thing to regard the child as a conscious creature that can apply his consciousness to acquiring knowledge and mastering skills – that is, as a learner. And we can – indeed we do – set up contexts or forms of life which mirror and pursue these different concerns. The distinction is *recognizable*.' And if our interlocutor did not immediately recognize it, we could teach him. In the same way, with reference to political education itself, we could teach (show) him the difference between regarding the child as a mere recipient and parrotter of a particular political ideology on the one hand, and encouraging the child to stand back from a number of ideologies and criticize them, thinking for himself and being concerned for truth in general rather than just one particular view; and we might mark this difference by 'indoctrination' on the one hand and 'education' on the other.

Suppose now that our interlocutor made the slightly more sophisticated move of recognizing the category as a possible one – or even as one actually used in practice – but maintaining that the establishment and use of categories was itself political or ideological. He might say, for instance, 'Yes, I grant that it is possible to distinguish in this way, and of course if you have the kind of ideology that stresses the importance of autonomy, reason, mutual criticism, free choice and so on – roughly, a liberal ideology – then you will wish to set up a category, and call it "education", and engage in various practices within it. But why should we do this? Isn't the question of whether we should do it an ideological or political question?' What should we reply to this?

Two basically different replies are possible. One is that the category is desirable: that there are good reasons for anyone, whatever his political or ideological persuasion, to use it. We might say, for instance, that in a world – which would surely be any world – where truth is not always obvious or easy to get, and in which lack of agreement leads to conflict and bloodshed, it is desirable to sit down and learn things so as to arrive at rational answers; and that children should be brought up (educated) to do this, rather than just to absorb and parrot particular answers given to them by other people. It is, indeed, hard to see how *some* kind of concern for truth and knowledge, in an arena in which particular ideologies are not taken as given, could not be regarded as at least sometimes desirable. This could be denied only by someone who thought, to put it briefly, that there was no such thing as truth or knowledge, in the normal senses of those terms: that is, by an extreme relativist. The idea that 'everything is political' does indeed often collapse rapidly into relativism. To criticize this more fully here – I have done so elsewhere (Wilson, 1986) – would take us too far from our main topic; suffice it to say that, in the absence of a belief in some kind of objective truth or reasonableness, even a debate about relativism itself is pointless.

The other reply is stronger: we could say that the category is inevitable or inexpellable for any human being, perhaps for any rational creature. Some categories – space, time, cause – are clearly of this sort; so might certain human enterprises be. Thus the idea of medicine, the title of an enterprise concerned with physical well-being, seems inexpellable for creatures who have bodies that they want to be in a fit state and minds that can think about how best to achieve this. Could there be a society which was not concerned with the learning of its children? It seems plausible to say that any society will necessarily have some values and truths to which it is attached, and which it thinks important for what it takes to be good reasons; and this in itself implies some desire to pass these on to its children, so that the children will have to engage in some sort of learning process. Moreover, since people (which includes children) are always liable to question and think for themselves, a minimal arena for education rather than mere indoctrination seems to be inevitable. Notions like showing, explaining and giving reasons for will be in place, and that is sufficient for at least an embryonic form of education.

That is, of course, an extremely brief and hurried explication of an important basic idea. It would be necessary to explicate the category of education in much more detail in order to do the job properly: to mark its limits more exactly, and to specify its goals, virtues, procedures, goods, reasons and concepts. But it may be enough to show that education is a suitable case for such treatment. The basic idea, however, needs bringing out more clearly. It is that, although many concepts, distinctions and categories are not necessary for human life, some at least are, and amongst these are categories marking basic human enterprises. 'Enterprise' is not perhaps an ideal term here: I have in mind certain general stances, interests or, as it were, pairs of spectacles which we put on when we wish to view life in a certain way, with regard to certain kinds of goods (*species boni*). Thus we have, and perhaps cannot avoid having, an interest in good appearance or beauty: we use words like 'neat', 'tidy', 'attractive', 'elegant' and so forth; we have a category, albeit ill-defined, called 'aesthetics'; and we gain some kind of good, or satisfy some interest, in this way – 'aesthetic pleasure'. Politics itself is a basic and inalienable enterprise of this kind: how could human beings not have some interest in the proper running of a social group or *polis*, since human beings are inevitably social creatures, and indeed could not grow up to be human except in the society of others? 'Morality' looks like another candidate; 'religion' another, though perhaps less plausible as a candidate for inevitability. Clearly our first step is to define the categories more clearly: only then will we be able to see what status each category has.

It will not, I hope, be too boring to point out that the same basic moves apply if we use 'ideology' instead of 'politics'. I have seen no clear account of what 'ideology' or 'ideological' are supposed to mean. But, to cut a long story short, they must either refer to some *specific* business or department of life – the kind of thing that Marxists, for instance, or Christians or Existentialists go in for, some reasonably well-formulated set of values and doctrines, some kind of 'ism' – or else they refer to *any* set of beliefs and values without qualification. The former seems the more plausible use: it would be odd, outside the pages of a sociological textbook, to describe my concern for my children, or interest in mathematics, or pleasure in doing crosswords, as 'ideological'. The term suggests some rather more high-minded, or high-temperature, or well-articulated, set of doctrines: it is not too far away from the ideas represented by 'faith' or 'creed'. But be that as it may, if *any* belief or value is to be called 'ideological' or part of an 'ideology', then of course educational beliefs and values will count as such along with the rest. That is, of course, an empty victory for those who wish to claim that education is necessarily ideological. On the other hand, if 'ideology' is used in a more restricted sense, then it will – like 'politics' – demarcate some category or enterprise that is not the same as the category or enterprise demarcated by 'education', and the arguments used above will apply. We may add here that it seems important, if we are going to play around with a category marked by 'ideology', to determine just what the category is and what the enterprise is supposed to be about – what its purpose is, how one performs well in it, what virtues are required and what vices to be avoided by someone going in for it. This is, generally speaking, as much neglected by aficionados of ideology as by aficionados of politics.

The practical importance of clarifying categories and enterprises is surely clear enough: only by distinguishing them, and allowing due space for each, can each be successfully practised. As a teacher I need to know what space I have for the enterprise of education (perhaps not much in Nazi Germany, for instance): what goals and values are inherent in the enterprise that I am obliged to forward; what virtues and skills I need to forward them effectively; what sort of training I need to acquire these. Sometimes the answers are tolerably obvious; sometimes not. (A parallel but more difficult case is the function and training of ministers of the church: the question arises 'Is there something specific, *sui generis*, which ministers of the church can be expert in which is not already taken care of by educators, psychotherapists, economists, doctors and others?' The same point arises with 'social work', whatever that is supposed to be.)

Many people will be impatient with this attempt to make (admittedly hard) distinctions at this level: they cling to the fashionable idea of everything being mixed up with everything else. So, indeed, at a practical level, everything is: no one denies that somebody paid as a teacher, for instance, will have to do plenty of things that do not normally count as teaching or educating – just as doctors have to fill in forms, which does not count as medicine. But the only hope of doing these different things well is to start by distinguishing them, together with their goods and reasons. The flexibility and suppleness which are required of those who practise these various enterprises come only with some understanding of the differences between them; it is the attempt to assimilate them all to a single enterprise – politics or some other – that leads to rigidity.

The resistances to these (perhaps rather obvious) procedural points are in themselves interesting. There is currently a strong dislike, amounting to hatred and alarm, directed against the whole business of distinguishing. We have spoken already of the current passion for 'integration' of school subjects and of pupils with other types of pupils. Part of the fear may be that any kind of distinction ('discrimination') or segregation produces ghettos, because distinctions lead too readily to evaluations which will condemn certain categories to unfair treatment, if not to outer darkness; and that fear is not wholly irrational, though we have always to remember with Aristotle that justice is not the same as equality or homogeneity. I suspect that the fear goes deeper; it is almost as if the mere act of distinguishing threatens the integrity of one's personality, arousing fears of the schizophrenic. Perhaps the current refusal to accept the values of any solid authority, the desire for 'liberation' above all things, leaves us with a kind of internal vacuum and uncertainty, so that we feel obliged, as it were, to huddle together for warmth rather like children abandoned by their parents. It is into just such a vacuum that new, and perhaps even more irrational, authorities are liable to step; and if we want to avoid that horror, we have to be somewhat bolder in the task of mapping out categories and enterprises according to the dictates of pure reason.

But, of course, it is just this idea of 'pure reason' which causes the alarm – again, perhaps because it suggests some sort of authoritarian demand which has to be resisted. We have to face the fact that many people dislike the very idea of transcendental categories, seeing them as some kind of doctrinal truths which may be forced on them if they are not careful. Certainly care has to be exercised, but we may be cautious, even suspicious, without being paranoid. Perhaps only the personal experience of truth-seeking in a context of fraternal trust will persuade such people that submission to reason is not like submission to a tyrant.

Chapter 4

Liberalism and Consensus

Finally, in this part of the book, I want to address the worries of those – very many – people who are genuinely uncertain about whether the idea of moral education as a form of thought in its own right is a *practical* one: that is, whether, whatever its intellectual merits in principle, it is psychologically *strong* enough for it to form a working basis in any society. Such people may not be simply wanting to reinforce their own partisan values, though that temptation must always be noticed and resisted; they may feel that *some*, perhaps almost *any*, set of partisan, first-order values is necessary to keep ourselves and/or others on the rails. That is a serious and respectable view, not normally faced squarely by those of liberal ideas and disposition.

I shall use the term 'liberal' without prejudice, though I hope to make clear in what follows that we are not talking about some specific or partisan ideology that this term might imply, but rather about certain principles and procedures of pure reason. This is important in setting the general scene, which is surely familiar enough. For a great many people the image of liberalism is essentially connected with what seem to be purely negative or at best procedural ideas. The liberal is in favour of such things as open-mindedness, absence of prejudice, tolerance, moderation and seeing both sides of a question. In an extreme version, he may even descend to relativism, and appear to think that no one opinion or practice is better or worse, more true or more false, than another. But in any case he seems to have no substantive or solid or non-vacuous set of values: by tolerating everything and seeing all sides of the case, he stands for nothing firm. He does not fight for any cause, but at best merely keeps the ring for others to fight in. This, it may be believed, is commonly not enough for most people, who will then demand some more substantive set of values, some cause to fight for. They should be prepared to define and defend 'the fundamental values of our western inheritance', or at the least to establish in society some kind of 'moral consensus'. Or they may demand something much more sharply defined, like the varieties of fundamentalism to which both Christians and adherents of Islam have recently become attached. The question then arises of whether this is inevitable, of whether liberalism is inevitably so vacuous that it cannot satisfy the demand for substantive values.

This picture, as I have said, is a very familiar one, and it would be foolish to dismiss it as pure fantasy. Perhaps it contains some important historical or sociological or psychological truths. Whether it contains *necessary* or *logical* truths, however, is another matter. Of course if 'liberalism' is so defined as to include the notion, whatever exactly that may be, of vacuity or insubstantiality, then the thesis becomes logically necessary; but that may be too easy and cheap a victory. For such a definition seems at least premature.

The first point that occurs to one is that, since liberals do in fact back certain values, it must be superficial – or at the very least, insufficient – to say merely that those values are 'negative'. For any injunction phrased in a negative sort of way, such as 'Don't lie' or 'Don't steal' can be rephrased positively, as 'Tell the truth' or 'Respect other people's property'. That is to say, there must be positive goods – truthfulness, or the enjoyment of one's own property – which give these negative injunctions some *point*. Behind the apparently negative injunctions and practices backed by liberals – free speech, religious toleration and so forth – there must be positive goods to which liberals are committed, and can be very powerfully committed. So, too, if we describe some liberal values as 'procedural': if we believe in voting rather than fighting, or in courts of law rather than duels or civil war, there must be certain (indeed fairly obvious) *advantages* flowing from these procedures. The benefits of peace are no less 'substantive' than the attractions of war; indeed, in certain obvious respects, they are clearly much more 'substantive'.

This line of argument, indeed, can easily lead us to see liberalism as one ideology amongst many, each with 'substantive', and hence controversial, values. Some prefer war to peace, the excitements of piracy to international laws about safety on the high seas, the collective dynamic of a partisan and fanatical crusade to the more easy-going tolerance of a liberal democracy. I do not, however, take that to be at the heart of liberalism – not, at least, in any sense of the term that is worth defending. For the merits and demerits of particular regimes or styles of life are, indeed, both controversial and highly context-dependent; only a fanatic, and no liberal, would insist that one particular regime suited all cases. The (true) liberal's main point is surely not in *that* sense 'substantive': I mean, he would not insist on a particular life-style or social set-up if (1) the members of that society preferred a quite different system and/or (2) there were practical arguments to show that the liberal's preferred system worked badly. The central thesis of the liberal is not ideological but logical or philosophical. He thinks, to put the matter far too briefly, that other human beings should be treated as ends in themselves, that so far as possible business should be done with them by negotiation and not by force or other kinds of non-rational pressure, that there is some sort of basic moral equality between individuals, and that from this flows the immense importance of rational procedures, or procedures of negotiation, between individuals – the whole apparatus of justice and reason. The principle of universalizability, of which some philosophers have made so much (see particularly Hare, 1981), lies at the heart of this idea; and this principle – in essence the Golden Rule, the idea that there is nothing specially privileged about one's own wants, desires, ideals or views – is meant as a principle of pure logic or reason, not as some kind of ideological or partisan creed.

A lot of philosophical ink has been expended on this question: the question, that is, of whether there are considerations of pure reason, or non-ideological considerations, which have or should have force for any person. A great deal turns here on what we are to mean by such terms as 'consideration', 'ideology' and, in particular, 'force': do we, for instance, look for something which has, as it were, motivational force or just logical or 'rational' force? Bernard Williams, for example, in a series of brilliant if somewhat depressing works has shown us some of the difficulties in applying pure reason to ethics; and I do not deny that many, no doubt most, of the key issues are as yet unresolved. But I want to insist that there are 'liberals' in this sense: that is, people who feel at least that there is a real and important distinction to be drawn at some level between (1) considerations that can or should apply to any person, or any person prepared to think seriously about ethics and language, and (2) particular or partisan values of a more substantive or less generalizable kind.

These at least are the kind of 'liberals' I am talking about in the present context; and it may help us to avoid becoming entangled in the above debate to put the matter hypothetically. We shall say, 'If – only if – there are such considerations, which would naturally include things like logical consistency, a recognition that there are other people in the world who have wants and desires, agreement that it is possible to make *mistakes* (a crucially important notion) in morality, and so on – or even if, at least, there are social groups who do in fact distinguish these considerations from more substantive disagreements, along the lines of (1) and (2) above – then we can raise our question "Is liberalism (in this sense) strong enough for a moral consensus?"'

We may also concede ground in another area, mentioned obliquely above: that is, in respect of motivational, as against purely 'rational', force. Most liberals, in this sense, such as Hare (1981), seek only for considerations that are rationally compelling, and then, as a partially separable enterprise, turn to the question of how, in education and elsewhere, to make them motivationally compelling also. Indeed, our question, the question about the psychological viability of liberalism (can it be strong enough?), could hardly arise otherwise. If, as perhaps Plato thought, we could find features that were at once logically and motivationally effective, we should be home and dry already. But it is hard to believe – particularly for any parent who is actually engaged in child rearing – that there will not sometimes be some gaps between reason and motivation.

We may legitimately turn, then, to the original question. If there are, or even if there are thought (by liberals) to be, certain absolute truths of reason or logic of the kind mentioned, we need to face the difficulty of how these truths, considerations, rational procedures, or what you will – treating other people as equals, tolerating their views, accepting the rules of criticism and rational debate, and so forth – can represent any more than, to put it in psychological terms, a burden on the self or the ego which will be, for many people, intolerable; even if, as of course is the case, obedience to them brings benefits in the long term. We seem to be stuck here with what is essentially a Freudian picture (most clearly painted in his *Civilisation and its Discontents*), according to which human beings are essentially self-centred ('autistic' might be a useful term here) and acquire such things as prudence and justice only with great difficulty and, as it were, against the grain. '*Of course*', it will be said, 'people ought to be reasonable, and of course this would bring them great benefits; but the fact is that reason is hard to practise and inevitably fragile, and if liberals take their stand on pure reason they must expect constant disappointments.' That is equally a Platonic position: Plato thought that only a few people were capable of serious rationality in society, and that the rest of us had better be trained to obey them.

If we remained stuck in this position, we should have to adopt a strategy very commonly, perhaps almost universally, adopted by governments and societies even in modern so-called 'liberal' countries. Abandoning J.S. Mill's crucial distinction between public and private morality – roughly, between actions that harm others and actions that do not – we should attempt only to get some kind of popular ('democratic') agreement on values. Thus, if the majority of people in the UK think homosexuality to be immoral, then heterosexuality would form part of the 'moral consensus' and homosexuality would be outlawed as intolerable; and so with all other values and practices, irrespective of any general Mill-like principles of tolerance. The consensus would then be as 'solid' or 'substantive' as people, moralizing in their natural non-liberal state of mind, wanted it to be. First-order moral judgements, untempered by any criteria of tolerance or universalizability, would simply be collected and institutionalized. It would be possible for people to say – as, of course, each one of us with a part of himself very much wants to say – something like 'Such-and-such a practice just *is* morally appalling, dreadful, obscene, intolerable; never mind whether it can be shown to do harm to others, or whether other views are possible, or whether a perfectly well-integrated society could exist with such practices, it just *ought not to be*, and we will outlaw it.' It would not help with our present problem to say, 'That involves an abandonment of rational procedures, and may also involve persecution and other similar evils of which we already have had more than enough experience', for the reply would then be something like 'Well, maybe so, but at least it gives a solid consensus; liberalism – rationality, if you like – is just not workable, even if we have to pay the kind of price you speak of.'

It is important to see that this claim need not, if properly presented, involve an abandonment of logic or rationality in a wider sense. Suppose that we all agree on the absolute priority of certain goods for society – survival, for instance – and suppose further that it can be empirically demonstrated that people will not fight for, or even work for, their country unless they have laws which prohibit and punish certain types of behaviour – sexual deviance, for instance – which *in themselves* do no obvious harm: then it would be reasonable, if regrettable, to have such laws. We should say, 'Yes, it is a pity we have to punish homosexuals (or whoever) – they don't really do any harm in themselves, but unfortunately unless the moral feelings of the majority are expressed and enforced in this way, they lose confidence in their society and the society goes down.' It could even be that all (potential) members of that society would agree or contract in advance, along Rawlsian lines (Rawls, 1972), to have sexual deviance punished in this way, since all would have survival as a priority; so the society would not even be unjust.

The crucial question, then, turns out to be something along the lines of 'Are there, in fact, certain types of behaviour or phenomenon which, although not harmful in themselves – that is, not inevitably harmful to any rational creature in the way that pain or fraud or theft is inevitably harmful – nevertheless are so psychologically important for human beings that they have to be treated as if they were harmful, in order to preserve vital social values or for other similar reasons?' That question of course is far from clear, but it is significant that it has not in general even been seriously faced (e.g. in the famous Hart–Devlin controversies in the 1960s), let alone answered. It may of course be said that the question is an empirical one, for psychologists or sociologists; and so, in part, it is. But there are also a number of essential philosophical points which have to be made.

Perhaps the most important of these concerns the immense difficulty in identifying certain features as (1) *important* enough and (2) *inevitably* important. It is not enough for (1) to show that a feature generates high-temperature reactions in a society, nor for (2) to show that it generates these reactions in all societies. Thus it is quite possible for people in some, perhaps all, societies to get very hot under the collar about, for instance, 'keeping women in their proper place', or about the awfulness of some sexual practices, or even about what kinds of food should be eaten; but that goes no way to show that these reactions are, as it were, written into human nature as such. We are all fallible mortals, liable to prejudice and fantasy and violent emotional reactions; if we do not want our deep feelings to be written off by blithe utilitarians as mere taboos, we shall have to do more than demonstrate their intensity or even their universality – *pace* certain anti-utilitarian philosophers who have stressed such universality (Wilson, 1979, with references). There may well be deep, and deeply emotional, problems in ourselves which the human race has yet to solve or perhaps even to face squarely.

A much better shot, but still not good enough, would come from a Freudian-type locker, or from any reasonably sophisticated theory of child development. We shall say, in some language or other (anti-Freudians must forgive the terminology here), something like 'Look, the human super-ego does not, and cannot, develop solely or even primarily by rational liberal instruction. Certain features, perhaps connected with keeping one's body clean (toilet-training), with sexuality, with some sort of restraint when eating and drinking, are bound to figure importantly and universally; bound to, because these are part of the inevitable furniture in the world of the young child. These features are not just tiresome taboos which can be grown out of, mere detritus which the adult liberal can easily shed; they are, as it were, symbolic for a person's whole moral effort and attitude. Thus it is not just accidental, or unnecessarily reactionary, that when people feel morally threatened in society they tend to concentrate on things like sex, food, dress, hair, cleanliness and so on – however little these things may seem to *harm*, in any utilitarian sense. Similarly, on a personal level, actions like shaving before breakfast or keeping one's hair tidy may in themselves seem comparatively insignificant; yet – as with old people, for instance – failure to perform these simple actions may represent a deep loss of confidence in life generally, perhaps an unwillingness to keep going. They are important because, developmentally speaking, they are *structural* features in the psyche, even if they are not structural in the real world, and we have to treat them as such, rather than dismiss them as some sort of Victorian hang-ups.'

There is much more force in this line of argument than most liberal thinkers, certainly most philosophers, have allowed; but it does not show what has to be shown against the liberal notion of moral consensus, that these features must be *enforced on adults*. The idea most clearly set out by Strawson (1974) of making a distinction between public morality, which has to be enforced if we are to do business with each other, and private morality, which each individual or group can practise on its own without demanding the conformity of others, can still be upheld. It is, to say the least, not clear that the structure of the individual psyche can be sustained only if that individual can enforce his developmental history on others. The paranoid, indeed, believes that he can only survive and be safe in a world which mirrors his own values, and will no doubt try to enforce them on others because he takes the mere existence of other values to be dangerous to him. But it is not inevitable that people are paranoid. Further, the liberal, in the manner of Strawson, will not only allow but encourage the existence of subgroups or enclaves – one might say, clubs – whose members willingly agree to enforce particular types of behaviour that cannot be shown to be demonstrably harmful to human beings as such; indeed, the psychological merit of such decentralized institutions as the home is precisely that they allow individuals latitude to live out their own preferred values, however neurotic or unreasonable. Allowance may also be made for those individuals who are incapable of any other life than that of the hermit or isolate. Such allowances provide a kind of playground, as it were, for those of us (no doubt all of us at times) who find it too strenuous to live all our lives according to Mill-like principles of tolerance.

Such considerations as these, albeit far too briefly stated, may be sufficient to show that there is no strictly logical inevitability in the weakness of liberalism. But they also show, as we saw earlier, that liberalism is psychologically vulnerable to paranoia, and the question remains of how the liberal is to display his goods in a sufficiently positive form to retain the individual's loyalty and emotional investment. It may still be thought that those goods, though in principle 'positive' rather than 'negative', are too remote, too hard to understand or to pursue, for them to attract the loyalty of more than a few people; people who, perhaps fairly predictably, will be psychologically secure, and to whom notions like tolerance, intellectual debate, autonomy and other much-canvassed liberal virtues make a ready appeal. But what about the masses of people who are socially oppressed, or intellectually feeble, or psychologically insecure? Does not almost any historical period suggest to us at once that these latter will not be likely to find the security they need in a liberal consensus?

As things stand I believe that to be clearly true, but that is because liberals have paid insufficient attention to the psychosocial background that must sustain liberalism. The essential constituents of that background are, fortunately, not far to seek. We must look first at the family, in which, if the child-rearing process is successful, paranoia is diminished by a parental attitude which has two essential features. (1) The parent feels affection towards the child, shares with him, rejoices and suffers with him, cares for him, loves him in his own right and irrespective of merit, and creates a structure for him which provides security by keeping anxiety at a minimum. But also (2) the parent mediates reality for the child, insists that he is subject to rules and discipline, that he works as well as plays, that he learns to treat others as equals and considers their interests, and that he has a sensible attitude to authority. These two together constitute love. Without (1), love lacks the affection and warmth and compassion which the child needs in a harsh world; without (2), love degenerates into a kind of false 'caring' which treats the child merely as a recipient, and prevents him from facing reality. It is, in fact, fairly easy to see undue emphasis being placed on (1) or (2) both in actual families and in institutions, including the wider society. In schools, for instance, current ideologies move uneasily between the twin poles of (1) 'caring' for children, particularly those who can be represented as belonging to oppressed minorities, whilst allowing a degree of indiscipline and laziness which cannot be rationally defended, and (2), perhaps less fashionable nowadays or perhaps coming back into fashion in the western world, a passion for work, discipline and self-help which may easily forget about the idiosyncratic, unconditional affection and tenderness which all people need.

The essential task of all institutions here (schools are only the most obvious example) is to provide a context which enables and encourages these two elements. Institutions which are designed purely to 'care' or purely to 'discipline' must fail. Everyone, however old, ill, stupid, handicapped or weak, requires the discipline of reality; everyone needs to do some work in the proper sense of that term – that is, to make some responsible contribution to the public good, whether paid or not. Equally, everyone, however young, strong, healthy and intelligent, requires the support of sympathy and affection. It is precisely the merging of these two elements which produces a mature person, the potential liberal: somebody who is strong enough and feels loved enough to enjoy doing business with and for other people. Such a person, to put the matter in analogical political terms, will both partake of socialism in its basic sense (*socius*, a friend or ally) and willingly participate in the pressures of reality (whether economic or other) that right-wing parties have constantly stressed. Neither the caricature of a 'wet' social worker who never blames his clients nor that of a hard entrepreneur who thinks only of economics is in place here.

The model of a game, so often used by philosophers in the last few decades, is very much in place in this context. For games are (1) meant to be *enjoyed*, to be pleasurable in themselves, and also (2) are *rule-governed*, involving the acceptance of authority and the equality of all players. Much that happens in good schools and families is on the analogy of a game: that is, a rule-governed activity (not just a creative mess of autistic individuals) which is attractive to the players (not just the stern demands of a non-negotiated authority). The players of a game are, crucially, *together* (whether or not the game is competitive) in their activity: they are sharing something which they all want to share, not unlike the psychologically even more basic cases of sharing food and drink, or mutual caresses. It is by such shared activities and rituals that a benevolent super-ego is built up and liberalism made possible. This is, of course, a form of communication; a simpler form than the more sophisticated intellectual discussions so prized by liberals, but all the more powerful and universally effective for that.

There are of course all sorts of communal tasks which, unlike games, are not hived off from reality but have external points, and all sorts of communal rituals and other activities which are neither games nor tasks. The problem for liberals, particularly in education, is to identify those forms of interaction, of doing business with other people, which are suitable for individuals of different ages, abilities and interests, and to make them sufficiently attractive and rewarding. Of course it is, or at least it seems, much easier to do this if there is already some kind of common structure or ideal: if, for instance, we are fighting a war against a common enemy, or are all adherents of a particular religion or political creed. But the temptation to seek for this kind of consensus must be resisted, if only because, *ex hypothesi* (since the consensus will be ideological), some people will be left out: it would no longer be a *liberal* consensus. It seems to us easier to revive old values, or to start some new partisan movement of 'liberation'. Even in our search for a sound psychological basis for liberalism, we are inclined to overlook the importance of the various ordinary, but immensely powerful, forms of 'doing business' with other people, and seek for something more dramatic or high temperature. But that line of approach merely repeats the problem.

These points, though important, may also seem to convey an

impression of naivety and to leave some problems unsolved, for *de facto*, as we all know, there is in many groups often just not enough fraternity or 'doing business' for us to rely on for liberalism to have a fighting chance. We do not have to think here of extreme cases, like the Nazis or the religious wars and persecutions of the Middle Ages; we need think only of the immense difficulty which adolescents, at least in our culture, have in trying to establish their own identities and at the same time preserve some sort of rational communication with their parents. This raises a question which is directly relevant to the problem of whether liberalism is 'strong enough': that is, how is the liberal to behave in such circumstances?

Of course the liberal (in Nazi Germany, for instance) may simply lack the power to affect matters to any considerable extent. He may protest, take various kinds of dramatic action, plead, argue and, in the last resort, decamp; he cannot control the norms or ethos of the group. But where he can – and this point is very important for educators – he must surely use his power to establish and enforce the procedures of reason wherever this is not counterproductive. There is nothing very original in this point: every parent knows that it is desirable to make his children (so far as he can) attend to, respect or at least be aware of rational procedures, (1) because otherwise other people are disadvantaged (the boy bullies his little sister, or whatever) and (2) because, anyway, the child needs in his own interest to be educated in that sort of way (what else, indeed, could 'education' properly mean?). At the same time he will appreciate the difficulties which children and adolescents, not to mention adults, have in this kind of learning, and will realize, as I said above, that if it is sold too hard or enforced too strongly, then what he does as a parent may be counterproductive. A *via media* has to be found between the context of non-directive psychotherapy, where no pressure is supposed to be used at all, and a more military context in which no allowance is made for the individual's difficulties, privacy and independence of spirit.

The important thing here – and a point which not all liberals have fully grasped – is that, whatever his *tactics*, the liberal educator must be thoroughly committed to his *aims*. A parent may not think it wise to enforce rational discussion on, say, a rebellious adolescent at every opportunity, but he will make it clear, at all times, that those are the norms and values which he firmly stands for. Certainly he will not make the (obvious but common) error of thinking that liberal *aims* necessitate liberal *methods*: there may well be a case for a very firm insistence, even against the natural grain of the pupil, on the pupil's submitting himself to the procedures of reason. Unless liberal educators themselves display in some form the strength of their commitment to liberalism, they are bound to appear wishy-washy. They have somehow not just to engender trust and fraternity by 'doing business' with others, but – and Socrates is a paradigm example here – to be anxious to stand up and be counted. That is hard not just because it may demand personal courage, but because it is difficult to make clear to unsophisticated and frightened people just what one is standing up *for*; liberal aims are less easily grasped than ideological ones, and gestures of personal courage are empty unless they also educate people. (Socrates at least had the advantage of a good publicity agent in Plato.)

Briefly, then, I am arguing that liberalism can thrive if, but only if, liberals – and again, particularly liberal educators – can (1) understand the logical and psychological bases that liberalism requires and (2) translate these into educational and social practice. Some understanding of analytic philosophy and post-Freudian psychology must surely be helpful here, and it is somewhat depressing that these intellectual tools are not often brought into play either in education or in society at large. That is, in itself, unsurprising, for the deployment of those tools is only possible for those who are already secure enough in their liberalism to prefer them to various kinds of ideology. Ultimately we are caught up in a largely deterministic circle: psychological security, in particular freedom from both the uncritical acceptance of authority and the paranoid rejection of authority in general, is required for the careful consideration of the problem, but only such careful consideration can lead to a solution which will increase such psychological security. Not everything is thus predetermined, however: insight and rationality can do something, and even if they cannot do much, their contribution is all the more precious.

CONCLUSIONS

I believe that any teacher, parent or other practitioner in education who has firmly grasped the points made earlier in this part – that is, one might say, anyone who has managed to retain enough conceptual clarity, common sense and freedom from fantasy in respect of the notions of authority, discipline, reason and education – should be able to draw his own conclusions about what sort of background is necessary as a precondition for moral education. He should also be able to see what practical moves are needed to establish that background – indeed, since he alone will be familiar with the local conditions in which he works, he will be better placed than I (or any other theoretical researcher) to determine such matters. However, it may help if I state briefly one or two conclusions which follow from, or are inherent in, what we have said so far.

There are two basic points which might be said to sum up the whole business:

1. The practice of moral education, as of any other kind of education, needs a firm and clear background of *authority* and *discipline*. This means that those in charge of the educational institutions – chiefly the teachers, who are the experts (if anyone is), with of course the assistance of parents and other interested parties – must be authoritative and powerful enough to enforce *obedience* upon their pupils. The rules of the institution must be clear, fully publicized, properly explained to the pupils and backed by sufficiently powerful sanctions to ensure obedience. In other words, we require a framework of legitimated order within which to educate. (I have discussed these notions more fully in Wilson, 1977 and Wilson and Cowell, 1990.)

2. The authority of educators must be bound and governed *not* by the criteria of any partisan religious, moral, political or other beliefs and values, or by any kind of ideology, but by the notion of education itself. Education has its own values, chiefly concerned with the pursuit of learning, truth and reason, and must not be contaminated by beliefs and values external to itself. The educational authority asks the question 'What rules will best help our pupils to *learn* more?' *not* 'What rules best instantiate or promote our particular ideological (moral, religious, political) values?' (This, too, is discussed more fully in Wilson, 1977 and 1979.)

It will be seen that we have, so far, discussed only the background or preconditions of moral education, not the process of moral education itself. But that background is extremely important. Characteristically, we have to admit, most schools and societies (and not a few families) do not in practice follow (1) and (2) above.

Either, as happens in most liberal societies, there is a loss of nerve about authority and discipline, with a good deal of resulting chaos, so that condition (1) is not realized; or they feel unable to establish any firm authority except on the basis of a partisan ideology, as happens in most totalitarian or absolutist societies (where Christianity, Islam, Communism, 'democracy' or some other ideological basis is taken as primary), so that (2) is not realized. It is hard to say which mistake is worse, but certainly these two mistakes lie at the root of our failure to get the preconditions of moral education properly set up – just as they lie at the root of our failure to understand what moral education itself is. It is primarily because we are confused about authority in this way, either (1) distrusting and virtually abandoning it altogether or (2) basing it not on educational and rational values but on ideology, that the groundwork of the whole subject is still not properly secured and we can take no effective steps forward.

As I have said, this is primarily due to our own inner fears and fantasies, which I have tried to conquer in what I have said so far in Part One. It is tempting at this point to go on to describe what, in practice, might be some features of a saner approach to education in general: for instance, an increased autonomy and greater power and responsibility given to teachers, so that they are more effectively in a parental position (*in loco parentis*); the ways in which teachers can initiate pupils into an understanding of the notions of authority and discipline; the specific values, and hence rules, which education (not ideology) necessitates; the part to be played by government and other central agencies; the specific virtues and training that educators require; and so forth. These have been discussed in literature already mentioned, however, and I shall be more than content here if educational practitioners will accept the general conclusions and devote their thought and practical efforts towards realizing them in the very different political and other conditions that prevail throughout the world. At least we can then establish a proper background for moral (and other) education, and can go on to consider moral education in its own right. This is what we shall now do in the following parts.

Part Two

The Philosophical Basis

Having obtained a clearer understanding of at least some of our prejudices, fantasies or hang-ups, we can return now with a more open and free mind to the questions posed at the beginning of this book. If we are to talk seriously about moral education, we need to know (1) what sort of ground we should put under the heading of 'moral' or 'morality', and (2) what are the criteria of success for performing well in that area, what kind of qualities or bits of equipment we need to count as being educated in morality. We shall still feel the temptation to backslide, pulled by one compulsion or another in one direction or another – perhaps still towards the idea of setting up some 'solid values' as an authority, some unquestioned *content* on which to base moral education, perhaps towards the more despairing ideas of relativism, perhaps in yet other directions. We shall need to be reminded, from time to time, of what it means to be *educated* in this (and other) areas, but we can now perhaps afford to allow ourselves to tackle (1) and (2) more directly.

In doing this we shall not just be trying to make sure that we have a proper basis for moral education which we can *then use for* educating our pupils. We shall also be trying to gain an understanding of morality which we can *pass on* to them. Some of us, naturally enough, may be impatient with the (often complex) philosophical arguments and descriptions of morality which I shall mention in what follows: we would like, as it were, to get the thing settled and then move rapidly to practical action. But it is crucially important that we appreciate to the full the form of life and thought with which we are concerned, and for this we have to grasp the basic issues as firmly and deeply as we can. Giving our pupils a proper idea of (1) what morality actually *is* and (2) what its basic principles are, is perhaps the most important task we have. Here, one might say, we are all pupils, all needing to immerse ourselves thoroughly in the nature of the subject. Hence I make no apology for going into the matter in some depth; even if what I say is wrong or inadequate, I hope at least to make the importance of the philosophical basis clear.

Chapter 5

The Meaning of 'Moral'

If someone were to say, 'Look, your book is about moral education, and it even has the word "moral" in the title, so before going any further I'd like to know what "moral" means', and a philosopher were to reply, 'Just shut up about that because what I want to do is to tell you how to live, or how words like "good" and "ought" work, or whether there is such a thing as moral knowledge, or what the point of morality is, or whether morality pays', we might think it a bit steep. Yet nearly all moral philosophers implicitly do just that. Why is this so?

Some philosophers seem to maintain that such an enterprise is in principle misguided: roughly, on the grounds that 'the concept of morality' (to quote a misleading phrase) is essentially mutable or 'contestable'. Any plausibility this view may have rests either on a confusion between words and concepts, or on a misunderstanding of the nature of concepts. To speak briefly (for a longer critique see Wilson, 1986), of course the meanings and associations of *words* may change; and of course our 'idea', in a loose psychological sense, of (for example) feminine beauty may change – we call different kinds of woman beautiful at different times. But 'the concept of feminine beauty', in one clear sense of such a phrase, means something like 'the range of meaning covered by the phrase "feminine beauty" as used by such-and-such a group of speakers'. A range of meaning is what it is; if it changes, it becomes a different range – a different concept. The word 'moral' may be ambiguous, or mean different things to different groups of speakers at different times; and people may call different things (behaviour) moral, just as they call different women beautiful and different things good. Perhaps this is all that these philosophers really want to say, but it is misleading to put it by saying that the *concepts* marked by 'moral' and 'beautiful' and 'good' (i.e. what a predetermined group of speakers means by the words) are contestable. We can 'contest' what the group means only in the sense that there may be philosophical or linguistic arguments about what the concept actually does mean (how the word is actually used). We can also, of course, argue about the facts: someone who thinks that, say, fornication corrupts the soul will count fornication as a moral issue, just as someone who thinks it harmless fun will not. That, again, is not a difference about what we *mean by* 'moral', but in part a difference about what the facts are. Similarly, the concept of health is shared both by those who, say, think it essential to clean one's teeth immediately after every meal and those who think it makes no difference to tooth decay.

Other writers take it for granted that there is no single and coherent concept marked by 'moral'. I say 'take it for granted', since such assertions are not backed by any adequate analytical argument from usage. They use this alleged ambiguity and vagueness as a licence to pursue their own particular philosophical interests and theories, in a way not much different from (and not much less destructive of public agreement than) that in which philosophers of earlier generations used it as a licence to promote their own particular moral values; to lay down what is to count as moral has, albeit indirectly and at one remove, just as strong a practical effect as to lay down what is morally right. In any case, even granted such ambiguity and vagueness (which I do not grant: see below), the question still arises of what categories and distinctions, amongst those that are or could be made, it would be wisest or most profitable to adopt; and about this they say little or nothing. Theoretical interests are allowed to prevail over taxonomic ones.

Others again profess an interest in establishing the actual usage of 'moral' but, when it comes to the point, lay down without argument a usage which fits the particular enterprise in which they happen to be interested. Thus Warnock at the end of one book (1967, pp. 75ff.) makes a strong and entirely justified

> plea for investigation of the word 'moral'; for if we do not investigate the sense and scope of this word, how do we know what the phenomena are which moral theory is to deal with? To be uninterested in the *word* is to be uninterested in the subject – in what it is that distinguishes this particular subject from others.

This makes it all the more disappointing that in a later book (Warnock, 1971), the title of which (*The Object of Morality*) might give grounds for hope, he makes no such investigation though he is eminently qualified to do so. In that book he simply *takes* (there is no other word) 'moral' to be limited to interpersonal morality: that is, to a department of life concerned exclusively with the regulation of a person's interests in reference to the interests of others. This enables him to say (pp. 78ff.) that such virtues as industriousness, courage and self-control are not moral virtues, since of course they can be deployed purely in one's own interest: 'they are virtues all of which a very bad man might have'. As a piece of taxonomy this is not convincing (see Wilson, 1971, pp. 251ff., and below), but it is pretty clear, from the absence of linguistic argument, that taxonomy does not interest him.

That an enquiry of this kind is almost universally absent from the work of leading moral philosophers of the older generation – philosophers brought up on, and sometimes by, J. L. Austin – is sufficiently remarkable. One searches in vain for it through the works of Hare, Warnock, Williams, Foot, Bambrough, Mackie, Anscombe and others. Other writers of a different persuasion (Phillips and Mounce, Winch, Beardsmore) say many illuminating things about morality – or at least about such concepts as integrity and purity of heart – but again show little interest in how the area may best be *defined*. Even in a book with the title of *The Definition of Morality* (Wallace and Walker, 1970) no contribution considers at length how the word is actually used. The reasons for this are not far to seek. Just as laymen often like to think of morality (religion, education, etc.) solely in terms of the particular moral codes (religions, educational systems, etc.) to which they themselves adhere, or which flourish in their own societies, so moral philosophers have their own particular philosophical interests which they wish to pursue under the heading of 'morality', and hence want to define, either tacitly or by stipulation, 'moral' in a way which fits those interests.

The most lucid and honest writers are overt about this: Hare, for instance, says (1981, p. 55) that 'the best policy will be to admit that the word is ambiguous and even vague', but I doubt whether it makes sense to describe *words* as 'vague'. There is, as I shall show, a certain sense in which 'moral' has a very general – I would rather say, a very *basic* – application, but no sense in which it is (even, so to speak, if it could logically be) vague. The idea that it is *ambiguous* is a bit more plausible. Most obviously, it has been pointed out that 'moral' can mean (1) virtuous in some prescriptive sense (opposed to 'immoral') or (2) connected with human character (or something of that kind, opposed to 'non-moral'). Certainly there are different forces, perhaps different uses, here; whether different senses (which I take to be required for a serious use of 'ambiguous', as with river banks and money banks) is more doubtful. 'Scientific' refers to a particular form of thought or department of knowledge; it may also refer, as a laudatory term, to a certain attitude or type of procedure – we say that a person is not approaching a problem 'scientifically'. Is that an ambiguity? The same goes for 'religious' and perhaps other terms like 'artistic'. Are there ambiguities here? I should say not, preferring a more stringent concept of ambiguity; but perhaps one should say rather that we can speak here of ambiguity if we want to and provided we recognize the distinctions. I do not propose to pursue this further, since we shall be exclusively concerned with the category-making sense of 'moral' (opposed to 'non-moral'); this discussion has been intended to show only that we cannot pre-empt the need for analysis by writing the term off as *obviously* ambiguous or vague.

Again, it may be thought (Wallace and Walker, 1970, pp. 4–5, 148) that 'moral' and 'morality' are ambiguous because we can speak of 'morality' *sans phrase* on the one hand, and of 'British (Polynesian, mediaeval, etc.) morality' on the other; similarly, it is sense to talk of my moral beliefs and principles, but not of my moral law or point of view. But this does not amount to an ambiguity in any serious sense: we can speak of 'science' *sans phrase* or of 'British (mediaeval, etc.) science' without being tempted to say that 'science' is ambiguous; and the reason why we cannot speak of 'my scientific truth' or 'his scientific point of view' has nothing to do with any ambiguity in 'scientific'. General enterprises like science and education take on or appear in particular local forms, without losing their essential nature, any more than the game of chess loses its nature, or the word 'chess' changes its sense, when we talk of British or Soviet chess.

If we clear the decks of theory and attend to usage, we may first be struck by the remarkable wideness of most dictionary definitions of 'moral', a wideness that at first sight seems to offer the taxonomist no help at all. We have entries like 'concerned with character or disposition' (*Concise Oxford*) and – still more general – 'of or belonging to the manners or conduct of men' (*Chambers*). Our natural reaction is to doubt whether any and every point of character, disposition, manners or conduct will count as moral. If we look up 'character', 'manners' and so on this is confirmed: their definitions are far too wide. Indeed some take us right back to where we started: the *Concise Oxford*, for instance, gives under 'character' the definition 'mental or moral nature', 'moral strength'. Nearly all philosophers have tried, overtly or tacitly, to narrow this down by, so to speak, *partitioning* morality or separating it off in some way from other features of character and conduct. Thus some claim that morality is concerned with a particular *content*: it is confined to certain kinds of goods only, and uses only certain kinds of reason. Some take it that morality has to do only with what is *overridingly* important in our dispositions, manners and conduct, without restrictions of content and reasons. Again, some hold that morality arises only when the interests of *other people* besides the moral agent are concerned, or when *society* puts some special kind of pressure on all its members to conform to a rule. It may seem that some kind of partition or separation is essential if we are to avoid the apparently excessive generality in our dictionaries; nevertheless I shall argue that all these moves are misconceived, though there is of course an element of truth in each.

We can see our way to a more satisfactory account by considering common usage. Fowler (1965, p. 370), remarking on features common to all dictionaries, speaks of the two phrases 'moral victory' and 'moral certainty', and says:

> It is so easy to see why m. victory should mean what it does, and so hard to see why m. certainty should, that anyone considering the point by the mere light of nature is tempted to guess that m. certainty is the illegitimate offspring of m. victory ... the OED quotations show that, on the contrary, it is much the older of the two phrases; and though this peculiar sense ... is hard to account for, it is established as idiomatic.

Now he ought not to think it altogether 'easy to see why m. victory should mean what it does'. For 'moral victory' does not mean that one side has triumphed in virtue, if not on the battlefield, or that it ought to have won because of its superior morality. Fowler, if that is what he thinks, is infected with a Kantian or Protestant idea of morality, to be discussed later. A 'moral victory' means that one side can for some reason regard what is overtly a defeat as having the psychological effect of a victory. A team defeated by pure chance, though its general play was superior; a boxer out of training who nevertheless manages to scrape up almost as many points as his well-trained opponent; the British army at Dunkirk, defeated but managing by good luck to save more than might have been expected; these are the sort of cases we think of. We could well substitute 'a *psychological* victory', and 'psychological', in its (slightly slangy but widespread) modern use, can very often be appropriately substituted for 'moral'. A moral certainty is in the same boat: it is something about which one is entitled to feel psychologically certain, even though strict logic or strict evidence might make for more doubt. Other phrases ('moral fibre', 'moral impossibility', 'moral support', 'moral courage') fit in here, and that this is not a quirk of modern English is shown by the appearance of many such phrases in other languages: *victoria moral* (Spanish), *moralischer Sieg* (German), *moralmente impossibile* (Italian), *certitude morale* (French) and so forth.

I am suggesting (no surprise to students of Plato or Aristotle, though the matter is not stated altogether clearly even by the latter: see, for instance, *Nicomachean Ethics*, 1103) that the central use of 'moral' refers to a certain set of underlying dispositions, to the basic ecology, as we may here briefly if obscurely put it, of human desires, emotions and deeds. Before trying to see how this works out in more detail, it is instructive to consider the Platonic parallel with health (for example, in *Republic*, 444). If we look up 'health' in the dictionary (I omit extensive quotation) we find definitions like 'a good state of the body'. Here too we might react by saying, 'But surely that is far too wide: surely it is good or desirable for the body to be beautiful, able to endure cold, capable of reaching a high standard in various athletic exercises, and many other things, yet these qualities, though they may partly depend on health, are nevertheless not defining characteristics of it.' And then we might be tempted either (1) to define 'health' descriptively – the bones and blood must be in such-and-such a state, etc., which will not do because Martians and plants can be healthy or unhealthy without having blood or bones, or (2) to say that 'health' refers only to what a man chooses to count as overridingly important about the body, which will not do because it leaves it open for him to prefer, say, physical beauty to freedom from cancer and dysentery, and to describe the former as 'healthy', which is absurd. We should rather say that health is *basic*; it *lies behind* beauty and physical skills, and cannot be partitioned or separated off from them.

As anything that affects the body *can* be regarded as a matter of health, so anything that affects the soul or character *can* be regarded as a matter of morals; the wide dictionary definitions ('character' and 'conduct') are accurate. When we object to these on the grounds that some things – etiquette or diet, for instance – are surely not moral matters, that is not a criticism of the dictionary definitions: there would be no *linguistic* objection so someone who said that eating pork, for instance, was a moral matter – provided always that he thought of it as affecting character and conduct in some significant way. Our objection is that it does not, and that therefore it can with propriety (but not *linguistic* propriety) be regarded only under other headings (health or diet, perhaps). In just such a way, arguments about whether something is or is not a political issue are not normally about whether it can be seen as having some effect on the state or society: almost anything *can* be thus seen. They are about whether its general effects are such that it *ought primarily* to be seen as political rather than in some other light: whether, for instance, we are to judge a piece of literature by its effect on society (politics), or its beauty (aesthetics), or its effects on individual character and conduct (morals), or its cost (economics), or under some other *species boni*.

I suspect that the basic mistake here is to make the primary connection of morality with action. The mistake is made because of a confusion between what is central to the meaning of 'moral' or 'morality' on the one hand, and what is, in various kinds of practice, of central moral importance on the other. It may be that (1) what men do to each other is more important, in some kinds of practice, than (2) what they feel towards each other or how their souls are basically constituted, though it at once becomes clear, because of the logical connections between action and motives, that the distinction between (1) and (2) is very hard to make; but that does not, of course, go any way at all towards showing this to be the most important element in the meaning of 'moral'.

In some ways what we do is primary; what we feel or desire, or how we conceive of the world, secondary. This is partly because what we do is often, not always, the most faithful representation of what we feel or desire, because actions speak louder than words – they are often better *evidence* than anything else; partly because what we do to other people (perhaps also to ourselves) is often more important than what we feel about other people (and perhaps also about ourselves); and partly because, when it comes to making moral rules, it is often easier to describe – and certainly to prescribe

– actions than feelings. Even these points, however, require amendments. Sometimes, at least, actions can be misleading or ambiguous; and we cannot understand actions properly (sometimes not at all) without understanding their antecedent intentions and desires – indeed it is impossible, in human action, to separate the two elements. Sometimes, again, people require of us that we feel in a certain way towards them – in sympathy, for instance – rather than that we perform any actions. There are moral rules and principles which relate to attitudes rather than actions: we are commanded to love one another, not or not only to perform loving actions.

There are other viewpoints from which what we do is secondary – just as, in medicine, the patient's overt behaviour or symptoms are secondary to the antecedent diseased state of his body. In this sense morality is primarily about our basic mental or spiritual make-up, about the health of our souls. The parallel with health is important, and words like 'soul' necessary, because, of course, no one wants to say that our 'detachable' mental powers, our skills and talents, are matters of morality, or at least not necessarily so. For just as a man can be physically healthy without being an athlete or immensely strong, so a man can be morally satisfactory without being a concert pianist or immensely clever. We are talking not of talents, but of basic dispositions. It is an open question, indeed, just what features of our mental make-up are 'basic' in this way (perhaps some degree, or kind, of intelligence should be counted in); but on any account some are not.

The idea that moral thought or judgement is most easily assimilated to the imperative mood and to prescription goes along, obviously enough, with the idea that morality is about action. Such an idea is deficient at the linguistic level, just as it is deficient phenomenologically and developmentally. 'Good' and 'bad' are experienced before 'ought' and 'right'; it would not be conceivable to imagine a child, or any growing rational creature, who had grasped the notion of following a rule, let alone a moral rule, before grasping the notion of the goodness (or desirability) or badness (undesirability) of certain things. Wanting comes before grasping the idea of standards of behaviour; indeed the latter makes no sense except in the light of the former. The first thing that strikes a person is that some state of affairs is desirable or undesirable; that there is something good or bad, pleasant or unpleasant, which impinges on him and in the light of which he wishes for some change. Correspondingly, the first thought he will have is a wish: he 'says in his heart', to use one philosopher's phrase, 'Would that such and such were so!' This is best represented by the optative mood, and the distinction is clearer in languages which have such a mood, as in classical Greek. The imperative comes in only when he conceives himself as an agent, bringing about the change. In the third person, commonly translated in English as 'let such and such happen', this distinction is blurred: that phrase may serve as a sort of imperative, but also as an optative expressing a wish. The distinction is in practice often fine, because of course people grow up quickly to see themselves as agents, not only as merely wishing for things; and, as has often been said, wanting (though not wishing) implies trying to get, as well as thinking something desirable and worth getting. But it exists: *sic volo, sic jubeo* expresses two ideas and not one.

The over-stringent connection of morality with action goes along with the idea of seeing morality as essentially a social device or institution. There is some attraction in following such writers as Strawson (1974) and Warnock (1971) in at least distinguishing the two realms of (1) social need (others' interests and other-regarding virtues) and (2) individual ideals (our own interests and the self-regarding virtues). But where this does not overtly and unfairly monopolize the word 'morality', as Warnock does, it still leaves the connection between the two realms unexplained. On our own account, accepting the parallel with health, we shall say that the person with a moral (psychological) disease may not only (1) affect others' interests, nor only (2) affect his own, but also (3) display (non-causative) *symptoms* of his disease, which fall into neither of the first two categories. (Some sexual behaviour, for instance, may harm others; some may harm oneself; but some may simply be symptomatic of an unsatisfactory psychological – that is, moral – state.) The connections here are as important as the distinctions. Similarly, although the logical inevitability of praise, blame, resentment and so forth is clear enough, and has been well demonstrated by Strawson (1974) amongst others, morality extends more widely. To use our parallel, it is as if a concern with *public* health – the spread of infectious disease, for instance – so predominated in a particular society as to connect the general idea of health with this public notion. In an age when almost everything is ascribed to or connected with 'society', this is perhaps not too surprising.

What is the importance of this for moral philosophy and education? The main point is not that philosophers have misunderstood what 'moral' means – that is just a symptom. Even their concentration, which goes hand in hand with this misunderstanding, on one department of morality (public morality, with particular reference to action and the will) would not so much matter in itself, if only other philosophers redressed the balance. The real trouble is that important areas of concern are not considered by moral philosophers because they are absent from our current conception of *morality*. What happens is that the thoughts and pressures from these areas are placed elsewhere, and put under other categories. In religion, literature, psychotherapy (at least of a Freudian variety), reflection on personal relationships, and most views (not only Marxist) about 'society' – a category that for many people has largely replaced 'religion' – these thoughts and pressures remain. Notions like original sin, the pessimism of Freud, the inescapable and (to us) unfair parameters of Aeschylus' *Agamemnon*, the despair and radicalism of much modern literature – all these of course survive. But by relegating them to other departments of life with non-moral titles it is as if, almost by a desperate act of will, we have tried to extricate from such thoughts a department called 'morality' in which there is a better hope of each and every individual performing well, freed – as much moral philosophy has been freed – from considerations about the meaning of life, salvation, Bunyan's slough of despond, despair, a sense of unreality and sin.

It is beyond my scope, and in any case irrelevant to my present purpose, to attempt any account of historical or sociological causes or correlations. We may find it more profitable, if we seek to educate ourselves, to locate this picture in developmental psychology. Roughly, we are talking about an idea of morality that is learned by children, and was learned by us as children, at a fairly early age. It arises from the clash between, on the one hand, a child so brought up that he has scope to challenge parental authority and, on the other, the rules (particularly negative rules) that all parents must impose on such a child. Not all children are brought up with much scope, licence or opportunity to do this, and it is a matter of some interest how far this connects with notions like that of the Oedipus complex and the rise of individualism, still absent in some cultures. But in any case this background incorporates the ideas that the child can always be 'good' if he tries; that being 'good' consists of obedience to an authority; and that the authority will be primarily concerned with certain fairly obvious public goods, such as order, truthfulness and elementary justice. The parent wants the child to be trouble-free in a social context, and this means restraining his aggression by a set of independently conceived rules. It is possible (and in many parts of the world often happens) that the child's individuality and aggression are given no chance, being more or less completely smothered by a set of rituals, by a particular way of life in which no challenge can be offered to parents or the ancestors that stand behind the parents, by a mixture of closely applied care for the child and a refusal to confront his own individual passions, and by an extremely elaborate system of behaviour which avoids any serious threat to the dignity, honour or 'face' of the various parties concerned. (Even the practice of overtly expressed *disagreement* is avoided in many cultures.) But where this does not happen – and arguably it happens less and less in a rapidly changing and shrinking world – the picture of morality is painted in these colours.

That picture corresponds more or less exactly with the way in which many adults view morality: the essential elements of action, the will, obedience, freedom, conscience and others are all there. Of course the picture, and the developmental stage of childhood in which it flourishes, is – so far as it goes – entirely reasonable; it is simply not complete. Omitted from it are such considerations as happiness, dignity, sin, despair, personal ideals and others already mentioned. In most cases the child is simply *left alone* with these. He picks them up, often in a fragmented and nearly always in an uncriticized 'brute' sort of way, from other sources: from whatever love and attention his parents may give him aside from 'morality', from the peer group, from the values of the wider society, and from his own inner reflections and strivings. They are not mediated to him in any effective or overt educational manner. In adolescence he may or may not throw off or rebel against the rule-morality that his parents have taught him, but whether he does or not, his extra-moral concerns are not catered for. Unsurprisingly he may find himself projecting his fears and uncertainty on to 'society', perhaps adopting some Marxist or other sociologically construed outlook; or seek hope in some religion which seems to offer it; or plough desperately through the twists and turns of individual personal relationships and involvements. But it is difficult for him to connect, or reconnect, the idea of morality with the other ideas which have been excluded from it.

How is this likely to affect the way in which any writings or teaching about morality are likely to be received? One natural reaction will be that a rebellious or contra-suggestible person will reject the idea of morality altogether (bound as it is, in his mind, to the way in which the term 'morality' is commonly construed); and that is, I think, the chief reason – there are others – why moral philosophy, as we have it, cuts little ice in some societies today. If he does not do this, he is still likely to view moral teaching in one of two ways. Either (1) he will want to be *told the answers*, as if doing well at morality were primarily a matter of eliciting the right set of rules and principles for behaviour; or else (2) he will think that the answers are already clear, and hope to find in moral teaching – or, more likely, in attachment to some person or creed – some kind of *motivation*, non-rational persuasion, exhortation or inspiration to do what (as he supposes) he already knows to be right.

This very common and very deep split is the most serious obstacle to the advance of practical morality, because it puts out of court right at the beginning the kind of learning which is, I shall argue, absolutely central to the moral life. If (1) we construe the moral philosopher as someone who can tell us, presumably by virtue of his powerful intellect, a set of rules and behavioural principles of which we had previously been ignorant, we shall be disappointed. Most of these are already quite well known; the trouble is, as some people will be quick to say, that they are not practised. Enlightenment in morality is not like advances made in physics or medicine or other kinds of theoretical knowledge, where we require only intellectual virtue and await strikingly new truths dispensed by expert research. But then we have available only the other half of our dichotomy, whereby we fly to the idea that (2) all we need is 'will-power' or 'determination' or 'inspiration'. Then we shall expect the philosopher – more probably, the guru or inspirational figure – to sweep us up in some appealing other-worldly mystique, wherein (as it were, in some kind of pre-Oedipal way) our problems are magically solved; or else we shall expect him to represent the voice of conscience, dourly reminding us of our duty and of what is to be 'good', perhaps with threats of punishment to back it up. But the basic reason why moral virtue is not practised has nothing directly to do with lack of 'will-power', though that concept has its place; it is to do with lack of understanding about what moral virtue is, about its importance for human life, and about the difficulties involved in weaving it into our own lives.

Morality, then, is about the state of the soul; or, if 'soul' is too unfashionable a word, about our basic emotional dispositions and mental health. A number of things follow from this, some of which we need not linger over. First, there will be whole areas of human life which some might not normally put under that heading, but which certainly ought to be there: to take an ever-topical example, sex. Some philosophers have doubted whether there can be a specifically sexual morality, but clearly sex plays a highly significant part in human life, and how a person stands in relation to it – I do not mean only what he *does* – will be a moral matter: to that extent the popular connection between sex and morality enshrines an accurate intuition. Secondly, morality is inescapable: it will not be open – as for Warnock (1971) it is open – for any rational person to say that he is not interested in morality. For no one can rationally be uninterested in the state of his own soul. Thirdly, morality will be of basic and in general overriding importance. That is not quite a tautology, since it is logically possible – that is, not incoherent – to be primarily concerned with non-moral features of one's own and other people's lives: with intellectual talents, for instance, or beauty, or physical strength. But the obvious point is that moral dispositions underlie and in a sense control these; it is these dispositions which allow or prevent such things from flourishing or being used. In order to *make space* for even the wildest ideals – say, an ideal which stresses the importance of courage in combat (never mind who dies), or of aesthetic achievement (never mind if the artist's children starve) – there has to be a background of dispositions in action that will sustain a world in which these things may happen. This will be true of any human enterprise, since any such enterprise (whether or not incorporating a particular ideal) requires this background for its success; we cannot pursue science, or politics, or medicine, or education, or the arts, or any such thing without there being people whose basic mental constitution, so to speak, is geared to allowing these practices and to forwarding them. Without love of truth, willingness to co-operate and accept criticism, determination and accuracy, and many other moral virtues, little of importance in human life can flourish.

How then should we proceed? On this view of morality, we should be naturally inclined to look with more favour on a long-standing tradition in moral philosophy which does in fact (or did originally) view morality as analogous to health, and seeks to elucidate those qualities of the soul which are necessary for human flourishing – that is, the moral *virtues*. This is, generally speaking, Plato's approach in the *Republic*; and a good deal of it survives both in Aristotle and in the Christian thought which incorporated and extended Aristotle's thinking (thus the idea of *salvation* is essentially the same as the idea of spiritual health, as the Latin *salvus* implies) and to a lesser extent in more recent moral philosophy.

It turns out, however, that the task of making a satisfactory list of moral virtues runs into a great many difficulties. One of the most basic of these is connected with the point that what we are going to count as a virtue must be, at least to some extent, dependent on some overall view about what sort of life we think men ought to lead, or what is to count as 'human flourishing', or something of that kind. But we have no tradition of agreement about what human flourishing is, so that we run into problems about (1) what concepts of virtue are parochial and what of permanent value, (2) what languages or traditions to draw on, (3) what basic facts of human psychology are relevant, (4) what connection to make between virtue and the will, (5) what *sort* of mental phenomena to classify as virtues (dispositions, capacities, etc.) and (6) what to do about the possibility that the virtues may conflict. I have tried to say something about each of these elsewhere (Wilson, 1987); suffice it to say here that the problems seem to me too severe to make them a satisfactory basis on which to proceed.

We may, as I have said, distinguish (1) between different *types* of virtue or bits of moral equipment. Thus we can distinguish between self-regarding and other-regarding virtues and vices, or between executive virtues (courage, determination) and non-executive or judgemental virtues (justice, wisdom). There are problems about these and other distinctions, but it is certainly possible to sketch out various types of person or 'character', in the manner of Aristotle or Theophrastus, who can be described as lacking or possessing this or that virtue or swathe of virtues. The *Nicomachean Ethics* does this on a broad canvas; Theophrastus' *Characters* are much more varied and detailed, thereby raising the question of just what criteria one is to use in adjudicating the number of virtues or 'characters', or the importance of the distinctions that may be used to produce a typology of them. All this, however, is different from trying to distinguish (2) various *arenas* or departments of life and morality in which human beings perform. Thus a very popular if rather broad distinction, perhaps first clearly stated by Strawson (1974), is between what one might call public or social morality on the one hand, and private morality or ideals or ways of life on the other. Other distinctions, similar to this in spirit but significantly different in certain respects, could be drawn: between cases where relationships among people are comparatively close and cases where they are impersonal or non-existent; between that part of morality which is concerned with other people's interests and that part which is concerned solely with one's own interest; or between those moral arenas which chiefly require some kind of *doing* (for instance, just and competent public administration) and those more to do with *feeling* and the emotions (certain aspects of personal relationships, and one's own attitude to life in general).

A good deal more could be said about these taxonomic problems, though I incline to believe that most of what can usefully be said for practical purposes would turn on what particular social roles or other arenas a person is supposed to be operating in (as an administrator, a spouse, a friend, a citizen and so on). We should have to produce some view about what roles or arenas he *ought* to operate in (though perhaps some are inevitable for him), as in (2) above, and then list the qualities he needs, as in (1). The production of such a view seems to me at present beyond our powers, for the reasons I gave before in reference to the virtues: in particular, because we do not yet know enough about the nature of man or human psychology to be able to go into that much detail. How public or private a life people should lead, whether they should all be husbands and wives if they have the chance, the comparative importance of egalitarian friendship as against having children of one's own, how much personal relationships are to count as against attachment to nature or the arts – these and other questions remain to be answered. It is probable that some overall view of the morally good life, if it can be sustained, will help us to answer them. But for the present we must proceed by different guidelines.

The most profitable approach, as things stand, seems to be that we should first consider what might be called the public arena, and confront the general question of how a person should stand in relation to other people and their wants, outlooks and interests; and in the first place, how he should *behave* or what he ought to *do* in this arena. This is, of course, to go back to the picture of morality as essentially connected with action, the will and other people, a picture I have criticized earlier as too partial or one-sided, but which nevertheless clearly has an important place in any moral life. This is in fact the arena to which many philosophers, particularly in recent years, have devoted most of their efforts, and there are a number of procedural advantages in beginning with it. First, for reasons given earlier, most people are likely to enter into morality as a whole by that route. Secondly, only the most extreme moral theory would claim that this arena ought to be avoided by all or even most people; and so long as there are societies or groups of people at all – which, since some of such groups are families, means so long as people continue to exist and reproduce their kind – the arena is plainly inevitable. Thirdly, and most important for our purpose, it can be shown how a consideration of reason and virtue in this arena leads us inescapably to a wider view of morality and the good life. We shall plunge, then, into this arena, remembering however that it is not the whole of morality but – albeit of immense practical import-ance – only the aspect of it which is likely to strike us most forcibly.

Chapter 6

Justice and Love

Why should we bother about other people? This is perhaps the question most often raised by educators, and more philosophical ink has perhaps been expended on this question (which I put in a deliberately vague form with the phrase 'bother about') than on any other question in morality. For philosophers who assume (1) that morality is primarily concerned with action (rather than with feeling and being) and (2) that only strictly deductive argument is either relevant or decisive in morality, the question that Plato raises in the *Republic* – roughly, 'Is justice profitable?' or 'Should one be the sort of person who gives weight to other people's interests?' – will characteristically be construed in a certain light. It will be construed as something like 'Are there logical constraints which compel any person to *behave* or *act* justly?' Attention will then be focused upon particular cases in which, at particular times, some person faces a choice between his own interests and those of other people; especially upon the legitimacy or illegitimacy of his using certain concepts or *words* (notoriously, 'ought') and upon whether or in what sense we can say that he has good *reason* for his choice to *do* something.

It is worth tracing, however sketchily, as a kind of preview, the way in which this construction is likely to affect (and has actually affected) the argument. Some philosophers, following Kant, will interpret 'reason' in a sense that divorces it fairly sharply from motivation, and claim that the notion of giving weight to others' interests is inherent in certain concepts marked by 'ought', 'right', 'good' and so on. (The principle of universalizability is one version of this claim.) Others will pick holes in this by various methods, all of which amount to a refusal to accept these limitations placed on the concepts: in particular it will be held that there are senses of 'ought' which escape them, and that the notion of having a reason for action cannot be divorced from the agent's own desires and interests. (The dialogue between these two parties can be followed in the writings of Hare, Winch, Foot, Williams, Mackie and elsewhere.)

Perhaps it will help to use a parallel. Suppose, which I take to be actually the case, that we have certain public criteria of a scientific nature which we commonly use to determine whether or not something is worthy of belief – for instance, whether or not I should believe that my nature is judicious because I was born under the sign of Libra. Suppose also that, though this is scientifically absurd, I need to believe it 'for reasons of my own', as one might say: it makes me happier, encourages me to be more judicious, gives me more self-confidence, perhaps saves me from a nervous breakdown. Now clearly there will be two different sets of answers to such questions as 'Ought I to believe...?' or 'Is it reasonable/rational to believe...?', depending on whether we refer the questions, and the words in them, to the public criteria of science or to the other criteria which operate in my particular case.

Neither set of answers seems ultimately satisfactory. For (1) of course we want to say (a) that *in general* the public criteria should be overriding – we want to ensure and enforce these criteria for belief as a permanent public institution; but we seem forced to admit (b) that no such criteria – not even those that might come under the heading of 'logic' or 'consistency' – should *always* be overriding. Is it not better that a person should contradict himself, or flout the evidence, or indulge his own fantasies, or whatever, if the only alternative is suicide or severe mental illness? Then (2), conversely, we can say (a) that these particular cases can always legitimately override the public criteria; but we must still feel (b) that this is somehow a pity, in some sense 'wrong' or 'not ideal', since we do not see the public criteria as something we can pick and choose at will, to suit ourselves. We do not want to say that it is absolutely all right for anyone simply to opt out of the public criteria for the benefit of his own integrity or happiness.

Just as there is no (serious) dispute about the general merits of scientific criteria for forming our empirical beliefs, so there is no (serious) dispute about the general desirability of justice and benevolence. There may be doubts about the delimitation of certain areas of applicability; it may be disputed whether or not it is in the general interest to have a *laissez-faire* or a socialist economy, to allow overriding duties towards one's own family as against the interests of others, to sacrifice the excitement of piracy and free-booting for the benefits of safe navigation and travel, and so forth. But these disputes are about the general or mutual desirability of certain regimes or styles of life, so to speak, and may still be *ultimately* governed by the principle of giving weight to others' interests, not just to one's own. In effect, we sit round a negotiating table trying to decide what regimes or styles will be best for all of us or most of us; and whilst of course we may make mistakes, we negotiate with the common good in mind. It is necessarily the case that justice, benevolence or some principle of helping and not harming each other pays off, since if it did not we should not describe them in such terms ('helping', etc.). To that extent, and in that sense, morality precisely *is* a device for our mutual profit.

If justice and benevolence are not thought to be inherently profitable for the individual, then we shall see the business of moral education as essentially *ad hoc* and use any stick or carrot to persuade individuals to immerse themselves in the moral form of life and thought. The notion of duty, perhaps in the form of a requirement to speak and act on a certain kind of language (the universalizable 'ought'), will be an obvious stick; the rewards of benevolence, of being nice to others so that they will be nice to you, will be an obvious carrot. But perhaps there is an argument of a different sort, to show that it pays a person to invest in this form of life for its own sake and intrinsically, not to gain other goods.

Discussions of reasons and justice, then, present us with a dilemma, roughly represented by the question 'Are we to take (1) the public form of thought, institutions and set of reasons that incorporate justice or interpersonal morality as basic, or (2) the private interest of each individual? Is our starting point to be the public mode, the "external" reasons that constrain individuals as members of a collective, or the individual rationality of those "internal" reasons which actually have motivational force for parti-cular people at particular times?' On behalf of (1), we can see how extremely difficult it is even to pose questions about the reasonable-ness of justice in such a way that they escape the public form. If we ask, 'Why should one (anyone, in the sense of "each of us", *unusquisque*) care about other people?' then the answer is obvious: if each of us undertakes to do this, it pays off in general all round.

The same applies to any question form which is supposed to produce publicly valid answers – that is, answers applicable to each and every individual: 'Why should *we*...?', 'Why should *a person*...?' and so on. That is, indeed, how the questions normally arise: we already assume the existence of a collective, a number of people discussing what each and every one of them ought to do. So deep-rooted in us is the idea not so much that justice is expected of us, but that reasons should be public and universal. Indeed it is not too monopolistic a move to say that 'reason' is connected with the public and universal (a person only *has* reason if there *is* reason), and that a person may indeed have 'internal' *motivations* but can hardly have purely 'internal' *reasons* in the sense of justifications: to *justify*, as the term implies, has some fairly tight connection with justice, which is a public notion.

It may be said, of course, that if we do start with that (public) basis we are left with a more serious problem about motivation: the public form may be there, and may even (again on public, collective grounds) be reasonable, but why should anyone go in for it? Here by 'anyone' we shall mean not each and every individual as a member of the collective (*unusquisque*), but some or any disconnected individual in some particular context (*quidam*). If such things as justice and altruism are against his own interests – and one may be tempted to think that this must sometimes be true – what reason, or motive, does the individual in this position have? Or what reason or motive can we give him? We are now *ex hypothesi* restricted to 'internal', motivating reasons.

That objection is not decisive as it stands. We shall be likely to reply, simply, that there is indeed a considerable (empirical) task to be performed by way of giving individuals adequate motivation to move from individual to moral (altruistic) rationality; but that, since the public form is (collectively) reasonable, there are no particular (or at least no immediate) philosophical difficulties about it. The task is justified because the public form is justified; we hire psychologists and others who will tell us how to develop the conscience, decrease alienation and self-deception, engender fraternity, produce an attachment to public forms of reasoning (in particular the principle of universalizability) and so forth. We should say that *there are reasons* – such a phrase being in the public domain – why a person's internal reasons should be brought into line with external reasons, the reasons why this should happen being external from the point of view of the disconnected individual, the *quidam*, but internal from the point of view of the member of the collective, the individual who is making some kind of public deal, the *unusquisque*, the person who has some stake in the community as a whole.

All this, however, starts from the idea of there being some 'we', some collective, which has priority over the individual 'I', the *quidam*. From the viewpoint of development psychology that idea is not unattractive: it is easy to see (Hamlyn, 1978) how the whole business of using a language and any form of reasoning, together with other central features of being human, can be generated only in some small collective – the family – in which other people count. It would be nice to think that each of us was irrecoverably landed with the importance of other people (without whose ministrations and parenting we could not have become human), were it not for the palpable fact that, whatever happened to us in an early stage of our lives, we are each of us quite capable of opting out of the collective and following our own individual interests: in a word, of being selfish. Why should some one of us in a particular context not opt out, if it is in his interest to do so? Why should he go in for the public form? And by this we shall now mean 'What reason has he?' not just 'What motivation can we give him?'

The crucial step in getting a person to enter the public form because it is reasonable (not because he already cares about other people, or has some 'internal reason', some piece of motivation, to do so) is often taken to involve some notion of consistency or impartiality. The basic idea here is simple enough, at least at first sight: we say to him, 'There is nothing special about *your* desires. If you think it right and proper that your hunger should be satisfied, that cannot be because it is yours; it must be because it is *a case of* satisfying hunger, so that other cases are on the same footing.' We here represent the person not just as moved to satisfy his hunger, but as thinking it right (proper, correct, reasonable, rational, a good thing) to do so. How far is that representation plausible?

I do not think its plausibility is determined only, or even chiefly, by a consideration of the meanings of particular words, for victory on either side is likely to be too quickly won. Thus it might be (has at length been) argued that, if a person uses words like 'ought' or 'right' about his proposed action, these words commit him to the public mode because in themselves they grant the same licence to others (universalizability). That is a quick victory on one side; but then the person will say either that he is using these words in a different, non-public sense, or that he will use other words which do not have the relevant implication. That victory too may be premature, however, because it may still be the case that, whatever words or senses of words he uses, he cannot in fact avoid the implication. The question is really a phenomenological one, if that term is of any use; a question about how human beings think, or are obliged by their humanity to think, when they satisfy their desires.

Here the ultimate victory seems at first sight to belong to the public mode. A person who wants or desires something is not like an animal who simply tries to get it, or is drawn to it like a moth to the light. He wants it *for a reason*. He thinks, however fleetingly or semi-consciously, that it will satisfy him in some way: give him pleasure, or safety, or power, or whatever. He may indeed not know – though in so far as he reflects, he is likely to have some sort of idea about – why he wants it or what he wants it for, but he believes that there is *something* about it which will satisfy him, something which makes his want more than an external compulsion which he could totally disown. This idea is concealed if we talk of his wants or choices in terms of prescriptions or imperatives; these indeed bring out the connection between his wanting and his acting so as to get what he wants, but they do not bring out the connection between his wanting and his believing that there is something good or desirable or satisfying about the object of his desire. It is this latter connection which makes his want subject to reason: if he comes to think himself mistaken about the desirability of what he wants, he changes the want.

One might put this by saying that there is something which he thinks himself to be *right about*: namely, the desirability of what he wants. What he may (or may not) be right about has nothing to do with his motivation, with the fact that it is *him* wanting it. If he is in doubt, he does not inspect the degree of his passion or the force of his desire; or, if he does, he does so only as a step towards trying to elicit what it is about the object that makes him feel so strongly. What he inspects is whether the object does in fact have some quality or feature which would satisfy him. He considers not whether he is hungry, but whether the fruit he sees is real, ripe fruit, and not made of wax or rotten.

Further, he is – to use a suitably neutral term – concerned with all this because he is concerned to get satisfaction. The 'because' here does not represent a purely mechanistic or animal-like process: he is not like a pig snuffling about to find the particular food that suits it. He is able to *conceive* of his satisfaction, in this or that instance, as itself desirable; and his ability to have this conception makes it possible for him, both in principle and (sometimes at least) in practice, to reject it. He may think, for instance, that he ought not to enjoy the feeling of being well-fed, or sexually gratified, or whatever; and it makes no difference that his reason for rejecting this can always be construed as the seeking of some other kind of satisfaction – pleasure at his own powers of self-abnegation, or something of that kind. The point remains that he does not just move blindly towards satisfaction, but conceives of it *as a good*, or thinks it *justified* (right, proper, reasonable, etc.).

It is at this point that universalizability or the public mode seems to get a grip on me, because my individual wants and general desire for satisfaction involve me, as a self-conscious and reflective being, in the idea that the world ought to be such a place that I can be satisfied and get what I want. Hence I strive *with reason*, not just with effort, to make it such a place; I am involved with justification and not just motivated. (Indeed, 'motivation' can be a very misleading term here, as is the terminology of 'internal reasons'. Human beings are characteristically 'motivated' or moved to seek certain things because they think it right or reasonable to do so, not as cars are moved by the internal combustion engine.) But now it cannot be simply because I am I, or because the satisfaction is my satisfaction, that I am justified. It can only be because I subscribe, or must if I am being consistent and reasonable subscribe, to the principle that wants or needs in general ought to be satisfied. Of course I can *say*, very loudly, 'I ought to have it because I, John Wilson, want it', but the 'because' will make no sense unless I can represent myself as one case of a general principle. That is clear enough if we start with the word 'ought', which means basically 'is owed' and has public force; but I hope also to have made it clear that the central point does not turn on the uses of particular words. It turns ultimately on the inevitable or inexpellable fact that, as a conceptualizing creature, I have either to endorse or not endorse my own search for satisfaction – and on the virtually inexpellable fact that I shall endorse it.

Virtually inexpellable, but perhaps not absolutely so. Philosophers have been characteristically concerned with the egoist or selfish person, who has strong wants of his own and has to be brought into the public mode so as to make space for the wants of others; and since most of us are perhaps like that, no doubt the target is appropriate. However, there are greater difficulties both in practice and in theory with another kind of person: the person who has virtually abandoned the search for satisfaction in his own case, who regards it as hopeless or illusory or in some way improper. We are talking here of the depressive, the guilt-ridden, the nihilistic, the self-destructive. If his own satisfaction is not significant, not worth endorsing, why should he care about other people's satisfaction? He may not want to spoil it by invading it with his own desires, since he has no strong desires at all; but, though in some contexts comparatively harmless, he is very far away from a proper moral state.

Here again we have to resist the idea that morality is centrally about, to put it briefly, getting naughty and selfish people to stop doing evil and harming others. In the public, political, everyday, surface-level world of course that is of the greatest importance. But from the theoretical, or a more basic, viewpoint the naughty and the selfish are just one case of moral inadequacy. The other, or one other, case is presented by the indifferent and the despairing. Both are examples of inability to love, which is why the notion of love turns out to be central. We are told to love our neighbours as ourselves, but if we do not love ourselves this injunction does not have much force. The importance of self-love is a commonplace in psychotherapy, and something which any sane parent or educator knows perfectly well by common sense, but it is curiously neglected in moral philosophy. We are too exclusively concerned with the distinction marked by 'unselfish' and 'selfish'; the distinction we need to attend to is that between one who loves and takes seriously all people, including himself, and one who is so wrapped up *in* himself – whether in despair, or the search for power, or whatever – that he attends properly neither to himself nor to others. ('Caring', or 'serious', and 'autistic' might mark this distinction.)

Indeed there may even be a conflict between the interests of a moralist who is primarily concerned that human interaction should be trouble-free and those of a moralist who is concerned with mental health or with getting people to be what they ought to be. For the difficulty with the indifferent or guilty or despairing is that they have, or seem to have, no particular desires of their own at all: they have, as it were, given up the search for happiness and meaning. Now certainly one way – some might argue that in empirical fact it can be the only way – of improving such people is to allow or encourage their unconscious anger and aggression to emerge: that will at least give them some sense of their own reality and worth. (Instead of lying about in defeated heaps, the Palestinian refugees or oppressed Bangladesh peasants or underprivileged blacks, or whoever, should take up arms and fight: that is the only way, at least as a first step, to acquiring dignity.) If that is right, it clearly conflicts with public desiderata such as peace and harmony.

Be that as it may, one point to make here is that there are some severe limitations on reason as an inducement to enter the public form. First, though we have not discussed this, it is not clear that one ought always to be consistent or impartial or reasonable, if it does not always pay; and secondly, a person's desires may be so weak that, though he may be brought to be reasonable and to universalize, he has nothing much to be reasonable and to universalize *with*. It is, I think, fairly clear even in advance that much more needs to be said about the notion of a person's *attachment* to other people, not just about the logical network which he must accept if he is to be reasonable. It is not so much that the network does not help us with the problem of motivation – how to persuade people to accept it – but that it is not and cannot be at all points comprehensive and effective.

Moreover, there are difficulties or at least limitations that apply to any formal system that attempts to bind individuals into the public mode. I have mentioned the case of the person who has too weak desires, but that is only one instance of a general question about what sorts of desire people ought to have. Any theory which *starts with* individual desires, and takes them as given, ought to be seen as a *political* rather than a moral theory. Sitting round a table, as a collective, we may for some purposes take our desires as given, and work out – attending to the logic of what Hare calls 'the moral concepts' (good, ought, right and so on) – what would in effect be a basic *constitution*, or principles of interpersonal procedure, which enabled us to negotiate our desires with each other. Justice is primarily a political notion. But in other contexts we may discuss with each other whether, in fact, our desires or preferences are correct or appropriate or wisely conceived, and for that we need a quite different kind of theory. We need to know not just how to negotiate our interests with other people, but what our interests actually are: what sort of construction to put on notions like 'happiness' or 'a good life', what the state of our souls ought to be.

Our present problem about entrance into the public mode is, in fact, just one example of our tendency as individuals to prefer our own conceptions of what is good, our private advantage and private worlds, to the public truth or the public facts of the public reasons. It is tempting to jump in too quickly here and write off, or write down, such cases as by definition 'irrational' or in extreme forms 'insane'; and so perhaps – so powerful is the influence of the public forms over our language – they may fairly be called. But we are not to be frightened by words, and we still want to know whether or not the individual is right in doing this. Why *should* he 'face reality' or operate in the public domain if it hurts too much? Is it not clear that many people are often happier – and happiness is surely worth something – being autistic? By what arguments does one think that they ought to be pressed into the public domain? Again, it will not do to say simply that *in general* the public forms of thought pay off, either to the individual or the collective, for that leaves open the option of shelving them on those (perhaps rare, though not all that rare) occasions when some public form does *not* pay.

The trouble here, I think, is the tendency to think that public forms must be shown to pay *instrumentally* or *extrinsically*. Somebody who simply used the natural sciences for external purposes – to exploit nature, make life more comfortable and so on – could comparatively easily opt out of them when they became painful: when they threatened some religious belief, for instance. But someone who was committed to science – and that means, also, having the prior commitment of wanting to understand the natural world as it is, not as we might choose to invent it – could not do this: his commitment would prevent him. In much the same sort of way, someone who sincerely loved or valued another person would find it difficult or impossible to view that person instrumentally, so that he could forget about the person's interests when necessary. The public forms, as I have rather clumsily called them, come into play because we tolerate some degree of commitment to certain realities: the reality of the physical world, the reality of other people who have desires and needs just as we ourselves have, and so forth. The forms simply incorporate the tools we need to institutionalize that commitment and put it to work. So what we need to ask is something like 'Are there internal (self-interested) reasons why an individual should be thus committed, reasons which make it profitable for him to be so, yet reasons which are intrinsic to being committed and not just instrumental?'

Like Plato, I think there are such reasons so far as justice is concerned, but I am bold enough to claim that Plato did not see clearly enough into the heart of them. I suspect that this was because he put the paradigm case or model of such commitment –

personal love – behind him, for reasons of his own (some of which are traceable in the *Symposium*). But however that may be, we should begin by considering such a case. A loves B, and we mean by this, of course, not just that A has some kind of passion directed to his image of B, but that he takes B seriously, knows what B is like, faces the reality of B, and is committed to *that* – to the real B. Now, what is there in this for A? Not, centrally, anything we might want to call 'pleasure': B may bring A a lot of grief, anxiety and so forth. Happiness? Here we rightly feel 'yes and no': no, if 'happiness' is tied too tightly to notions like contentment, security and lack of anxiety; but yes, if it involves also the idea of an enriched consciousness and a meaningful existence. (A full analysis would end in a 'yes', in my view: see Wilson, 1979.) The idea of life being worth living, 'meaningful', in any case *preferable* (A would not *do without* B, however much grief B caused him)? Certainly that; and that, after all, is the kind of thing we are after in seeking intrinsic reasons for commitment.

Before going more fully into the ways in which love, happiness and a satisfactory life interlock with each other, let us see how far this sheds light on our present problem. There are, as I see it, two residual difficulties (even when we are clear, as I hope later to get clear, about why love is so fundamental to morality and life in general), as follows:

1. Are we to represent the person who loves as under some kind of compulsion, *incapable* of opting out of his love and care for the other, even on those occasions when they operate to his severe disadvantage (in death, for instance)? Or are we to say he *chooses* to continue his love and care even in such cases? Some philosophers (notoriously Williams) have made great play with the way in which people's particular 'projects' (as he calls them), or local loyalties and commitments, 'take up psychological space', so that people cannot be expected to operate as impersonal utilitarian calculators – their 'integrity' would not allow it. But it is never very clear, in all this, whether it is being said that (a) people *could* not opt out of their particular commitments, or (b) people *ought* not to do so, or perhaps both. This is our present question.

The answer must surely be that they (sometimes) could, but do not want to and – other things being equal, particularly the happiness of other people with their own commitments – ought not to. We can easily envisage (no doubt they may actually exist) drugs or other devices which would obliterate A's love for B, even though their use might obliterate much else in A: his love might form a considerable part of his identity, if that means anything sufficiently clear, or of what makes life meaningful to him, but it is quite clear that he could, in principle, choose to opt out of it. The point is that he does not want to, even when it hurts, and this has something to do with the way in which love keeps one in touch with reality, which in turn has to do with the greater importance for all men of being in touch with reality than of reality having a certain kind of tone (pleasantness). So we need not regard it as somehow a *pity* that A is saddled with this compulsion. It is not that, by and large or in general, love or altruism pays off, so that we need (as Hare puts it, 1981, p. 197) 'firm dispositions of character' which make it difficult for us to opt out of it and keep us up to the moral mark, even in cases where it does not pay off; we are saying, boldly, that it *always* pays off. And that makes it a reasonable (too weak a term, as we shall see) way of life.

2. Then there is the more intractable problem of what counts as reasonable when we do *not* love. If A loves B, all is well because there is a certain sort of (intrinsic) 'reward' in maintaining this posture at all costs. But we are not able, or not willing, to love many people; yet we want an argument to show the reasonableness of being just to them, in some (perhaps low-temperature) sense caring for them, perhaps behaving as if we loved them. Can this still be represented as intrinsically rewarding? Of course we may back such behaviour as leading us towards loving them, and hence getting the rewards of love, but that line of thought will not do enough work. In what way does it pay us to behave well towards people we positively dislike?

The answer here must again have to do with the priority of reality over pleasure, or what looks like pleasure. To recognize that another person has rights (and hence must be treated justly) is, at least, to live in the real world: to accept the world as it is rather than distorting it for our own purposes. To use a somewhat gruesome but perhaps paradigmatic example, we might ask why it is more satisfactory to relate to members of the opposite sex as they actually are, rather than make love to rubber dolls or engage in masturbatory fantasies. It is not easy to pin down just what *species boni* is missing in such fantasies, and extremely easy to say what the difficulties are on the other side (real people are difficult, often tiresome, in any case not tailor-made to our own desires). But what Iris Murdoch (1970) calls 'the familiar rat-runs of fantasy' rapidly come to seem to us – and not always because of the pressure from guilt feelings – worn out, lacking in substance, desperate, boring, frenetic, somehow hopeless. It is as if – or it is in fact that – only real people will do, and that may have something to do with the way in which real people, notoriously parents, figure as love objects in our early lives. The fantasies and dreams that we spin out of our own minds inevitably lack body and substance; precisely by not bumping up against the real, precisely by being tailor-made, they are thin and unsatisfying even in the comparatively short run – in much the same way as a superficially attractive tune wears out our interest and pleasure long before a more complex piece of music which we have to *confront* and *work at* in order to appreciate.

One way of putting this is to mention again the immense importance to us, over and above pleasure, of feeling safe in our own existence. This is more than just a matter of not feeling alone; it is a matter of *having a world to live in*. The child, like the adult, is reassured in his existence not by inputs of pleasure from nowhere in particular, but by seeing himself as part of an objective reality. Perhaps paradoxically, feeling safe in one's own existence is not a matter of extending one's power and fantasies over the real world; indeed if one's fantasies were actually to overtake the real world, or that world to become infinitely malleable, it would be alarming and devastating. There would be no structure to exist in. Safety consists precisely in the rejection of autism, in being able to come to terms with and accept the world as it is, even in its nastier aspects; not – this has to be stressed – either because it is one's moral duty (in an old-fashioned sense) to do so, nor because the world is likely to trip one up if one does not come to terms with it, but because one can only stay sane and secure by doing so.

This is, I think, ultimately what justifies psychotherapeutic practice, as it justifies the acceptance of moral reasoning. It is not that we should 'accept reality' because that is somehow a nobler thing to do, even if it makes us unhappy, or because we shall get into trouble with the police otherwise; still less because we are so to be frightened by the words 'neurotic' or 'psychotic' that we are bullied into accepting some concept of 'mental health' which is not based on what is ultimately satisfactory to human beings – a kind of enforced conformism. Reality, to put it rather dramatically, is the only food we have: nothing else is ultimately edible, and though we may use drugs instead of food we ought always to prefer food when we are capable of eating it. Of course none of us is very capable, and there are many instances in which we simply *cannot* behave justly or altruistically, just as we cannot love: it is not just a matter of trying. But if we cannot, we cannot; the philosopher can only show us why we should take every opportunity of doing so when we can, and every opportunity of improving ourselves so that there are more contexts in which we can. Much (not all) of the actual improvement can only be done for us, or with us, by others: by people who care for us, understand us and are willing to help us face the facts more bravely. That is perhaps the most important thing that people – and not only psychotherapists – can do for each other.

All that will sound rather vague to some philosophical ears: let us see if we can put one or two of the relevant points more crisply. It is a striking fact that if A genuinely loves B, A will prefer to die in B's place. There is nothing irrational about this: A has invested his feelings so much in B that it is preferable to him that B should survive rather than himself. If we now raise the question 'Is it *better* for him?' or 'Is it in his *interests*?' we can see that there is a clear sense in which we have to say 'yes', even though A will be dead. His interests, we might say, *exist in* B whom he loves. In other words, we have to take seriously the idea that A's good, or interest, is not circumscribed by what happens to A. (Indeed, a fairly obvious idea: A cares for or values all sorts of things that are not within himself.)

Now suppose a case not of love but of justice. A does not much like or care for C, but in this case it is reasonable (in the public mode, interpersonally) for A to sacrifice himself for C's benefit – to give C and C's family food which A wants and needs, or whatever. We ask why (in the private mode) he should do this: what is there in it for him? Now either (1) C's interests do count, or weigh, with A: he cares, or invests his feelings, at least to the extent of wanting C's needs to be satisfied: and in that case there is no problem – it can be regarded, so to speak, as a luke-warm case of love, as with B in the earlier example, and some of A's (low-temperature) interests will exist in C. Or (2) C's interests do not count or weigh with A: A has no interest in doing justice. This is the hard case. We ask whether it is in A's interests to do justice, and it seems that we have to answer 'no'. It does not in any sense pay him because he makes no invest-ment in C whatsoever. But we may ask this question in two senses. 'Doing justice' might mean the actual *behaviour* of giving C the food, and there seems no (internal) reason for A to do that. But it might mean adopting an *attitude* towards C which involves things like recognizing his common humanity, sympathizing with his plight, in short doing justice to him as a human being in that situation; and now we shall say that this does pay A, on the grounds that it pays human beings to invest their emotions outside themselves. And then A, with this attitude, will behave justly.

That does not settle the matter, since it seems that we may still ask the same question about the mere behaviour. If he cannot, or will not, adopt the right attitude to C, is there now any reason for his giving C the food? It might clear our minds here to take a parallel. Suppose there is a man who does not yet get any satisfaction from works of art, and who inherits some first-rate paintings or whatever. Why should he not smash them up for firewood? Well, first we say that if he adopted the right attitude to them, learned about art and so on he would find himself investing emotionally in them, so that it would not be in his interests to smash them up. Then, suppose he says that he does not want to adopt that attitude; now we shall say he is silly because he deprives himself of great joy. Then he says that he cannot adopt it: it takes time to find joy in works of art, and he is going rapidly blind or going to die or whatever. In this case there is indeed, so far as I can see, no (internal) reason for his preserving them.

It is very important to see that this parallel does *not* hold good with people. I used the example of art to drive a wedge between (1) adopting an initial attitude towards something as a potential source of satisfaction and (2) actually (after a time) coming to invest in it emotionally. It was rational of the man not to preserve the paintings because, although he could do (1), he could not do (2): it takes time to learn to enjoy art. But this is not true of human beings, at least in relation to their common humanity. The origins and growth of any human being (see Hamlyn, 1978, and further below) are so bound up with his interaction with other human beings that the case is different. There is no question of having to *learn* how to see other people as like oneself, with equally important desires and needs – or at least not in the same sense as one has to learn to understand quadratic equations or Dante's *Inferno*. One has rather to *remember* that they are human like oneself; also to *imagine* what it must be like (remembering from one's own case, or putting oneself in another's shoes) to be C in C's situation. There is a clear sense in which one can under normal circumstances choose or decide to do this, and the doing of it immediately makes C into something valuable, something A has – just *by* adopting the attitude – invested in, so that his interests now exist outside of himself, in C and C's interests.

But what if A really *cannot* adopt that attitude? Perhaps he is drugged or coerced or his mind filled with propaganda or whatever, so that it is beyond his power to see C as a fellow creature. It is, actually, quite difficult to think of cases where adopting the attitude really is impossible for A: nearly all the reasons one thinks of are ones to do with A's own ideas, feelings, prior attitudes and so forth, so that 'the origin of it is in the person', as Aristotle has it, and it is not a matter of external compulsion. Nevertheless, and skirting all the problems about free will, let us say that A cannot. Well then, he cannot; which means that he has no motivation to act justly, and perhaps plenty of motivation to act unjustly; which means that he cannot act justly. In so far as 'ought' implies 'can', it makes no sense to say that he ought (because he cannot); in so far as it does not, the only sense it makes to say that he ought is that he ought not to be in that position, or be that sort of person, in the first place. That is true, and there *are* internal reasons for A's being a juster person.

We suffer from two illusions that make us resist this line of argument (which, in broad outline, is the line adopted by Plato in the last books of the *Republic* and by Freud in *Beyond the Pleasure Principle*). One is comparatively easy to describe: it is the illusion that we know well enough what to count as pleasure and pain, happiness and misery, profit and loss in our lives. But in fact self-ascriptions even of pleasure and happiness are not incorrigible: we can deceive ourselves and (sometimes) recognize that we have deceived ourselves about when we are happy (Wilson, 1979). In particular, we are apt to think that we are happy when we can retain and hold steady the precarious balance that constitutes our conscious minds, a balance between our unconscious emotions and the real world. We take that fragile identity to be our 'true selves', as a person might take the tip of an iceberg to be the iceberg even though the nature and being of that tip is swayed and determined by the larger part that is submerged. We often *do not know*, chiefly because we cannot afford to know, what pains and pressures we suffer from, and are apt to ascribe them too freely to how we are situated in the world rather than to how we are basically constituted. A realistic view of the human condition should remind us that this inner constitution is, inevitably and systematically, beset by very grave difficulties and obscurities: to use a pedestrian term, our moral ecology is *mismanaged*. Even the most obvious pain which comes from the outside world – the horror of torture, for instance – may be less than the pain which we constantly inflict on ourselves, however little we can help it.

The other illusion is harder to pin down, though it stems from the same source. We are apt to think 'But surely, at least sometimes, it *must* be better not to face the demands of reason and reality; there are, after all, many cases where we should count it as just cruel to undeceive people who are in a happy state of illusion. Do we not often need to turn away from truth in order to avoid pain, to survive, to keep ourselves intact?' The last phrase gives the game away. As I have tried to argue, there are indeed plenty of cases where we *cannot afford* to do justice to external demands, and in those cases there is nothing to say except that we cannot, any more than a sick person can jump six feet. We all know what it is like trying to persuade someone to abandon a deeply rooted illusion or compulsion: we meet a brick wall. Neurotic and psychotic symptoms, if we may use these vague terms, are, as it were, the best that the psyche can do in its sick state: if, *per impossibile*, the person were to abandon them, he would have nothing between him and chaos. Because we have, as conscious creatures, to cling to a particular idea of free will and action, we imagine that there is some kind of *choice* at stake here, a choice about which we can moralize. We sustain this illusion because our conscious minds are, as it were, caught between two worlds: on the one hand, we feel the inner pressures from our unconscious that for the most part determine both what we are like and what we are capable of doing (and perceiving), but on the other we recognize to some extent the justice of external demands and feel that we can and ought to meet them. And so – in principle, so to speak – we can: that is, we have the opportunity, nothing external to ourselves is stopping us. But we do not always have the resources.

We conclude, then, that the logical starting point for interpersonal morality must be the individual's own interests. It is not enough, as some philosophers seem to think, simply to say in the manner of Wittgenstein that there *is* a public form of reason and practice quite familiar to us, for that leaves open the question of why a person should go in for this form. At the same time – and thinking now as educators rather than (or as well as) philosophers – we must not suppose that the best psychological or pedagogic starting point lies in the same place. The roots of love are very deep; we are not to imagine children as rational egoists, to whom an appeal can only be made via self-interest. A large part of them is already – that is, well before the age of reason, whatever that may be – invested in the interests of some other people: 'Honour thy father and mother, that thy days may be long in the land' offers an unnecessarily utilitarian reason. To some extent children are already in the public mode. It is this, I think, together with some other fairly obvious bits of natural human equipment, particularly the ability to grasp the concept of a person and to put oneself in another person's shoes, which gives arguments about the rationality of altruism a somewhat unreal air. It is tempting, though perhaps too quick, to say that *we all know very well* what is reasonable and unreasonable here. We *know* that other people count, that they are people like us, that their needs are as important as our own: basically we accept the public form, however much and often we like to wriggle out of it in particular cases. For the most part, the educator confronts not rational egoists totally disconnected from the public mode, but individuals who are mixed bundles of love and hate (not often indifference), selfishness and altruism.

Even if we were dealing solely with rational egoists, it would not follow that the most effective way of inducing them into the public form was by rational argument: various forms of practice and experience would almost certainly be better starting points. There is a whole range of methods running from the 'abstract' method of strictly logical argument, via encapsulations of that argument in stories and parables, through role-play and other devices that help the imagination, to the practical experience of being wanted, valued and loved, or even just hugged and cuddled. Nevertheless – and this takes us back to the beginning – it is essential that, whatever mix of methods is used, at the end of the day the individual fully appreciates the logical points: centrally, here, the point that the public form is in his private interest. For there will be many times in his life when particular pieces of motivation fail, and when he will be tempted to renege on the whole business: to ask, as people obscurely do, 'Why should I be moral?' So he needs to know the answer to this, in order to keep himself going. Of course that is only a necessary condition for keeping himself going, not a sufficient one. It is necessary because if he cannot reasonably believe that there is a satisfactory answer he will have no reason for arming himself with the other equipment necessary for keeping going: in particular, what may be put under the heading of 'faith' or 'hope' – roughly, the virtues of having sufficient trust in the merits and profit of the public form to keep on pursuing it in the teeth of despair or a hostile world. Faith must not be irrational, and hope must be seen not to be vain: that is the importance of the conceptual arguments, however and wherever we are to fit them into any educational programme.

This may also help us to see our way out of a dichotomy which continues to afflict moral philosophers as well as others, roughly represented by the question 'Do we want the individual (1) to attach himself to other people, to care for them, love them as far as he can, at least be interested in them and respect them as equals, or (2) to attach himself to some impersonal ideal, represented by "duty" or "justice" or "being reasonable"?' Each seems to have well-known advantages and disadvantages. Caring or sentiment seems more natural, less bleak and more fundamental (why should anyone bother to be reasonable or just towards others if he does not *care* for them?); on the other hand, it seems fragile, at the mercy of the eddies of sentiment, unprincipled. Duty seems more permanent, ever-present, a guide for all seasons, reliable; but it also seems arid, heartless, too removed from human motivation, at times even irrelevant. We may also say, rightly, that caring fits some contexts (close relationships, for instance) better than duty seems to; and vice versa (in administration or other impersonal contexts we want justice, not sentiment). Most of us in fact work with an uneasy mixture of the two.

To say that we need both is not ultimately satisfactory, because a big part of the trouble is precisely that we see them as basically different and disconnected. Suppose there is a person who spends a lot of time looking through telescopes, watching eclipses, reading about the solar system and so on; now, shall we say he is devoted to the stars or to astronomy? Clearly this makes no sense: someone who is seriously interested in the stars – I mean, who does not just look at them sometimes and make up fantasies about them – is necessarily interested in astronomy, because 'astronomy' is the word we use to mark the way in which such serious interest displays itself. Suppose A spends a lot of time with B, takes pleasure in B's company, likes learning about B and working out what is in B's interests, wants to do his fair share of work with B in some co-operative activity, restrains himself from harming B and so on; shall we say that he cares for B or that he cares for justice and duty in relation to B? Clearly we shall say both; or rather that to be seriously interested in, concerned with, any object for its own sake – to set oneself to face and work with the reality of any object – involves both some kind of desire and some kind of rules and principles. The phrase 'doing justice to' something or someone serves as a useful gap-bridger here: to do justice to a meal, an author or a friend is to take that object seriously with both one's feelings and one's principles. One has to *appreciate* the object, to *respect* it.

We have the illusion that our world or set of objects is divided in two: on the one hand, we have those people whom we love or feel affection towards (which seems to be something out of our control), and on the other there are all the other people about whom we feel nothing but to whom we can, if we are principled enough, at least do justice (which is in our control). The distinction is, at least, far too sharp. If we put sufficient pressure on the notion marked by 'love', distinguishing it from various forms of physical attraction or concealed narcissism, and bringing it into the realm of serious concern for something; and if we put the same pressure on 'duty' or 'justice', distinguishing it from a reluctant set of overt behaviour patterns and moving it closer to the same idea of concern for what the object is like and actually merits ('duty' = 'giving the object its due'); then, having done this, we shall be less inclined to distinguish in this way. The really important distinction is between genuinely serious concern on the one hand, and other ways of approaching objects on the other.

We are misled here, partly perhaps by a romantic (perhaps quite modern) notion of personal love, but certainly by the idea of pleasure. It is as if we relegated pleasure to the sphere of the personal and the idiosyncratic: we enjoy caring for and being nice to those we happen to love, but for the rest we do our duty without hoping for any reward except that of a 'good conscience', which here seems somewhat contrived. But again, we have to remind ourselves of the very strong, if non-romantic, pleasure in doing justice to (doing our duty by) those objects which we take seriously: in trying to get a piece of work right, a room tidy, a party guest properly attended to and made to feel at home, a helper properly rewarded. All these cases are disregarded and separated off too sharply from the idea of caring, because we suffer from a split which goes back in the history of ideas to Luther and Kant, and further back still to Aristotle and Plato, both of whom sometimes regarded pleasure with deep suspicion. The split creates for us two worlds: a world of duty which we must not expect to enjoy, and another world in which we are free from moral or other pressures to do just what we like and enjoy it. By paying our taxes to the former world, we are licensed to make free in the latter. It is like a child who has first to take his medicine and can then choose a sweet. Many people, perhaps all of us in some degree, do indeed live in this split condition, but we must not be tempted to regard it as God-given. If we hang on tightly enough to those cases of genuine love, serious concern, which are within our experience and which, as it were, heal the breach by showing it to be unreal, we can resist the temptation.

Cases of genuine love, when we reflect on them in our own experience, do not come about (at least not directly) by acts of will or moral effort; they appear more as acts of grace bestowed upon us by chance or a benevolent deity. But that too is misleading. The crucially important feature here is *being free to love*, not so wrapped up in one's own fears and compulsions and autistic interests that one cannot bestow serious attention on the object. It is not a matter of direct effort, but neither is it a sort of divine bonus; it is what naturally happens when the human mind can make space for it. Love is the *natural condition* of the human mind, the normal and proper way in which it meshes with reality. Because we tend to look at the extreme, high-temperature, romantic cases, we suppose it to be a sort of magic, but when we remember the down-to-earth cases in which we love our cat or our fireside, we can see clearly enough that this is possible chiefly because of the absence of any internal distraction. We are able to *attend properly* to the object, and such attention turns into, perhaps is itself, a form of love and caring. If we cannot enjoy such space, we are driven into the split mentioned earlier: we have either to do our duty in a desperate and unrewarded sort of way and/or to clutch at pleasure equally desperately. Both are autistic: the unrewarded doing of duty is bound to be primarily a matter of satisfying one's own guilt rather than actually helping other people, and the pleasure that does not flow from properly perceived objects rapidly becomes no pleasure at all – it is more a kind of rebellious demonstration of one's own existence than something seriously *enjoyed*, for, if one is autistic, there is nothing *there to* enjoy.

The logical importance of love, or that acknowledgement of the existence of other people which is the basis of love, can also be seen if we put as much pressure as possible on the idea of being reasonable or rational. Thus Hare, right at the beginning of his book (1981, p. 1) says that 'It suffices now to say that we are all often faced with moral questions, some more tormenting than others; and that most of us, when we have to answer these questions, do some thinking about them', and that the improvement achieved in our thinking by moral philosophy will be in 'rationality'. Rationality he takes to be primarily 'a property of thought directed to the answering of questions' (p. 214). Now it is surely clear that a great many people in a great many situations do not *ask questions* at all, let alone be tormented, about their moral behaviour; they just carry on, often under the influence of some more or less overt and all-embracing faith, creed, outlook or ideal, often under pressure from their own perhaps unconscious desires and emotions when these are not rationalized into any overt structure or belief. They do not ask, for instance, 'Is it actually right to put this Jew in the gas chamber? Ought I to do it? Is it a good thing?' They assume that they ought to do it, because it is part of the master plan, or the will of the Führer, or what they have been ordered to do, or necessary for the achievement of racial purity, or whatever. What might indeed be stark and tormenting questions framed in terms of 'right', 'ought' and so on are avoided because these terms are swallowed up, as it were, in the overall outlook. So long as what one does is 'progressive', or 'fulfils Arab destiny', or is 'in line with modern thought', or is 'truly Christian', or whatever, one has no need, apparently, to ask whether it is *right.*

We can only catch such people by *getting* them to ask questions, not by assuming that they ask them already. If we think, surely rightly, that we are entitled as philosophers or educators to do this – that it is reasonable for us to do it – then we must have a concept of rationality or reasonableness which lies *behind* the one mentioned above. Rationality must involve not just *having* 'actions, desires or moral systems which survive maximal criticism by facts and logic' (Hare, 1981, p. 214), but *desiring* such criticism. Arguably 'reasonable' fits this and other criteria I shall mention better than 'rational' does. When we talk of a reasonable person we think partly of his relationship to other *people*. The reasonable person, then, has a commitment to reason which goes beyond being open to the particular points that the moral philosopher can make to anyone who asks moral questions. He wants to ask questions and get criticism, and it is *because* of this that he is prepared to listen to the moral philosopher.

It is important to see that there is a sort of vicious circle here. We want wicked and selfish people to take other people seriously; to do that, we want them to consider the logic of the moral concepts; to do *that*, we want them to ask questions and have some commitment to reason in general; but that, finally, involves that they take other people seriously. For reason is essentially dialectic: it involves listening to other people's views and answering them, joining and competing with them in the search for truth. A child could not learn how to think, or even to talk, if he did not experience this process, as mediated to him by adults. Unless he trusts other people and takes them seriously, he cannot learn to reason. Everything, therefore, turns ultimately on whether it is better for him to face the world or not, better to do business with reality or retreat from it. The quick answer to this is that it is better for him if he can love the world and feel at home in it; otherwise the inevitable fact is that he will not and cannot face it – and there is no kind of logical reasoning that has any claim upon him.

There is a connection here with the legitimacy of different kinds of argument in morality. We have seen how far one may get by deploying the requirement of logical consistency, but of course it is always open for a person to refuse (sometimes) to be consistent. Such a refusal may be merely pig-headed, unreasonable in the widest sense of that term, but it may also incorporate a genuine demand. Even the apparently self-contradictory question 'Why should I be reasonable?' may make sense. As we have seen, it is not obviously absurd or wrong for a person simply to *opt out of* the public mode if it becomes too painful for him or if that mode does not in some way reward him sufficiently.

At this point there is a temptation to abandon the question to psychologists or others; it is taken for granted that we have the right to enforce the public mode, because it pays off all round, and need only find adequate 'motivation' to ensure that individuals live up to it. But, quite apart from the dubiousness of any such right if it is not grounded on some concept of reason which is anterior to and embraces the reason enshrined in the public mode, since it is precisely the public mode that is being put in question, not just *any* kind of 'motivation' will pass muster. We can, in effect, bribe or threaten people to behave altruistically, and that will result in their better behaviour, but the price we pay is a certain corruption of the will, since they should not be behaving for *those* motives. It is hard to know how to weigh these features against each other, but in any case we should do better to rely on the right motives, if only we can clarify them and make them work.

If a boy is indifferent to his sister's interests, we can (1) attempt to recall him to reason by deploying the principle of universalizability, or by showing in some other way that he is acting inconsistently. But we can also (2) point out to him the advantages of being nice to her rather than indifferent. Some of these advantages would be extrinsic – being punished or given sweets – but some would be intrinsic. We could try to persuade him that he would be happier in relation to his sister, that it would pay him to treat her as an end in herself, as having rights, as somebody who was interesting and lovable for her own sake. Such persuasion would not take the form of deductive argument; it might take many forms – reminding him of experiences shared together, suggesting mutually profitable forms of interaction, even saying, 'Look how pretty she is!' The idea behind all this is to persuade him to *value* his sister, and in fact we learn to value other people, to treat them as ends in themselves, by *many different* ways quite apart from extrinsic rewards and punishments.

This also brings us back to the importance of attending to language and achieving clarity. The most obvious, and ultimately the most important, reason why we need to be clear about the meanings of words is that we cannot communicate with each other unless we understand each other. I call this the most important reason because there is a great temptation, more usually unconscious than conscious, to prefer autism to communication. By 'autism' I mean, as the reader will already have gathered, a type of behaviour which is ungoverned by any kind of public or interpersonal rules, standards or criteria: 'autistic' is a term of art here, which may have the advantage of avoiding the rather too specific connotations of such terms as 'egocentric' and 'self-centred'. It is, in this sense, autistic to engage in daydreams or fantasies about, for example, sex or power, as opposed to attempting to communicate and come to terms with actual men or women in a sexual context or in the context of doing some job. 'Facing reality', to use a cliché, is obviously hard work and in some ways not immediately rewarding because reality does not fit our own immediate desires; hence we are tempted, in our talk as well as our other behaviour, to distort or disregard the real world in favour of our own fantasies.

All that is obvious enough in a general form, but the importance of communication, of *doing business together*, has to be constantly stressed. Thus it may be the case – sometimes it plainly is the case –

that certain terms have no fixed or standard meaning, or that we need to change the meaning they now have, or that we need to invent new terms. But when this is so, there is still a crucial difference between the person who says, to put it roughly, 'Good, so I can mean what I choose by these terms and need not be bound by any public or impersonal considerations' and the person who says, 'Very well, we need to get together and decide together what this or that term shall mean in our talk with each other, or what changes it would be wisest to make, or what new terms would best serve our purposes.' The former leads directly, at an intellectual or sophisticated level, to the erection of systems of belief which represent elaborations of a person's own personal desires and fantasies, and which therefore have little or no connection with truth or reality, both of which are essentially public notions: one may think of the unreality, evidenced by the autistic jargon, of Nazi philosophy or of other sectarian intellectual systems. The latter leads, in a more pedestrian but also more fruitful way, to the establishing of sensible agreements, conventions, categories and methods by which we can do business together. It is not too much to say, though I shall not pursue the point here, that the unwillingness to attend to and respect the meanings of words is a symptom of an unwillingness to respect truth and reality; and that this unwillingness can be overcome only if a person is capable of tolerating the real world sufficiently to want to work with it – in particular, perhaps, if he is capable of tolerating the reality of other people with other points of view. We should, indeed, hope for more than tolerance and respect, since those are hardly sufficient incentives to reach agreement; they might lead only to an agreement to differ, though this is not itself unimportant. For further progress we need something like enthusiasm for the world and its inhabitants, ultimately something like affection or *love* for them.

Part Three

The Moral Components and Assessment

Chapter 7

The General Approach

In Part Two I hope to have clarified at least some essential aspects of the philosophical basis or groundwork for moral education, with particular reference to the central notions of justice, love and insight. These notions, I have claimed, are inescapable for anyone who wants to take the moral life seriously; or, indeed, for developing the sort of seriousness we ought to have. They are not the personal property of any particular set of moral beliefs, or religious or political or ideological creeds, but simply an expansion of what we have to attend to if we want to be educated in this area, or to have thoughts and feelings which will count as reasonable, or to engage in action which can be justified by reason. I have also claimed that these notions can form the basis not only of interpersonal morality (justice), but of those wider elements in the notion marked by 'moral' that have more to do with ideals and mental health. But we now need to develop this idea further, for the notions as they stand are excessively general. It is not much good trying to educate people in morality by saying, 'Be just', or 'Develop the ability to love', or 'Have more insight'; we need to break these notions down into as many specific parts or aspects as possible.

The connection of education with the development of reason suggests that 'being reasonable' (about the moral area) may stand as a general description of what we are looking for. Here it is natural to begin by trying to consider what we mean when we call *people*, rather than *beliefs*, rational or irrational. When we describe somebody as 'irrational', 'unreasonable', 'intolerant', 'prejudiced', 'insane', etc., we do not (or should not) refer primarily to the truth or falsehood of his beliefs. A person may hold beliefs which are perfectly correct in an unreasonable, intolerant, prejudiced or insane *manner* – and, of course, vice versa. We are talking about the *way in which* or the *reasons for which* he comes to believe, and continues to believe, rather than *what* he believes. A 'reasonable' person is not essentially a person who believes x, y and z, but a person who is prepared to listen to argument, attend to facts, to logic, to the meanings of words and so on.

To put it another way, we can draw a distinction between the merits of a person when playing a particular role and the correctness or incorrectness of his beliefs. For instance, we can talk about a 'good scientist', meaning, roughly, a person who observes the physical world closely and patiently, who frames hypotheses intelligently and submits them to experimental tests, and who is prepared to abide by the relevant evidence. More obscurely, but still intelligibly, a 'good literary critic' is someone who is widely and deeply read in literature, is well versed in certain studies which are relevant to literature (perhaps the history of the period, or the life of the author) and shows an acute perception of human nature and the literary forms which portray it. We can categorize individuals – schoolboys, for instance – as 'good at' these activities without necessarily maintaining that their scientific or literary opinions are, in any particular case, correct. We mean rather that they are good at following certain rules of procedure, or principles of thought, which are relevant to their field of study; in much the same way as somebody can be a good bridge-player without necessarily making all his contracts, or a good barrister without winning all his cases.

What is it, then, to be 'good' at morality? I have said that we ought *not* to try to answer this question by saying, 'Holding the right moral views.' If we say this, we shall find ourselves asking next, 'But what *are* the right moral views?' and to this question we may fail to find an answer. We may fail for two reasons: first, because we shall not be clear about the criteria by which we can judge; and secondly, because we still might not know which actual views were right, even if we knew what we meant by calling a view 'right' – we might, for instance, not have enough factual information to decide between conflicting views. We should rather ask 'What are the rules of procedure, or the canons of relevance, which we actually use to assess the merits of a moral view?' or 'What sort of demands do we make on a person who puts forward a moral view, when we want him to justify it?'

After all, we are in a not very dissimilar position as regards scientific views. We have a fairly good idea of what rules and criteria govern the activity of science, and how scientific arguments and justifications are supposed to work. But this does not mean that we never hold mistaken scientific beliefs, however careful we try to be in attending to the rules and criteria – we may have overlooked some vital fact, or our instruments may not be good enough to collect all the evidence we need. Nor does it mean that our scientific beliefs can be shown to follow *logically* from certain pieces of evidence, that they are *necessarily* true. Yet we can still talk about 'proof', 'knowledge' and 'certainty' in science as in logic or mathematics. And so we can in morals. These words will relate to different rules of procedure according to the activity. Different activities have different standards, but this does not mean that one is inferior to another; they are just different.

With some of the rules of procedure in morality we are perfectly familiar because they are rules which enter into other activities besides morality. Briefly they are:

1.   That we should stick to the laws of logic.
2.   That we should use language correctly.
3.   That we should attend to the facts.

Many examples have been given of these kinds of rationality: they may be found elsewhere, and I will not repeat them here. But these particular principles are not peculiar to morality. We need to find out what other qualities and procedures are important to this area of human life.

To put this another way, hitherto we have been trying to avoid one general danger, the danger of putting forward particular moral values or partisan views of morality as a basis for moral education. Here we have to deal with another equally common and dangerous practice: the tendency to talk *in global terms* about what it is to be 'morally educated'. It is very easy to try to give quick, complete answers. Thus I have so far given the answer 'being reasonable about morality', but this is wholly inadequate as it stands, for, although it is not partisan, it is too general: plainly 'being reasonable' involves all sorts of very different qualities, skills, abilities, attitudes and so on. Similarly, to talk globally of trying to make our pupils more 'concerned', 'sensitive', 'aware', 'mature', 'responsible' and so on is of little use. We want to know more precise details and to break down the notion of 'being reasonable in morality' into a precise set of qualities.

Such a set of qualities would also answer the questions 'How can we tell (verify) when, and in what respects, a person is morally educated?' or, moving now towards a more practical concern, 'How can we *assess* (evaluate, determine, check up on) moral education?' Here I make no apology for using a method which appeared, in a somewhat primitive and undeveloped form, in earlier works (including Wilson *et al.*, 1967): that of trying to specify particular qualities or attributes which merit titles of their own. This is, I believe, not to introduce unnecessary jargon or technical terms, but simply an attempt to be really clear and specific about each individual attribute.

There are, however, some important points that need to be made in advance. The first of these concerns the applicability of the moral components to the wider area of morality: that is, not just to interpersonal morality but to ideals in general and perhaps religious outlooks in particular. The second concerns some methodological problems in the assessment of the components, which is directly relevant to understanding what function they are intended to perform. We shall look briefly at both of these.

RELIGION AND OTHER PERSONAL IDEALS

It is already clear that, if we are not to base moral education on some partisan set of ideological beliefs and values, we shall have to construct a list of qualities, attributes, skills, abilities and other features which can be shown to be both (1) relevant to the area covered by 'moral' and (2) necessary for any person who is willing to take the area seriously, and demanded of him by pure reason. In other words, it will be these components or bits of equipment, as we may call them, which form the basis of moral education, and to which (rather than to any ideology or anything else) we want our pupils and ourselves to give their ultimate allegiance.

Before going on to list these, however, it is important to see that they must be relevant not only to interpersonal morality – that is, to that part of morality which is concerned with justice and proper behaviour towards other people – but also to religious and other ideals, ways of life, general outlooks on the world, and other governing pictures or principles. We may hope that some at least of these incorporate the central ideas of our components in respect of interpersonal morality – notions like justice, fraternity, treating others as equals, and so forth – but they often go deeper than that, since they represent the ways in which individuals try to achieve security and make sense of their personal lives. We are here very much, as I see it, in the field of mental health, or the education of the emotions. For whether a person takes up a particular ideology, religion, ideal or outlook on life is largely a function of his emotions – in particular his unconscious emotions, which, as we have seen in Part One, affect his conscious beliefs and behaviour very powerfully.

Clearly a proper demonstration and enlargement of this would require a book in itself (I have in fact attempted this task in Wilson, 1971, to which I refer any reader who is likely to have grave doubts). Briefly, people can only be educated in respect of these emotional investments (religious and other) not or not only by historical, theological, literary, sociological or other study, but by coming to develop insight and understanding of their own and other people's emotions. This seems to me the central task not only of any serious religious education but of education in all cognate fields, such as personal relationships, health and politics, in which the emotions play a (the) major part. Here again, as in education for interpersonal morality, the educator will not take sides for or against religion (still less for or against any particular religion), or any other ideal, ideology or emotional investment. What he will try to do will be to develop those components which are particularly concerned with insight and understanding.

These qualities, to be discussed under the technical heading of EMP (empathy or insight) in the list of components that follows shortly, of course merit a much longer treatment, particularly in respect of the unconscious (Wilson, 1971, pp. 121ff.), the meaning of 'insight' (pp. 227ff.) and possible methods of practical education of the emotions (pp. 241ff.). Here I want to say only that those who subscribe to particular religious or other outlooks, and also those who subscribe (at least consciously) to none, have to take these ideas seriously, for they form the only possible rational basis for education in that wider aspect of morality which goes beyond justice. I have also argued that the notion of love has an overriding and central part to play, and this, fortunately, also connects with another of our components (PHIL), the ability and willingness to be concerned for other people, and for other entities in the world besides people. I should like the reader, then, to appreciate that the list of components is intended to cover – albeit in a skeletal form, and recognizing the need for much further explication – *all* the ground that we have delineated by 'morality'. The connections between morality, in the narrow sense, and religious and other ideals (also discussed in Wilson, 1971) are complex but very strong, and it is particularly important that we should not allow ourselves to suppose that the dictates of religious or other ideology can reasonably prevail over the authority which the components ought to have.

PROBLEMS OF ASSESSMENT

In attempting to assess human (rational) behaviour we have to assess a person or research subject (S) in terms of the *reasons* and the *rules* or principles S follows when he performs the action. This cannot be done merely by observing overt physical movements – by just taking photographs, as it were. We have to know 'what goes on in S's head', what 'overriding syllogism' S is following at the time. It may seem that the researcher can easily guess (induce) this from S's overt behaviour, and under certain conditions this may be true. But these conditions are not easy to establish, and, in any case, we should certainly require cross-checks in the standard form of verification for human reasons and intentions – namely, by *asking* S what his reasons and intentions were. This method of verification raises important problems of sincerity and rationalization, but we cannot do without it.

This point cuts deeper than might be supposed, and I shall reinforce it by three examples:

1. Suppose we are trying to assess various Ss for generosity. We observe them passing by a beggar, in turn. Each puts his hand in his pocket and gives the beggar £1. S1, however, does this because he is sorry for the beggar; S2 because he wants to show off to his girlfriend; S3 because he thinks this will gain him a reward in the next world; S4 to get rid of his guilt feelings; and so on. We can, if we like, say that their behaviour or actions were generous, but obviously they are not, in any serious sense, equally generous people, for they are following different rules and syllogisms.

2. Suppose now that we are trying to assess Ss for 'honesty', and put

them in situations where they can cheat. S1 cheats because he doesn't see anything wrong with cheating anyway; S2 cheats to gain an advantage; S3 cheats because he wants to disobey the authorities (when he can get away with it); S4 does not cheat because there is someone around (even if not watching) who makes him feel guilty; S5 does not cheat because he is the son of a gentleman, and 'gentlemen's sons don't cheat' except in some circumstances; S6 does not cheat because it seems to him more fun to abide by the rules; and so on. Now we can say that Ss 1–3 cheated and Ss 4–6 did not cheat, but without further verification that is *all* we can say, and it is not much if we are really interested in *honesty*.

3. Suppose we are assessing S for his tendency to kill. Concealed in bushes with telescope, we discover that S kills foxes, single individuals with pistols whom he meets at dawn, and foreigners – sometimes on alien soil, sometimes in his own country. 'This is "situation-specific"', we conclude. So far as *killing* is concerned, so good. But, of course, S is a gentleman who engages in fox-hunting, duelling and, when honour requires, war. He follows, and follows consistently or 'generally', an overriding principle or syllogism of the form 'I ought to act honourably; this is an honourable action; therefore do this.' This S does not do what he regards as 'murder', which is probably (for him) dishonourable.

From this, two points follow. First, if we predefine and thereby limit the area of morality to specific situations (the 'public norms' of honesty, truth-telling, etc.), we shall be apt to overlook different types of reason. Secondly, unless we find out 'what goes on in S's head', we shall be apt to forget the importance of what *concepts* S uses in his behaviour. Thus we may operate with the simple pair 'honest'/'dishonesty', whereas S is operating with 'honour'/ 'dishonourable', or some quite different pair. When S meets a situation, S will *see* the situation *as* (describe it to himself as) this or that, and 'this or that' may be almost anything. You call it murder; I call it revenge; Siegfried calls it exercise; Hitler calls it purifying the state; and so on. The description that S gives may be caused *by* S's overriding principles, or it may be the cause *of* S's choice of one principle rather than another. (S1, a Pharisee, is on the look-out for trouble-makers, being frightened about his authority, so he identifies Jesus as a trouble-maker rather than under the description of an 'innocent man'. S2, another Pharisee, has it brought to his attention that Jesus is a trouble-maker and this arouses his fears, sparking off a 'put down trouble-makers' syllogism rather than an 'acquit the innocent' one.)

Rather than elaborate these problems, it will be more profitable to try to make a fairly comprehensive list of the different aspects of moral thought and behaviour which any serious assessor must attend to. These 'aspects', 'components' or 'constituents' are not psychological entities, 'factors', 'traits', 'constructs' or anything of that kind. They will be derived not from any theory or hypothesis about 'mental mechanisms', but simply from a consideration of *what it means* to think and act morally, and from what is necessarily implied by this. I stress this because the whole burden of my criticism is that empirical researchers have been too hasty in their approach; they have not succeeded in bridging the vital gap between what is normally meant by moral thought and action on the one hand, and practical assessment and empirical evidence on the other – partly because they have not realized just how wide the gap is.

Basically, the making of such a list will be no more than an elaboration of those aspects of thought and behaviour which are relevant to S's following an overriding principle or 'practical syllogism'. But there are many such aspects, and the serious researcher ought at least to be interested in the following:

1. What concepts S *has* (e.g. of 'other people', 'honour', 'honesty', etc.).
2. What concepts S *thinks he ought to use* in his behaviour: that is, what rules or principles he thinks he ought to follow. (I may have the concept of 'honour' without thinking that I ought to use it when deciding how to act.)
3. What *feelings* or emotions S has under normal conditions that support his belief that he should use these concepts and principles. (I may have the concept of 'honour', think in a general or theoretical way that I ought to use it, etc., but have no feelings attached to it – I do not feel remorse when I fail to deploy it, for instance.)
4. What knowledge or awareness S has of the surrounding circumstances. This would include:
    (a) S's ability to identify his own and others' emotions.
    (b) S's knowledge of the 'hard' facts relevant to what he decides to do.

5. What 'know-how' or 'social skills' S has in dealing with people, since much of S's moral behaviour may turn on this.
6. Whether S *brings to bear* the above on those situations with which he is actually confronted in 'real life'. This would include:
    (a) Whether S notices or is alert to the situation, and describes it in a way related to the concepts in (1) and (2) above, or in some other way.
    (b) Whether S makes full or partial use of his knowledge and awareness in (4) and (5) above.
    (c) Whether S actually *does* use the principles he claims as right ((2) above), supported by his feelings ((3) above), so as to make a sincere *decision* to act in a certain way; or whether he uses other principles.
7. Whether S *does* actually act in accordance with his decision.

I think it would be mistaken for any researcher to form a priori opinions on the comparative importance of some of these aspects as against others. One reason for this is that they are in an important sense cumulative: thus S has a concept, thinks he ought to use it, feels he ought to use it, has various kinds of knowledge and skill relevant to using it, brings these to bear when facing a 'real life' situation, and acts on this basis. Differences, whether we call them 'successes' or 'failures', may occur at any point. To ask how 'important' those differences are is already to have adopted some viewpoint about the importance of a certain type of research. Thus if we have already decided to make it our main concern to discover whether S performs certain overt actions, never mind why he does, then we shall be tempted to concentrate on (7), but this would be an error even in its own terms: moral thought and action are, as I have tried to show, too intimately connected both logically and empirically to allow of such an approach.

Chapter 8

The Moral Components

I have argued that the researcher ought to use something like a set of 'moral components', both on grounds of research strategy and on more strictly philosophical grounds. Here I want to stress the importance, for both kinds of researcher, of giving these clear titles and definitions. The odd-sounding titles we shall use – PHIL, EMP, GIG and so on – are more than merely convenient. First, they wean us from vague 'global' terms such as 'sensitivity', 'awareness', 'maturity', 'a responsible attitude' and so forth. Secondly, they force us to be clear about their definitions, so that we are sure about what we are trying to assess. Thirdly, they force us to try to cover all the ground – to identify, putting it negatively, what can go wrong with S's moral thought and behaviour, to clarify all the logical types of failure.

I make no apology, then, for asking the reader to become familiar with this simple terminology; indeed I would warn the reader against any radically dissimilar approach. I do not claim that the following list is either at all points complete or at all points conceptually watertight. Much may remain to be done, even at the purely conceptual level. But I think it will stand as a sensible basis for research, and that it is sufficiently well developed for empirical researchers to use as a framework. I shall explain the logic, status and assessment methods relevant to each component in following sections; here I shall simply list them.

PHIL(HC)   Having the concept of a 'person'.
PHIL(CC)   Claiming to use this concept in an

	overriding, prescriptive and univer- salized (O, P and U) principle.
PHIL(RSF)(DO and PO)	Having feelings which support this principle, either of a 'duty-orien- tated' (DO) or a 'person-orientated' (PO) kind.
EMP(1)(Cs)	Being able, in practice, to identify emotions, etc. in oneself, when these are at a conscious level.
EMP(1)(Ucs)	Ditto, when the emotions are at an unconscious level.
EMP(2)(Cs)	Ditto, in other people, when at a conscious level.
EMP(2)(Ucs)	Ditto, when at an unconscious level.
GIG(1)(KF)	Knowing other ('hard') facts rele- vant to moral decisions.
GIG(1)(KS)	Knowing sources of facts (where to find out) as above.
GIG(2)(VC)	'Knowing how' – a 'skill' element in dealing with moral situations, as evinced in verbal communication with others.
GIG(2)(NVC)	Ditto, in non-verbal com- munication.
KRAT(1)(RA)	Being, in practice, 'relevantly alert' to (noticing) moral situations, and seeing them as such (describing them in terms of PHIL, etc. above).
KRAT(1)(TT)	Thinking thoroughly about such situations, and bringing to bear whatever PHIL, EMP and GIG one has.
KRAT(1)(OPU)	As a result of the foregoing, making an overriding, prescriptive and universalized decision to act in others' interests.
KRAT(2)	Being sufficiently wholehearted, free from unconscious counter- motivation, etc. to carry out (when able) the above decision in practice.

We shall now take a closer look at these components and how to assess for them. A full understanding of each is essential, and I would ask the reader to go through the following sections with care, for without a firm grasp of the components, the later remarks on assessment methods and the sketches of assessments will be at best misleading and at worst incomprehensible.

PHIL

Under the heading PHIL we have to make sense of the area often described in such terms as 'concern for others', 'sympathy', 'sense of fair play' and 'respect for other people'. As this is one of the most important components, so also it is most liable to confusion and vagueness. I shall try to break it down into a number of logically distinct parts.

1. Having the concept of a 'person'

The first thing that seems to be required is that S should have a clear concept of a 'person' or the 'other', in the sense demanded by morality. Briefly, this concept involves a criterion of similarity in virtue of which all 'rational animate creatures' are put into the same category. By 'rational animate creatures', I mean all entities who are (in the full sense) language-users, and to whom we can correctly ascribe such terms as 'will', 'emotion', 'intention', 'purpose' and 'consciousness'. Such creatures will also have wants, needs and desires in a fuller, or at least a different, sense than that in which we may say that plants or machines or animals have wants, needs and desires.

Of course there are both logical and empirical difficulties here. We may be logically uncertain about whether, say, dolphins and chimpanzees are to count as 'rational animate creatures', even if we know all the empirical facts about them; and/or we may be empirically uncertain about the facts – do dolphins really have a language? But the vast majority of cases are clear, and the concept can be established clearly enough to enable us to know, for instance, what sorts of entity discovered on Mars would in principle count as 'people' in the required sense. Similarly, we may be doubtful about the age at which infants can be said to count as 'people', but at least the concept allows us to dismiss as irrelevant such considerations as sex, skin-colour, race, height and creed.

It is important that we should remember what is meant by 'having the concept of'. As I use the phrase, it will refer solely to S's ability to conceive of all 'people' as forming one class and, given the facts, to identify any 'person' as a member of that class. This ability is verified by S's being able to *say*, to himself and in principle to others, something like 'This entity has intentions and needs, uses language, etc., therefore it counts as a person.' S must not merely react or behave differently towards people and non-people, but must do so for a reason – namely, because he sees them as different in terms of this criterion. Nor is there any requirement that S must have an 'image', 'mental picture', 'idea', 'set' or anything else that suggests the existence of some 'psychological entity' or the working of some 'psychological mechanism'. That way lies confusion.

Equally, 'having the concept of' does not imply either of two things which even philosophers have sometimes seemed to imply. First, it does not imply that S has what I shall call the 'practical' ability to identify cases of the concept. One may have the concept of an alkali without, in laboratory practice, having the ability to identify an alkali; of checkmate, without being very good, over the chess-board, at recognizing cases of checkmate. Suppose that some of the entities on Mars are people, but that in practice it is difficult to distinguish these entities from robots or other non-rational artefacts. Then S may have the concept of a person so long as he can say, '*If* this entity can really talk, feel, intend, etc., then it counts as a person', and he may add 'though without more experience and practice (or sharper eyesight or other "practical" abilities) I find it hard to recognize which entities are of this kind.' Secondly, and more simply (although not less importantly for research), *having* the concept does not entail *using* or wanting to use the concept. I have the concept 'made of wood', but I do not normally see my room as divided between wooden and non-wooden objects. I shall only *use* the concept in certain circumstances, e.g. if I am frightened of woodworm or fire.

In assessing Ss for 'having the concept of a person', shall we allow ourselves to say that an S has 'some of the concept', or 'part of the concept', or 'is on the way towards having the concept'? The answer is 'no' to the first two, but 'yes' to the third. Suppose S begins by counting all bipeds, but not one-legged men or rational Martians, as people. Then we try to push him a stage further, and he counts all men but still not Martians. Then, finally, he includes all rational, animate creatures. What we should say here is that, at the first stages, he has *a* concept but it is not *the* concept (the concept we want him to have). 'Person' for him means, first, 'all bipeds', then perhaps 'all men on earth'. It is not till the last stage that he has *the* concept. Before then, he does not in any serious sense have 'part of' it; he just has a different concept. If our interests are in the empirical learning process, and if we have some kind of picture of stages of learning through which S has to go if he is to end up with the concept, we can certainly say such things as 'He is on the way towards getting the concept' or 'He has nearly got it.' But this is a very different matter. In assessing whether someone has the concept or not, we must say, 'Either he has it or he hasn't.'

2.   Claiming the concept as a moral principle

This aspect of PHIL is much more difficult. I have written 'claiming', not 'using' or 'applying', the concept because I want to exclude from this aspect certain things better assessed elsewhere. I want to exclude the question of whether S uses the concept of 'other people's interests' when S is actually faced with the necessity or opportunity for moral decision and action 'in the field': that is, not in any artificial test situation but in the outside world. S may, or may not, use this as his overriding criterion for *deciding* what to do, and, again, S may or may not feel the criterion as strong, or overriding, enough for S actually to *behave* in accordance with it. Both these are important, but I am not concerned with them here. I am concerned rather with whether S in general – one might say, in principle or as part of his moral theory – thinks that this is the criterion which he ought to use, whether S claims it as the sort of reason that ought to influence him.

This does not, however, excuse us from so constructing our assessments that we can be sure that S claims – or, in this very restricted context, 'applies' – this criterion as a genuinely prescriptive, overriding and universal one. It will be best to illustrate this and the preceding points by an example. Suppose we present S with a story describing a situation in which other people's interests are involved, and in which he may use them as a criterion for decision and action. We then ask S what he thinks ought to be done, and we suppose that S says that other people's interests should be satisfied. Then (1) this does not (and is not intended to) tell us whether S *would* in fact use this criterion if he were, in real life, the agent *either* (a) in his decision-making *or* (b) in his actual behaviour. All it tells us is that S thinks he ought to use it, that S claims it as his principle. But (2) we need to know more than this. (a) S must mean his 'ought' prescriptively: that is, as *committing* him, S, to action. S must mean something like 'It isn't just that this would be a good thing to do; I think that, in such a situation, I ought to commit myself to (order myself to, prescribe to myself) such decision and action.' (b) S must mean his 'ought' overridingly: S must think that this is what he ought to do *more than anything else*. (c) S must mean his 'ought' universally: S must think that he, *and anyone else* similarly placed, ought to do it.

It is easy to see from this, without going into too much detail, that we have both certain limitations and certain detailed obligations, for testing in this area. First, we must *avoid* trying to find out what S would in fact ('in the field') decide to do – or, of course, what S thinks anyone else would in fact decide to do. Secondly, we must *ensure* that we do not rest content with knowing what S thinks some other agent ought to do, or what S thinks that he (S) but not some other agent ought to do, or what S's judgement on actual decisions (given in the story) is, or what S thinks would be 'nice to happen' but not (prescriptively) ought to be done. All these considerations will affect the form of our tests and assessments.

As we have said, we are here concerned with S's beliefs, basic principles or 'moral theory', and to get at this, we have to *exclude* 'in-the-field' factors. In our terminology, to get at PHIL we have to exclude KRAT(1) and KRAT(2) factors. Hence the form of our assessment must be such as to allow S to reflect, at leisure, on what he thinks ought to be done – on what criterion he thinks appropriate, whether that of other people's interests or some other. It is, indeed, necessary to ensure, particularly if S is a young child with low verbal ability, that S *understands* the story or other test form; in that sense, the situation must be 'made real' to him. But it is equally necessary to ensure that it is not too life-like. If, for instance, we used some game or simulation situation instead of a pencil-and-paper story, S would be more likely to be carried away by 'in-the-field' (KRAT(1) and (2)) factors, although we could of course use a simulation situation, or a film, or puppets, or some other non-verbal presentation, provided we allowed S time to reflect on it. But we have throughout to remember that our aim is to get at S's *general* moral views.

In order to do this we shall of course have to present S with other options, with other criteria besides the 'other people's interests' criterion. This means that we shall present him with conflict situations, in which he may be tempted to opt for other criteria. We need for this an adequate typology of what other criteria are likely to operate. This will be of particular importance in determining whether S's views are overriding, and we can only determine this by making available not only the practical syllogism in which we are interested ('One ought to act in others' interests; this is in others' interests; therefore do this'), but also other practical syllogisms (e.g. 'One ought to seek one's own advantage', 'One ought not to lose face', 'One ought not to disobey authority', 'One ought to act the way one's friends do', etc. as major premises).

We have also to remember that the test form will be primarily concerned not with what specific action S thinks right, but with S's *reasons*: that is, with whether S chooses the action in virtue of the criterion of others' interests. It is very easy to forget this point in an endeavour to keep test stories simple and easily scorable. We may ask numerous questions of the form 'What should Johnny do?' or 'What ought you to do?', forgetting that the answers to these are relevant *only* if we can be certain that they show the operation of a certain reason or criterion, and this need not be so. Even in conflict situations, S may have all kinds of reasons for choosing what is (accidentally) the 'right answer' in terms of others' interests, reasons quite disconnected logically from that criterion. We have to make sure that the criterion is actually being used.

Now it is fairly obvious that few if any Ss will always get the 'right answer' for the right reasons. An S will to some extent, or in some spheres, or in some situations, claim the criterion of others' interests, but in other situations deploy some other criterion. How are we to cater for this, either in devising or scoring the assessments? To this there is no simple answer. What we have to do is to make sensible guesses about the possible categories in which Ss may vary in their application of the criterion. For example, it is a fairly safe bet that some Ss will apply it in situations concerned with members of their own family or gang, but not outside: to whites but not to blacks, and so on. We have here a category or dimension which we shall call *range*, and I shall now go on, not without some hesitation, to sketch out this and other such factors. I must stress, however, that although all these categories (and no doubt others) need to be tried out in assessment, it is at present quite unclear which of them will turn out to be of the most practical significance.

(a)   Range

This concerns the numbers and classes of people for whom S applies the criterion. Important categories here may be *similarity* to S (in age, sex, social class, tastes, etc.); *social distance* (whether the other is a family- or gang- or class-member); *social behaviour* of the other (whether 'nice' or 'nasty'); *appearance* or *manner* of the other (physical attraction, accent, etc.); *social status* of the other; *age* or *sex* of the other.

(b)   Situation similarity

This turns on whether S has himself been in situations like that given in the story, where S has needed others to attend to his interests (e.g. S has often needed financial help himself, and is perhaps more likely to say that a story person should have it).

(c)   Situation experience

This concerns whether S has experienced situations similar to the story situation (irrespective of whether S has himself been in a position of need, as in (b) above).

(d)   Harming and helping

An S may perform well at not-harming, but badly at helping, or vice versa.

(e)   Subject matter

The empirical *type* of harm or help may be important. Among these types we may list:

(i)   'bodily' (violence, food, sex)
(ii)   'property' (stealing, lending money)
(iii)   'nuisance/kindness' (excessive noise, baby-sitting without payment)
(iv)   'words' (slander, cheering someone up)
(v)   'contract' (lying, keeping promises, punctuality, debts).

(f)   Scope/distribution

S may use the criterion well in distributing 'goods' to others, but badly when allowing others power or scope (in voting, decision making), or vice versa.

(g)   Visible immediacy

S may use the criterion well when the results are visibly immediate, badly when the results – though immediate in point of time – cannot be seen: e.g. not stealing from friends, but stealing from the railways or the taxpayer.

(h)   Temporal immediacy

As above, but in respect of time: e.g. S may be concerned about the good of others now or for the immediate future, but not about the eventual results of pollution, overpopulation, etc.

It should be clear that these categories are by no means exhaustive. But they are important, not only for PHIL but for other components also, and we shall find ourselves referring to them as we proceed. I have not extended them, chiefly because the most sensible procedure is to begin by trying out tests and assessments that take these at least into account, and then (with the help of interviews and information derived from conversation and behavioural observation) to become clearer about which categories are most significant. Only by spreading the net wide enough shall we ever be in a position to give S a *general* rating for this aspect of PHIL, and even this may prove unwise, for S's claim to the criterion may be *so* specific to particular situations (or other types of category) that we may be able to do no more than rate S within the various categories.

I have not added the point made earlier about conflict situations and the possibility of other 'overriding syllogisms' to the list above because this point is of a different order of importance. The list contains a selection of *other* factors that may affect S's use of the criterion, and some of these other factors will themselves be such as to generate other 'overriding syllogisms' for S. But it should now go without saying that we must, above all, take care to include in our stories, or whatever presentations we use, the various 'pulls' of guilt, honour, self-advantage and so forth.

It should also be unnecessary to say that, since we are concerned here with one aspect of PHIL only, we must control for other components (as well as, of course, for other variables such as IQ and reading ability). Thus we are here interested in what S *thinks* to be in the other's interests; whether S is correct or not may turn on his factual knowledge (GIG) or knowledge of others' emotions (EMP). We may best control for these by so simplifying the story that all Ss may be presumed to have adequate EMP and GIG. We cannot wholly exclude S's 'bring-to-bear' component (KRAT(1)), since we are after all getting S to bring his knowledge and principles to bear in one, albeit very restricted, situation: namely, the test situation. But by giving S plenty of time, and keeping the presentation simple enough, nearly all Ss should have sufficient KRAT(1) for us to feel secure. We are, in effect, doing the 'bringing to bear' for S, precisely by presenting him with the test (plus whatever incentives are required to ensure that S does it properly).

3. Rule-supporting feelings

We turn now to a very different aspect of PHIL. Let us assume that S has the required concept of a person, and claims this concept as a moral principle of rule of behaviour. It may still be the case that S has little or no *feeling* attached to this rule, and little or no tendency to *act* in accordance with it. We are here concerned with the former (feeling), but the general point requires a brief discussion.

It is perfectly true that, if an S said that he believed he ought to decide and act by the criterion of others' interests, but rarely or never did so, and rarely or never showed remorse, guilt or sorrow at not having done so, or pleasure or self-approval when he did so –

then, in this (rare) case, we should be tempted to say that S could not have really meant what he first said. 'Could not', not because there is a tight logical entailment between believing that one ought to do something on the one hand, and doing it and having certain feelings on the other – there need be no such entailment unless we force one – but because characteristically (rather than necessarily) humans tend to do, and to have certain feelings about, what they think they ought to do. Hence we should be justly suspicious, to say the least, of the S quoted above. But it is still possible, indeed common, *in certain cases* for an S to assent sincerely to our criterion, and yet neither to act on it nor to have certain feelings about it.

For these reasons it is necessary to deal with the feelings and actions under separate headings. This is all the more required of us because in section (2) above we were concerned solely with what we called S's 'moral theory', his intellectual opinion, so to speak, about what criterion he thought he ought to use – as an overriding and prescriptive criterion, certainly, but not necessarily as the one he actually *did* use. We need, then, to find out how far the criterion actually *is* supported by some kind of commitment on S's part. We shall here deal with the extent of what I call S's 'rule-supporting feelings'; S's 'rule-derived' decisions and actions will come under KRAT(1) and (2).

Note further that we are concerned with S's feelings only in so far as they are subordinated to the rule about others' interests. The feelings must be for the other *as for* a being with rights, interests, needs, etc. It is *about the other's interests* that he must feel (and act), not about the other under some other description or in some other light. For instance, I may hold as a principle that others' interests should be satisfied: I may satisfy the interests of an attractive blonde, and I may also have strong feelings about her. But my feelings are not about her *as* a source of needs or interests, and I am not here acting *on* my principle, but am only moved to act in what happens to be in accordance with it. My sexual feelings for the blonde are not 'rule-supporting' feelings. Again, there may be something about the sight of a cripple which moves me in some way (I feel embarrassed or guilty) such that I give him money, but I am not necessarily giving him money because his interests require that I should.

Nevertheless we must distinguish here between two types of feeling, which I shall call 'duty-orientated' (DO) and 'person-orientated' (PO). This distinction is not between the S who uses the rule about others' interests as a criterion for action and the S who does not: both must govern their actions by the rule. The latter S could not be said to have PHIL or to show genuine benevolence or love, however sentimental or affectionate or strongly moved he might be towards another person, precisely because he does not control his behaviour by the rule. Nor, again, is the distinction between the S who will do his (contractual) duty but no more, and the S who will go further, for our concept of others' interests extends indefinitely beyond any contractual duty (though not excluding it). The 'duty-orientated' S may look after the interests of the starving Chinese as well as of his family; the 'person-orientated' S may only look after his family. The distinction is rather in the *kind* of feelings that accompany S's obedience to the rule.

This difference of kind does not lie in the *strength* of the feeling. An S who is DO may feel very strongly (in a Kantian sort of way) about the importance of doing his duty, of attending to the rule about others' interests, but what he will lack is the PO feelings which should, in *some* cases at least, accompany his attention to others. For those latter feelings we use words like 'sympathy', 'love', 'affection', 'identification with others'. Perhaps a good way of putting it is to say that S should *take pleasure* in the other, that S should be happy not that he has done his duty, but that the other is happy.

The importance of this aspect of PHIL is clear. Briefly, there are many contexts in human life – particularly in such close relationships as marriage and child rearing – where others' interests are served not so much by action as by feeling of a PO type. Wives and children, for instance, may care less about getting presents than about their husbands' or fathers' affection. This is not to say that there may not be other contexts (e.g. having to conduct a surgical operation or organize relief supplies to disaster areas) where affection either does not count or positively inhibits the effective performance of the required task.

We have, then, to assess these DO and PO feelings. It is worth noting that we cannot assess them simply by observing what S does. S may have the relevant feelings, yet those feelings may not be overriding: they may not issue in action. For instance, S1 may be very sorry for the Jews in Nazi Germany, yet be even more frightened of what might happen to him if he actually helped them; S2 may be less sorry for the Jews, but because he has no fear at all may actually help the Jews. Here S1's PHIL feelings are stronger than S2's but do not issue in action. We have, then, to assess the DO and PO feelings independently of behaviour – though this is not, of course, to say that we cannot use behavioural observations to induce such feelings, provided we are sure that our inductions are correct.

One important difference between assessment in this area and that in section (2) above is that we cannot do other than try to assess the feelings of S 'in the field': that is, we are trying to get at what S feels in real-life situations. Our presentations, therefore, will not be designed so much to give S leisure to reflect, since reflection is not relevant: what we want to know is how much rule-supporting feeling actually attaches itself to the criterion of others' interests. Apart from field observation, therefore, we shall be inclined to use simulation or participation situations, practical experiments, visual media and other methods that try to reproduce real-life situations as far as possible.

What then are these 'rule-supporting' feelings? Chief among them will be *remorse* or *guilt* when S does not follow a rule, *self-approbation* or *pleasure* when S does follow it, *disapproval* when S sees someone else not following the rule, *sorrow* or *regret* or *pity* in respect of the person whose needs are unsatisfied, and *approval* and *pleasure* at rule keeping and the other's satisfaction. These and other relevant feelings have their characteristic beliefs, symptoms and actions (weeping, making restitution, smiles, frowns, etc.) and can be assessed, although with difficulty. Such difficulty should make us incline towards many different kinds of assessment (self-reporting, interviews, behavioural observation, reporting from peers and others who know S well, and so on), and towards those contexts of assessment which seem best able to give us the information we need.

Summary

Above we have distinguished three sub-components of PHIL, the third of which is divided into two. These were:

1. Having the concept of a 'person': PHIL(HC).
2. Claiming the concept as a moral principle: PHIL(CC).

3. Having rule-supporting feelings, 'duty-orientated' or 'person-orientated': PHIL(RSF)(DO) and PHIL(RSF)(PO).

EMP

Under the heading EMP we are concerned with the area often described in such terms as 'emotional awareness', 'sensitivity', 'insight' and 'empathy'.

1. Having the concepts of emotion

To have the concept of an emotion is a necessary precondition for being able, in practice, to identify the emotion. S must know what jealousy *is* if S is to be able to know that so-and-so is jealous. This at once raises questions about what emotions are, and what the particular emotions are. I and other writers have dealt with these elsewhere; here I shall give merely what is likely to be of use to empirical researchers and others.

First, there are important distinctions between emotions and other similar mental phenomena which we may prefer to call 'moods', 'states of mind', 'motives', 'wants' or, more generally, 'feelings'. Emotions, necessarily or characteristically, have *targets* (not just causes) and have a 'cognitive core' consisting of a *belief*: 'moods' (happiness, depression, etc.) do not. Under EMP in general we shall include not only emotions in the strict sense, but 'wants', 'moods', etc. as well. However, the distinction will obviously be important for testing purposes.

Secondly, the concept of an emotion is usually made up of the following elements:

(a) a belief (that X is dangerous)
(b) involuntary or semi-voluntary symptoms (trembling, going pale), including certain postures, gestures, facial expressions, etc.
(c) intentional action (running away, trying to avoid attention).

Emotions may be recognized, in ourselves and others, by these three ways. They may also, under normal conditions, be recognized by the *surrounding circumstances*. Thus, to fit the example of fear above, we can induce that X feels fear if we know that a bull is chasing X, or an avalanche is coming towards X, and that X is aware of this.

Thirdly, to have the concept of a particular emotion (as was pointed out under PHIL earlier) involves being able to classify the phenomena in (a), (b) and (c) above under a single criterion. Usually the grasp of an emotion concept will be represented by an ordinary word – 'anger', 'fear', 'remorse', etc. But this is not a necessary condition. If we ask S what X is feeling, and S says, 'Well, it's what people feel when someone else has something nice which they feel is somehow rightfully theirs: such people tend to say such-and-such and act in such-and-such ways', etc., then it does not matter that S does not know the *word* 'jealousy': he has the concept. Also it is not required, just for having the concept, that S is any good at identifying emotions in practice. In order to test for this (as for PHIL(HC)) we should have to 'hold the information steady', so to speak: that is, ensure that Ss all had the same information, in order to find out whether they could classify it under appropriate concepts.

Fourthly, there are, of course, a number of very different emotions and hence different concepts. S may have the concepts of fear, anger and hate, but not of remorse or pride. We shall have to assess for all emotion concepts, or at least for a representative sample (if we know what a representative sample would look like). This is not as bad as it sounds, for the number of basic emotions and moods is finite and in fact fairly small. What we require for this is a reliable taxonomy of the emotions, a task that badly needs undertaking. But the empirical researcher will not go far wrong if he starts, at least, by devising assessments for the most common and obvious emotions.

Finally, it may seem odd to suggest that there can be Ss who do not have the concepts of such emotions as fear and anger: only mythical heroes, or those very ignorant of English, ask 'What is fear?' No doubt this is generally true. But it is not at all clear, at least in some cases, whether a 'psychopathic' S (whatever this means) merely does not *feel*, say, remorse, or whether he also lacks the *concept*. Further, there may be many Ss who lack the concepts for the more complex emotions (jealousy and envy, remorse and regret, pride and vanity), emotions about which, indeed, we may require to get a good deal clearer than we are. Both for research and, ultimately, for teaching purposes, this aspect of EMP is far from unimportant.

2. Being able to identify one's own emotions (conscious and unconscious) and other people's (conscious and unconscious)

We are dealing here with what we shall later demarcate as four separate sub-components of EMP, but the relevant logical points are too closely connected to separate. The reader will find them discussed fully elsewhere (Wilson, 1971).

First, we are talking about *abilities*. Can S, in practice, correctly say, for instance, 'I am feeling insecure', 'He is jealous', 'She is frightened'? S may have this ability, but may not bring it to bear (for lack of KRAT(1)). To test this ability we should have to hold the 'motivation' – that is, simply, how much incentive S has to use the ability – constant. This is a problem usually either not faced or not solved in much psychological research (for instance, in intelligence tests).

Secondly, we are not concerned with *how* S knows what he or others feel. There is a temptation to think that S has a different *kind* of knowledge in his own case – a 'direct', 'self-authenticating', 'intuitive' or 'certain' knowledge. This is not so. S is differently placed for acquiring knowledge of his own feelings as against other people's, but this placing has both advantages and disadvantages. Sometimes S will know better than other people what he feels, or what they feel; sometimes not. We are concerned only with *whether* he knows.

Thirdly, S's knowledge is bound to consist in noting, and probably in correlating, the various aspects of emotions that we noticed above: that is, the belief, symptoms, actions and surrounding circumstances that go to make up the emotion. Our assessment will be based largely on this. S will be able or unable to induce from, say, facial expressions or postures to beliefs, or from beliefs to actions, or from actions to symptoms. Not much is known about the ways in which this ability operates, but obviously assessors must make use of any relevant research.

Fourthly, it is likely that Ss will perform variably, depending on the particular emotion, the context in which they are called on to identify it, the people of whom they predicate the emotion, and so forth, as well as being more or less good at making inductions from the various signs of emotion mentioned above. We shall need, then, a list not unlike that given for PHIL(CC), which takes account of the various areas, contexts, classes of people and so forth. Thus S1 may be no good at identifying emotions in women; S2 baffled by the over-40s; S3 inept when dealing with societies of people whose facial expressions are in some respects unlike those common in our own culture; and so on.

Fifthly, it needs to be made plain that we are not only concerned with this ability in face-to-face situations. The morally educated S must know what a person would be likely to feel, or to have felt, in the (real or imaginary) future or past. He must be able to *imagine*, as well as in some sense *see*, the emotions of himself and others. This plainly involves different, and in some ways easier, methods of assessment.

Sixthly, and this is connected with our second point above, it is not of course required that S actually *feel* the emotions which he knows to exist in the other person. It may be, indeed, that those Ss who can 'put themselves in other people's shoes' are in fact better at EMP (and perhaps at PHIL also) if they can do this in a strong sense: that is, *have* something like the other's feelings ('empathy'?) rather than just being able to state correctly what the other feels. This may be highly relevant to *methods* of developing EMP and PHIL, but it is not what we are testing for here.

Finally, the distinction between conscious and unconscious emotions requires a brief note. Sidestepping many problems, I shall here mean by 'conscious' emotions those which the person who has the emotion would *not* require any lengthy process of psychotherapy to recognize, and those which he is not prevented from knowing by any deep-laid defences or resistances. For instance, suppose I am angry. I may not be conscious of my anger in the sense of being able to say at once 'Yes, I'm angry', but I could without too much difficulty see that I was trembling, shouting and attacking, and perhaps that I believed someone was thwarting me. If I have difficulty, I lack EMP in respect of my conscious emotions: I am not good, in practice, at noting and correlating the symptoms, actions, etc. of anger in myself (or perhaps in others). The 'raw material' is available to me, but I do not make use of it. On the other hand, the 'raw material' of unconscious emotions (in myself and others) is more subtle and hidden: neither I nor they could reasonably be expected to have it available and to hand immediately. Yet I may induce unconscious emotions, if I have a lot of EMP in this particular area. Naturally Ss may vary a great deal depending on whether it is their own or others' conscious or unconscious emotions: hence we divide this into four sub-components.

The distinction between conscious and unconscious is not an

absolute one: we might rather talk in terms of degrees of availability. Nevertheless, a rough distinction between the two may be made, similar to that which we shall make when dealing with KRAT(1) and KRAT(2). It is sense, though untidy, to talk of what is 'normally' available to consciousness, just as it is sense to talk of 'bringing to bear' (KRAT(1)) one's conscious principles and faculties, though there may be unconscious 'parts of oneself' which one has not 'brought to bear'. It would be unobjectionable, perhaps, if we collapsed these four sub-components into two, abolishing the conscious–unconscious distinction and giving a range of assessments that ran from the 'immediately available' to the 'deeply hidden'. But I should be inclined to keep the fourfold division firmly in mind.

A more serious difficulty may be that assessors may not know, in the case of unconscious emotions, what the 'right answers' are. The very existence of unconscious emotions and the sense of that phrase are both disputed, and what unconscious emotions are felt by whom, and on what occasions, is disputed much more. Nevertheless, there seem to be some clear cases. There is, for instance, the adolescent who (unconsciously) feels insecure, impotent and frightened, and who behaves like a 'tough guy', keeps measuring his strength against authority, and so forth, perhaps consciously feeling nothing but contempt and hatred for the adult world of which he is secretly envious and scared. There is the Casanova who consciously despises women, but unconsciously is in desperate need of them. There is the 'nice chap' who consciously likes other people, but unconsciously fears them and tries to placate them. Of course, assessors would have to agree, and to agree for good reasons, on the 'right answers'. But this whole area is of such importance to moral education that the attempt seems well worth making.

Summary

We have distinguished four sub-components of EMP. These were:

1. Being able to identify conscious emotions in oneself: EMP(1)(Cs).
2. Being able to identify unconscious emotions in oneself: EMP(1)(Ucs).
3. Being able to identify conscious emotions in others: EMP(2)(Cs).

4. Being able to identify unconscious emotions in others: EMP(2)(Ucs).

GIG

This is perhaps the easiest component to deal with, and we can be fairly brief.

1. Knowing relevant 'hard' facts and sources of facts

Under this heading we exclude EMP, which deserved a separate treatment. By 'hard' facts I intend to exclude awareness of emotions and moods (EMP) but to include sensations (an S who does not know that a hard slap on the back may hurt a girl lacks this quality). Most of the 'relevant facts', however, will not be directly concerned with sensations of people, but with the following basic categories.

(a)   Facts relating to health, safety, etc.

This is a large category, and includes what drugs are addictive, elementary biology, first aid, contraceptive devices, the danger of certain machines (cars, electrical devices, etc.), what to do in case of fire, and so on.

(b)   Laws, social norms, conventions, etc.

This includes what may be called 'social facts': not only the law of the land, but also the conventions and etiquette of particular social groups with which S may be in contact, the particular powers and scope of various authorities, the workings of particular institutions, social rules and so on.

(c)   Facts about individuals or groups in need

S needs to know not just what is (as a matter of 'hard' fact) required in general to satisfy others' interests, but also about the existence of various others who are in need. It is relevant that there are old people, starving people, etc. either in other countries or in some other way removed from S's immediate environment.

It is not altogether easy to draw a sharp distinction between this quality and EMP. Under EMP we include awareness of wants as well as emotions, and it might be argued that this overlaps in certain cases – perhaps particularly in (b) above. Nevertheless, knowledge of laws, conventions and expectations can be roughly distinguished from awareness of wants. In practice we can reasonably confine ourselves here to the 'hard' facts relating to *need* or *requirements*. Whether a person *wants* a certain medicine if he is ill, or wants the kind of politeness that is conventional in his group, is here irrelevant: S will still find it useful to know what medicine the person *needs* or what is socially appropriate.

In reference to (c), we need also to remember that EMP is relevant only when S knows that a person exists, and knows something about him (so that he has, as it were, some chance of knowing what the person feels). It is the 'hard' knowledge of the person's (or group's) existence and circumstances with which we are concerned under (c).

Turning to 'sources' of facts, I intend here to make some allowance, so to speak, for those who happen to be ill informed in particular areas. S may not know much about medicine, but it will make a big difference whether he approaches the doctor or the witch-doctor when he or another is ill. He may not know much about science, but it is important whether he asks the physicist or the priest. Ss who are children or teenagers may rely on their friends as sources of knowledge, rather than their parents or teachers. In general, what we are after here is some awareness on S's part that X or Y is the *kind* of thing that comes under some general heading ('economics', 'medicine', 'science'): that there is some expertise here. Straightforward sources of knowledge, such as the encyclopaedia, are also not to be despised. The three general groups given above will operate for this kind of knowledge also: it is the same facts that we want him either himself to know, or to know how to find out.

To some extent, it will be true that 'relevant' knowledge is different for different Ss. It does not count much against my moral education if I do not know the conventions current among pygmy tribes, or much against a pygmy's if he does not know the social expectations of an Oxford sherry party. If S's own group is at semi-starvation level, S may be pardoned for not taking a great interest in the needs of what count as poor people in the UK. In this respect (and perhaps in this only) our tests are trying to measure something which is not demanded *in the same form* of all cultures. But it is still *equally* demanded. In other words, 'relevant facts' are equally important for me and for pygmies, but the content of this title will be different; whereas, for other components, not only the general quality but the specific content will be the same (emotions, having interests, 'relevant alertness', etc. are common to all societies). In any case, since there are many fundamental similarities between human beings in respect of these 'hard' facts, particularly in the area of health and safety, much of the test content will be common. (When we meet Martians it may be another matter.)

2.   'Knowing how': non-propositional skills in dealing with people

In relationships with people there is an important 'skill' element, which may be present or absent independently of the propositional knowledge of EMP, or of the 'hard-fact' knowledge mentioned just above. We are talking here of a skill which cannot be wholly learned by learning the truth or reasons of various propositions, but which might be picked up in practice or by imitation, like learning to swim. I am thinking here of such contexts as apologizing, cheering someone up, displaying sympathy, and giving or receiving orders. Of course propositional knowledge may improve S's abilities in such contexts, but we are here concerned to assess only the 'skill' element, so that such knowledge must be held constant. We have also, of course, to hold constant the motivational factors (KRAT(1)), for we are interested only in S's ability – whether he can, not whether he wants to.

These skills may be divided into (a) verbal communication skills and (b) non-verbal communication skills. (a) is about whether S says the right thing (when apologizing, ordering, etc.); (b) about whether he says it in the right tone of voice, with the right stance, gestures, etc. Both (a) and (b) are concerned with what S *does*, but not with what S does deliberately. For example, S1 may (unconsciously) always stand the right distance away from the person he talks to, smile at the right time, etc., and this will count as well as S2's deliberate taking up of position and smiling. If S3, however, is liked or disliked for what he *is* (badly dressed, ugly, dwarfish), this does not count. The distinction is a fine one, but may be drawn well enough in practice. We have to draw it in order to demarcate this quality at all, for it is something in respect of which people can be trained or educated, and we must exclude cases where Ss may be more or less acceptable to others for quite different reasons. (Being an attractive blonde is not a social skill.)

Summary

We have distinguished:

1. Knowledge of relevant 'hard' facts: GIG(1)(KF).
2. Knowledge of sources of facts: GIG(1)(KS).
3. 'Knowing how', or 'social skills' of verbal communication: GIG(2)(VC).
4. Ditto for non-verbal communication: GIG(2)(NVC).

KRAT(1)

We have here perhaps the most complicated of the components. In dealing with PHIL, we first wanted to know whether S had the concept of a person in the required sense (PHIL(HC)), and then whether S thought he ought to apply this concept in the sense of acting in accordance with others' interests (PHIL(CC)). Both these components could be described as 'cognitive', in that we are not concerned with any feelings or tendencies to act or behaviour on the part of S, except in the possible but unusual case of an S who said he thought he ought to act in others' interests, but never (or hardly ever) did so – in this case we should have doubts about S's sincerity. There is, then, no very tight conceptual connection between PHIL(HC) and (CC) and S's actual feelings or behaviour in 'real life'.

With PHIL(RSF), however, there is a stronger connection. An S who has some feelings, whether of a 'duty-orientated' or 'person-orientated' kind (DO or PO), that support the rule of acting in others' interests *eo ipso* has some motive or incentive for doing so. And the stronger the feelings – the more PHIL(RSF) – the more we should normally expect that he did so. But there is still not a necessary conceptual connection here. First, S may have the feelings, but not have them as rule-supporting feelings *in practice*. That is, it may be that when S considers, in the abstract, what he thinks he ought in general to do, he has feelings which support the PHIL(CC) rule, but that when he is called upon to decide and act in real life, he either does not have these feelings or does not have them *as* rule-supporting feelings. Secondly, S may have the feelings as RSF, but the feelings are not powerful enough for them to be overriding, in the sense of issuing in *action*. Yet they may still be powerful. S1 has a strong incentive to help a person, but he has a stronger feeling of embarrassment and so fails to do so. S2 has a weaker incentive but no embarrassment, and so helps the person.

For these (and other) reasons we need a separate component, which we call KRAT(1). This is generally concerned with 'bringing to bear' the previous components when S is actually faced with the need for decision and action, with whether S's attitudes and abilities and attainments, listed under PHIL, EMP and GIG, are 'alive' in real-life situations. It is clearly possible that they should be inert. This is easy to see in the case of EMP and GIG: S may have emotional awareness, the ability to identify others' feelings, but not actually use it (through laziness, nervousness or many other reasons); and S may know all the relevant facts, and have all the 'social skills', but not make use of the knowledge and skills when it comes to the point. As we have seen, this applies to PHIL also. We all know many Ss who quite genuinely hold, as a sincere moral theory, that they ought to act in others' interests, and who (to a greater or lesser degree) have genuine feelings which relate to and to some degree activate this rule, but who, nonetheless, sometimes or even often fail to follow the rule in practice.

Failure to follow the rule in practice may be of two kinds. Either S fails even to reach the stage of making a proper *decision*, and this is what we are concerned with under KRAT(1); or else he makes a decision, but fails to carry it out even though it was within his power, and this we shall leave to KRAT(2). The 'decision' we are talking about here, however, needs to be specified more fully. It is not just a question of S thinking that X ought to be done 'in principle', as it were; it is a question of S's committing himself to action in making the decision. We shall expand on this later; here I want to show the width and nature of the gap that KRAT(1) has to fill, between S's just 'having' PHIL, EMP and GIG, and S's making what I have so far called only a 'proper' decision.

The first way in which S can fail to bridge the gap is simply by not being *alert* or not *noticing* that a decision is required. S may be in a day-dream or so intent on his own ends that he does not even realize that a moral situation confronts him. By a 'moral situation' here I mean a situation in which others' interests are at stake and S can act in their favour. This shows that what we require here is not just that S should be, as it were, generally 'alert', but that he should be *relevantly* alert: that is, alert to certain classes of situation. Moreover, he would not count as being 'relevantly alert' if he did not see the situation *under the right description*. If some poor chap is being pelted with stones, S may notice this and say 'How amusing!', and whilst there might perhaps be a correct description under which it *was* amusing, nevertheless we want S to see it as a case of another person in need of help, suffering, etc. We shall describe this part of KRAT(1) as 'relevant alertness', and call it KRAT(1)(RA).

The second type of failure, closely connected but distinguishable, is if S fails to *think thoroughly* about the situation to which he has alerted himself. A bell rings in S's mind, so to speak, whenever it might seem as if others' interests were at stake, but then S might not bother to think much further about the situation. He might fail to make full and proper use of his PHIL, EMP and GIG – particularly, in this sub-component, of his EMP and GIG. S should ask himself questions like 'What does this person really feel? Is it really a desire to help him that I myself feel, or some other desire? What facts do I know, or could I find out, that would make my help effective?', and so on. (I do not imply, of course, that S has to do all this *consciously*.) Here it is important to note that S will summon up *any* ability, skill, attainment, etc. that he possesses – e.g. not just what he does know, but what he could find out. This part of KRAT(1) we shall call 'thinking thoroughly' – KRAT(1)(TT).

Thirdly, when S reaches the stage of making a decision, he may fail in three ways. (a) His decision may not be the result of his PHIL being *overriding*. Despite his KRAT(1)(RA) and (TT), there may still be some other overriding syllogism derived from his own self-interest, or his inner feelings of guilt, or whatever, which prevents him from deciding in accordance with, and because of, the PHIL principle about others' interests. (b) His decision may not be thoroughly *prescriptive*: that is, S may think in a general sort of way that X ought to be done, but not that *he himself* ought to do it. S is required, as it were, to command or prescribe the required action to himself: to commit himself to acting. (c) His decision may be such that he thinks that *he* ought to do X, but not that X is the thing that *anyone* in a similar position ought to do. S's rule must not be a rule for himself alone, but must be universalizable. (These last two requirements might perhaps be put by saying that S must mean 'ought' in a full sense.) From the requirement that S's decision should be overriding, prescriptive and universalizable we shall describe this aspect of KRAT(1) as KRAT(1)(OPU).

The assessment of KRAT(1), in its RA, TT and OPU aspects, is beset by similar complications to those of PHIL(CC): that is, there is likely to be a great variety of performance depending on various categories (the type of situation, the people involved, etc.). But we have also an added difficulty. S's decision to act can, obviously, be to some extent verified by seeing how S actually does act. However, we need to know that S acts *as a result of* this kind of decision; we need to know what 'goes on in S's head'. So mere observation of behaviour, even coupled with assessments of PHIL(CC) and (RSF) will not be enough: we shall need interviews, cross-questioning of S, and so forth. Such methods will be even more necessary if we are to distinguish whether S lacks the RA, TT or OPU elements of KRAT(1), and, in the latter case, we should need to know whether it was the O, P or U element that was lacking.

A few lines above I mentioned the problems caused by variety of context or situation. For KRAT(1) there will be some important additions to be made to the list given for PHIL(CC). This is obviously because, in the latter case, there are no serious problems about the *context in which* S 'claims the concept', though of course there are problems about the *internal* situation (e.g. the elements in the story) about which S is asked to judge. Thus a test for PHIL(CC) might be in the form of a story in which S's 'peer group' or friends pull one way and others' interests another way. But the peer group is not present in person when S chooses one or the other criterion. With KRAT(1), however, this is not so. S's peers are present, perhaps, looking at him, jeering, shouting 'Come on!', leaving him isolated and so on, and this is a very different matter.

What we are looking for here are categories and contexts which, we guess, so alter the surrounding circumstances of S's decision that we should expect very different 'scores' for KRAT(1) in different categories. Perhaps, in particular, we are looking for *special* or *atypical* circumstances. We may reasonably entertain the concept of S 'normally' bringing to bear, or not bringing to bear, his PHIL, EMP and GIG so as to reach a decision, and go on to determine the 'special circumstances' which encourage S to behave abnormally. S's 'normal score', of course, will depend on general features of S's personality, his 'rule-supporting feelings', general attitude to other people and so on: these are not 'special circumstances' in any sense. If S is characteristically nervous of other people, over-anxious, apathetic, hostile, etc., then this will affect (rightly) his 'normal' score.

The following categories, which may be taken just as general categories analogous to those suggested for PHIL(CC) or as 'special circumstance' categories, seem to be possibly relevant for assessment.

(a) Influence of 'potent' others

I use this jargon term to refer to 'others' who might, for normal Ss, exercise particular influence on decision-making 'in the field': e.g. S's peer group, his parents or other authority figures, his girlfriend, his dependants. These will affect S's KRAT(1) in ways more familiar to the social psychologist than to myself.

(b) Influence of locale

It is likely to make a big difference whether S's decision is taken in his own country or abroad; at home or at school; at work or at play; conceivably, in a crowded city or in the open country; and so on.

(c) Influence of immediately prior experience

If S has, for instance, just scored a notable success at school or, conversely, been severely rebuked in front of his classmates, won a sweepstake or had a row with his wife, seen an amusing film or been bored to tears by X's conversation – these and suchlike will affect the issue.

(d) Influence of temporary 'moods'

It will matter whether S feels depressed at that particular time, elated, 'unreal' and so on. There are temporary moods of this kind which are *not* caused by immediately prior experiences (as in (c)).

I am only too aware that the above four categories are very unsophisticated. There will be borderline cases and cross-categoriza-
tions. For example, if S is *with* his peer group *in* a football stadium
when his favoured team has just lost, *and* S is 'in a bad mood' that
day anyway, this seems to bring in all four categories.

KRAT(2)

If S has KRAT(1), as well as the other components, he reaches the
stage of making a 'proper' decision to act in others' interests. But he
may still not do so. It is both logically and empirically possible for S
to make a sincere and genuine decision and not to carry it out even
though he could do so. If we put enough weight (against normal
usage) on such concepts as sincerity, genuineness, wholehearted-
ness, 'bringing to bear', 'prescriptive', etc., then we can deny that
this is true, and say that S will necessarily act unless he is prevented.
But I have argued that to do this is to direct our attention away from
a very important class of cases which is of particular interest to the
researcher.

   This is the class of cases in which S has made a 'proper' (sincere,
etc.) decision, but does not carry it out, *not* because he is in any
simple sense prevented, as if his hands were tied behind his back,
but because there is some unconscious counter-motivation or
counter-syllogism. On what seems to me to be the correct view of
the unconscious, we shall say that there is a part of S – so unknown
to himself that we cannot properly speak of S's decision as 'insin-
cere' – that is *following different rules*; or we can say, if we like, that
S himself (unconsciously) follows different rules, as a result of
unconscious beliefs and emotions. This is, obviously, a very different view of the unconscious than that held by some, particularly by
those who regard it as a clumsy way of talking about conditioned
reflexes, 'imprinting', etc. In my view, it is often the case not that S
cannot, but that in an important sense S does not *want* to, perform
the required action.

   Since the unconscious is, on this view, in principle educable, and
since there is a sense (which I shall not expand here) in which S is
responsible and perhaps 'to blame' for the rules he unconsciously
follows, and since, further, this class of cases seems to me very
large, it would be a mistake to exclude it from consideration. We
are, then, dealing with cases in which S has got as far as KRAT(1)

but then simply does not (does not want to, rather than cannot) do what he ought, or what he has sincerely decided. But it will be immediately apparent that there is very little the philosopher can say about this class of cases. We could, no doubt, attempt some kind of taxonomy of the various unconscious counter-syllogisms that may be operating, but this seems rather a task for the clinical psychologist or psychoanalyst.

For our purposes of assessment, all we can do (and it is enough) is to identify that it is in *this* area that S fails. We shall describe the area as KRAT(2) because of its similarity with KRAT(1). We can assess it, at least by any direct form of assessment, only by determining that S has made a 'proper' decision, by assuring ourselves that there is no straightforward prevention of S's acting, and then by seeing whether S does or does not act. If S does not, he lacks KRAT(2). We shall, of course, take care to confine ourselves to standard cases, where a 'normal' or reasonably well-integrated person (I shall not enlarge on these phrases here) would be expected to carry out his decision.

STATUS OF THE COMPONENTS

I have pointed out earlier that the component titles are not intended to stand for any kind of psychological entity: for 'factors', 'forces', 'mechanisms', 'innate abilities' or anything else of that kind. When we score S for 'having' or 'lacking' PHIL, EMP, etc., we are simply answering questions of the general form 'Is it true of S that...?' We are not answering any questions about *why* this is true or untrue, about what mechanisms or forces make it true or untrue. This is quite a different enterprise, no less important, but one which in my view it would be hard to undertake successfully unless and until our present enterprise is successfully concluded. In other words, until we know the answers to the general question 'Is it true of S that...?', I do not see that we have much chance of propounding clear and plausible hypotheses about the underlying causes, for we shall not even have clearly identified the phenomena we want to explain.

This needs stressing because empirical research lives in a world densely populated by various entities or 'constructs'. I am thinking here not only of such terms as 'social class', 'ego-strength' and 'super-ego', but of words seemingly more relevant to our present interests – 'ability', 'capacity', 'competence', 'motivation', 'attainment' and so on. I confess to extreme confusion about the meaning of such words as used by empirical researchers, confusion perhaps not unshared by the researchers themselves. Nevertheless, there will be a standing temptation, to which I as well as others may succumb, to describe our components by the use of such terms. The temptation is hard to resist because at least some of them (for instance, 'ability') are normal English words and would be the most natural terms to use in certain descriptions.

In what immediately follows I want to clarify the status of each component in terms of the question 'Is it true of S that...?' If I can do this, we need not become entangled in the undergrowth of quasi-technical terms, nor ambiguously specify this component as an 'attainment', or that as an 'ability', or the other as a 'motivational factor'. To put this another way, on the one hand, we need to be absolutely clear about what we are testing for under the heading of each component. We must be able to say of any evidence that turns up in our assessment, 'This is (is not) part of *what we mean by* "having PHIL" (EMP, GIG, etc.).' On the other hand, we must steer clear of thinking that there is some underlying *thing* for which we are testing, as if our assessment were only valid if it got at this underlying thing. We are concerned with what PHIL, EMP, etc. are by definition.

PHIL(HC)   If S has the concept of a person, then S *can do* certain things (most obviously identify, once he knows the facts, certain instances as falling under the concept). There is no question of S's *wanting* ('being motivated') to do this, or of S's being the sort of person who, with time and teaching, may get to be able to do it ('innate ability'? 'potential'?). S has simply got to be able to do it, at the time of assessment, *if* he wants to or is induced to.

PHIL(CC)   If S claims the concept as his overriding moral principle, and thinks that he ought to use others' interests as the criterion of decision and action, then this is simply something that S *does*. We are not concerned with cases where S *cannot* do this owing to some preventing factor outside S's control (for instance, S is under hypnosis or threatened at gun-point or drugged). So we are concerned with what S *does when he can*. (We shall be careful, however, to interpret 'he can' in a wide sense to include S's unconscious desires, beliefs and emotions.) The context of assessment must be one in which S *can do what he wants*; we then assess what S actually does.

PHIL(RSF)
(DO and PO)

If S has DO and/or PO feelings, then again he simply *has* them. There is no question of his being able to have them, or wanting to have them, though again we must be sure that they are *his* feelings: that is, feelings which arise out of his perception and thinking, not feelings induced against his will.

Feelings, in the present sense of emotions, not sensations, are logically made up of characteristic beliefs, symptoms and tendencies to action. (This was discussed more fully under EMP.) Thus an S who evinces the DO feeling of remorse will believe he has done wrong, show symptoms of guilt and perhaps tend to apologize or make restitution; and so with other DO and PO feelings. Verification of these three elements is required if it is to be true of S that he feels X or Y, and the verification will vary with the particular feeling.

EMP(HC)

This is analogous to PHIL(HC), in that we are here concerned only with whether S has the concepts of various emotions (moods, feelings, 'states of mind', etc.). It has to be true of S that he can, if he wants, bring certain phenomena – beliefs, symptoms, actions, circumstances – under the same criterion. The criterion would normally be represented by a word – 'jealousy', 'pride', etc. – and full knowledge of the meaning of such words would be a sufficient condition for S's having the concept (but not a necessary condition: he may have the concept under some other heading). Whether S can in practice, or in practice wants to, identify particular emotions is not in question.

EMP(1)(Cs)
EMP(1)(Ucs)
EMP(2)(Cs)
EMP(2)(Ucs)

All these are concerned with whether S *can*, *in practice*, identify emotions: that is, whether he can recognize and correlate the various evidences of emotion in himself and others, in respect of conscious and unconscious emotions. They are not concerned with whether S actually *does* do this, for S may not want or be induced to do it, yet still be able to do it. Lack of incentive is lack of KRAT(1); we are here interested in the presence or absence of ability.

GIG(1)(KF)
GIG(1)(KS)

Both of these are concerned with whether S does actually know relevant facts and sources for relevant facts. No sense is to be attributed to saying 'Does S *want* to know?' Some sense may be attributed to saying 'Does S want to *remember* the facts?', but we are not concerned with *why* S knows or does not know, only with whether S actually has the knowledge (can consistently produce the right answers for his own or others' benefit).

GIG(2)(VC)
GIG(2)(NVC)

These are components of 'knowing how', and may fairly be called 'skills'. S must be good at (skilled in, competent at) behaving in certain ways, verbally and non-verbally. Neither propositional knowledge ('knowing that') nor motivation is here in question.

KRAT(1)(RA)
KRAT(1)(TT)
KRAT(1)(OPU)

These again are all things which S does or does not do. Is it true that S attends relevantly (RA) to real-life situations; that he attends to and thinks thoroughly about them (TT); that he ends up by making an overriding, prescriptive and universalized decision to take action

(OPU)? Here too S must be able to do these things: we are not concerned with cases in which some external compulsion prevents him.

KRAT(2)   Here we need to know only whether S in fact carries out his decision – again, provided he could carry it out, and not permitting situations of compulsion.

We may now be able, perhaps without too much risk of confusion, to categorize these components under various headings that may be useful to empirical researchers. I shall eschew, and would advise the reader to eschew, such terms as 'cognitive', 'affective' and 'motivational'. But it may help to give a quick sketch under three headings, as follows:

1. Knowing

The following components seem to be concerned with different kinds of knowing:

PHIL(HC)   Knowing what counts as a person.

EMP(HC)   Knowing what counts as anger, jealousy, etc.

EMP(1)(Cs)
EMP(1)(Ucs)
EMP(2)(Cs)
EMP(2)(Ucs)   Knowing when X feels anger, jealousy, etc.

GIG(1)(KF)
GIG(1)(KS)   Knowing that some drugs are addictive, etc.

GIG(2)(VC)
GIG(2)(NVC)   Knowing how to apologize, welcome, etc.

2. Doing

PHIL(CC)   What S does here is to *claim* the others' interests rule as his moral principle.

KRAT(1)(RA)	What S does is to notice, to be relevantly alert.
KRAT(1)(TT)	What S does is to think thoroughly.
KRAT(1)(OPU)	What S does is to make a 'proper' decision to act.
KRAT(2)	What S does is to take action.

3. Feeling

PHIL(RSF)
  (DO and PO)

Having a feeling (emotion) is, as we saw when discussing EMP, partly to have a *belief* and partly to have a tendency to *act*, so that to this extent we are dealing with something that S *does*. Nevertheless certain *symptoms* are also conceptually required and are from some viewpoints the central aspect of emotions, so this merits a separate heading. Emotions, we might say, are neither things we know nor things we do, but things we suffer (or that happen to us).

Part Four

Practical Methods

I feel a strong temptation to stop the book at this point and turn the whole matter over to teachers, parents and other practical educators, with the assistance of empirical workers (psychologists and sociologists). For, it might be said, the job of the theoretical writer, the philosopher or whoever, is finished once the aims have been made as clear as possible and some indication given about methods of assessment, as I have tried to do in earlier parts of this book. More importantly, it could be said that *any* practical method must depend for its efficacy on so many variables that nothing much general can be said. What we need to do or say to a child (or adult), any way in which we can influence him, will surely be very much a matter of the particular nature of the child, or ourselves, or the context in which we are operating. The child might need a cuddle, or a discussion, or some severe punishment, or some sort of curricular instruction, or some social experience, or practically anything. Surely the people actually dealing with the child, provided that – a crucial proviso – they are clear about the aims, will be best placed to decide such matters.

I believe this argument is sound, and if I could inject one piece of advice into the minds of practical educators it would be along the lines of 'First get *really clear* about the aims, about the details and meaning of each moral component. Clear your minds of the sort of prejudices and fantasies we have looked at in Part One and elsewhere – in particular of your own attachment to particular moral and religious or other ideologies, or to a despairing relativism. Especially try to adopt a reasonable attitude to the notions of authority and education. Then – well, you alone know the local conditions: the kind of children you are dealing with, the sorts of moves and methods you feel most at home with and can deploy most enthusiastically, the conditions under which you work. *You* are now the experts. Try not to despair at the complexity of the task, and try to remember that things can be changed, however slowly. Look at the moral components, and launch whatever methods *you* think are likely to improve them in your children.' The same, I would like to add, could be said *mutatis mutandis* to empirical researchers: something like 'Take the moral components as your working basis, and see what you can tell us by means of experiment (or any other means that your disciplines provide you with) about how to improve individuals or groups in respect of these components.' I must admit to some disappointment that not much work of this kind has been undertaken, partly perhaps because psychologists and sociologists pay insufficient attention to the philosophical basis. This is but one instance of a vast gap in communication between analytic philosophy and the empirical disciplines, on which I have written elsewhere (1972).

However, I shall not in fact leave it at that because there are practical methods which are absolutely required by the aims, either by way of straightforward logical derivation or by way of common sense. I shall outline one or two of these, but I shall first try to say something general about 'methods'. For here, as in the subject generally, we are likely to be afflicted by prejudice and fantasy. Fashions in methods of moral education ('PSE', 'value education' or whatever) come and go, and it is understandably hard for teachers to clear their minds of current trends: we need to take a long step backwards and consider 'methods' in general.

The intelligent reader, if asked whether moral education should be done by 'academic' methods (classroom periods) or 'social' arrangements (creating a good 'atmosphere' in the school), would dismiss the question as silly. He would say, rightly, that we need both. But before we dismiss it, we need to understand fully why it is silly. For on this understanding depends our grasp of what *kinds* of benefit we can expect from new social arrangements in schools, and how these benefits connect with more 'academic' learning.

First, it is worth remembering that there are many not-so-intelligent readers or non-readers who would *not* dismiss the question as silly, but would answer it along various doctrinaire lines. Some, apparently regarding the word 'education' as virtually synonymous with 'what goes on in the classroom', will be inclined to suppose that 'moral education' must, somehow, be some form of classroom instruction: rather like 'RE' or 'RI' periods, but (we hope) better. They think, perhaps, in terms of discussions about controversial moral issues: teaching important facts about the law, or old people, or war, or sex, or air pollution; or 'bringing morals into' other already established classroom subjects, such as history or literature. Others, who seem to think that morality is something that in some mysterious way *rubs off* on children, will tend to assume that nothing important can be done by direct teaching. It is all a matter of 'setting a good example', 'having the right sort of tradition', 'a good school atmosphere', etc.

The positive suggestions of both these groups may be very sensible, but it is fatally easy to be wedded to *one* particular approach – and to remain wedded, even though one may be forced to admit in argument that both are necessary. Often what lies behind such doctrinaire thinking is some (perhaps unconscious) *model* of 'how children learn to be moral', a model which would not survive a firm grasp of our very various 'moral components'. For instance, there are those who suppose that children learn primarily by *example*: if they have 'good people' (teachers) to imitate, all will be well. Others suppose that morality is essentially like factual knowledge, and can be taught like it: there are certain 'moral laws', which perhaps we can elucidate by dressing them up in fables or stories ('... and the moral of *that* is, "Do as you would be done by"'). Others again seem to believe that particular experiences or locales exert a strong influence in themselves: put their pupils on board a sailing ship, or on a mountaineering expedition, or amid the flowers and fields of nature, and moral virtue will somehow flow into them ('If a man can tackle a mountain he can tackle Life').

Some of these pictures may seem obviously old-fashioned or naive, but the doctrinaire tendency persists just as strongly in contemporary educational fashion. I will give three examples of this:

1.   Many writers identify the '*authoritarian role*' of the teacher as the chief obstacle to moral learning and development. The claim is that teachers are perceived by pupils as 'authorities' who dictate beliefs and values to them *ex cathedra*, whereas what the teachers ought to be doing is to act in a more 'permissive', 'democratic', 'liberal' or 'egalitarian' way, not in an 'authoritarian role'. Some seem even to maintain that, in the course of discussion on moral problems, the teacher should not express personal views at all, but act as a 'neutral chairman'. The pupils should not be given 'right answers', but should be encouraged to adopt their own moral values by their own thought processes and exchange of argument.

Of course, in morality as in any other field of rational thought and action, our objective is to develop the pupils' autonomy. Simply giving the 'right answers' is as educationally inadequate here as it is in the field of mathematics, where the pupil could look them up for himself at the back of the textbook. But it does not follow from this that the teacher has no 'rational authority', or that he should never adopt an 'authoritarian role'. Indeed, if we are to talk seriously of moral *education*, then our objective will partly be to teach the pupils to think in certain (reasonable) ways and not in certain other (unreasonable) ways. If we do not at least have a clear idea of an appropriate *methodology* – roughly a right way of 'doing morals' – and a clear idea of success and failure in morality, then we have no business to attempt moral education at all. Our discussions will be mere free-for-alls, with no question of *truth* or *correctness* or *rationality* at stake. As with other forms of thought, the teacher has of course to get the pupils to think rather than merely obey, but he has to get them to think in a certain style, and in accordance with certain rules and criteria.

In terms of our moral components, the pupil must naturally make up his own mind about what is right and wrong. If he does not, words like 'right', 'wrong' and 'ought' will lack prescriptive force, and simply mean for him 'what teacher expects' or 'what society wants'. This will not develop his KRAT(1): his judgements will not translate themselves into effective decision and action. Equally the pupil must see for himself the reasons which make concern for others (PHIL) a justifiable moral principle. But on the other hand, these reasons have to be *taught*, and there must be some 'authority' to teach them: that is, somebody who is clear about what they are and good at passing them on to pupils. More obviously, relevant facts about moral situations (GIG) or about the feelings of others (EMP) may be more clearly understood by 'authorities' than by laymen.

Hence both in morality and in other areas of education, it is silly to ask such questions as 'Should the teacher play an "authoritarian" or a "democratic" role?', for the obvious answer is that he should play *many different* roles. Everything depends on what is being taught, on what sort of context the teaching and learning demands. It is as ridiculous to suggest that I can lecture on the facts about air pollution or the psychology of race prejudice without being in some sense 'authoritarian', as to suggest that I can join in a seminar discussion among equals without being in some sense 'egalitarian' or 'democratic'. A glance at the list of moral components is enough to show that these and many other contexts are required, so that many roles are required to fit them.

2.   Some claim that only *'real-life' experiences* are effective in moral learning: that anything 'artificial', or which does not 'stem from the child's immediate concern' or 'arise from the child's life situation' will never work. The pupil 'learns by living': 'life and experience are the true teachers'. This is an understandable reaction against certain highly artificial or old-fashioned types of education, but it will not do as a general theory.

If we took it seriously, we should not set out to *educate* the child at all. We should simply let him live and have experiences. In fact, of course, we *control* his experiences in such a way that the child learns to reflect on them, understand them, and adopt certain rules and principles in relation to them. All this we know perfectly well already, and we can only understand the theory under discussion if we take it to be emphasizing the importance of certain criteria in relation to our control of the child's experiences – briefly, that the more closely these are related to the child's own 'natural' concerns, the better.

But what does this amount to? If we consider an example outside the moral area, such as the learning of mathematics or history, it is at once obvious that the child cannot learn anything at all except by stepping *outside* and *beyond* his 'natural' experience. We may, perhaps for good psychological reasons, wish to start with 'real-life' situations: the child may be interested in the number of children in his class, or in what his grandmother did when she was a girl. We may *use* these to develop his thinking in the fields of mathematics and history. But such development cannot occur unless the child is encouraged to drop, or at least go beyond, his immediate 'real-life' concerns and grasp facts and concepts which are *not* part of those concerns – concepts about addition and subtraction, the measurement of time by centuries, and all that goes to make up what we mean by 'mathematics' and 'history'.

So too with morality. If we consider awareness of others' feelings (EMP), for instance, it is apparent that we shall need to make use *both* of 'real-life' contexts *and* of more 'academic' or 'abstract' learning situations. We use the pupil's immediate experiences – what he thinks his father or classmate is feeling, whether he believes that teacher is cross with him, and so on – *in order to* encourage him to go beyond them and improve his EMP generally. We teach him, perhaps, about the various emotions *in general* – their characteristic symptoms, facial expressions, etc. – by using examples and by other methods, so that he can develop an ability which he can then bring to bear on his practical living. We cannot say a priori how much we need 'real-life' contexts and how much we need 'academic' contexts: this will depend on the pupil, as well as on the merits of particular methods.

3.   A further claim is that the '*social mix*' or clientele of the school is sufficient, or at least necessary, to do much of the work of the moral educator for him. In one common contemporary form, the claim is that by merely mixing different pupils, of different ability and different social class, we shall achieve a more 'democratic', or

'egalitarian', or 'tolerant', or 'concerned' school society (in our terms, the pupils will develop more PHIL). By contrast, it is said, to segregate ability groups or social classes is bound to produce a more intolerant and prejudiced attitude, just as the segregation of white and black produces race prejudice.

However, not only is there no empirical evidence for this, but it is a priori highly unlikely that the 'social mix' theory puts its finger on the main point. At a (nameless) international school, an interviewer said to the children of one (nameless) country, 'I suppose mixing with all these different races and nationalities must make you understand and like them more? I expect it's opened your eyes, hasn't it?' The children said words to the effect, 'It certainly has. Before, in our country, we used to quite like the——ians and the——ish: they were different from us, but fun to be with sometimes. But now we have to mix with them every day – well, they're awful. I shan't want to live near them when I grow up.' And so said all the other racial groups.

Equally, one might add, it is not clear that the *amount of mixing* between, say, men and women, or old people and young people, produces more tolerance, concern or liking. (It is tempting to argue the opposite.) The point here, however, is not to frame hypotheses, but to see that teaching PHIL is *by its nature* more complex than such doctrinaire hypotheses allow. The amount of mixing, whatever it is to be, is plainly relevant, but it can do no more than make *possible* the learning of PHIL. For to have PHIL is not just to 'get used to' the existence of others who are of a different colour, or IQ, or social class, or age, or hair-style, from oneself; nor even to 'understand' such others. PHIL involves understanding the *reasons for which* the other's needs and wants count equally with one's own. And this is not something which 'social mix', even in principle, can achieve by itself.

This last example in particular will, I hope, show something of the complexity of the relationship between the 'academic' and 'social' contexts of learning. But there is still one more doctrinaire hurdle to surmount. Many people, who will already have appreciated the general points made above, may be inclined to react by saying something like 'Yes, we understand all this. We understand that neither pure "academic" contexts nor purely "social" contexts are enough. We understand that we must not be wedded to particular models of moral learning, nor expect direct results merely by making changes in one particular direction. We need *both* "academic" *and* "social" contexts.'

All this is true, but it is not enough, for it is apt to lead to (or incorporate) the idea that the two types of context can be *dissociated* from each other. Thus, to take an extreme example, one might imagine a headmaster saying, 'Right, we need both academic and social contexts. Very well, we can fix the academic ones OK: we will have classroom periods about emotions, and politics and economics, and moral values. Now how about the social contexts? Well, people speak highly about the Outward Bound courses, school cruises, various kinds of summer camps, and so on: I must arrange for my pupils to be sent on these. Then they will have had both kinds of moral learning.'

This is a silly though not, I think, uncommon way of dealing with the problem. We can see what is likely to happen. The pupils will learn something in their 'academic' contexts, but it is unlikely to transfer to their actual behaviour; conversely, they will acquire certain behaviour patterns (perhaps in a sense 'learn') from climbing mountains or going on canoe trips, but if the contexts remain purely 'social' they will not grasp the *reasons* and *principles* required by moral education. Thus I can *both* be taught in a classroom that consideration of other people is morally good, *and* pull my weight in a football team or on a sailing ship, and *still* not acquire a generalized principle of PHIL which will affect my behaviour on land or off the games field. In the former context the reasons are 'unreal', not connected with my experience: in the latter there may be no reasons given at all, or the reasons may be the wrong ones (to win the game or keep the ship afloat). This leads to the first of two more positive points I want to make.

CROSS-REFERENCE FROM 'ACADEMIC' TO 'SOCIAL'

What we must have in mind, whenever we are thinking generally about 'methods of moral education' is a picture of a *range* of different methods which can be placed for convenience on a dimension labelled 'real-life' at one end and 'theoretical' on the other. Thus, getting pupils to co-operate on some 'real-life' task such as sailing a ship would stand at one extreme; explaining to them the ('abstract' or 'philosophical' but very important) reasons why one ought to be concerned about others' interests at the other.

But as we have seen, this is not enough. We have to make sure that the range of different methods, and the different contexts which they require, are *connected*. By 'connected' we must mean not necessarily that they are given to the same children, or run by the same teacher, or occur during the same school term or year; we must mean that the same *point*, the same *things learned*, become clear to the pupils in *all* the contexts. In order to ensure this, we have to have a very clear idea ourselves of which things they are actually supposed to be learning, and we also have to arrange our methods so that this becomes as clear to the pupils as it should be to us.

Both these are more difficult than they might seem. To use our previous example, suppose we conceive the 'sailing-ship' experience as a matter of 'encouraging self-reliance and responsibility', 'getting pupils to work together', etc., and suppose we add to this an academic context in which we tell them the parable of the Good Samaritan, point out the virtues of loving one's neighbour and so on. Now here our *own* picture of the point of the two contexts is confused: they have no real connection in our minds, except in the vaguest possible terms. If, on the other hand, we described the point of the 'sailing-ship' context in terms of 'getting pupils to experience and appreciate the value and equality of other human beings', claiming perhaps that this 'value and equality' becomes clearer to pupils in this sort of 'real-life' context, then we should already have brought the point nearer to the (same) point of the academic 'Good Samaritan' context.

In order to get clear pictures of the points of various contexts, I can only recommend that the teacher gains as firm a grasp as possible of the moral components. A proper understanding of what PHIL, EMP, etc. *mean* is the only thing that will arm him against muddle – not just philosophical muddle, but the practical muddle and ineffectiveness that arises from the lack of clear objectives in choosing contexts. This point stands even if empirical research eventually shows that certain contexts 'work', in the sense of increasing certain components, for it will be necessary for their 'working' that the teacher, who controls the contexts, understands what he is trying to do. It is not the ropes and the sails, or the opening of Bibles, or any other environmental feature in itself that does the trick; it is the way in which the teacher encourages the children to learn from these features and what they generate.

Even when the teacher is clear, it is essential that he makes the children equally clear. This can only be done by what I have called 'cross-references' from one context to another. By this I mean that ways must be found of getting the pupils to *put together* the various contexts. For example, we do not *just* put them in a sailing-ship and let 'life teach them'; we discuss the experience while they are on the ship, take films and tape-recordings of how they behave, consider what general principles emerge, etc. We do not just tell them to love their neighbours; we use examples, illustrations from books, films and real life; we get them to role-play and act such illustrations for themselves, engage in simulation situations and take part in 'real-life' contexts (back to the sailing-ship).

Cross-referencing will enable us to use contexts which affect the development of all the components, and if we use contexts through-out the whole range along the 'theoretical'–'real-life' dimension, we shall be saved from many fruitless worries about whether any *one* context does the job – the answer being that of course it does not, but that it will help to do this job in conjunction with other contexts. To take a simple example, suppose we use 'old people' as a topic title for part of our moral education. Then we can get the children to learn the 'hard' facts about the conditions under which old people live (GIG), to understand why they are just as important as anyone else (PHIL), to develop understanding of how old people feel (EMP), and connected with all this to make decisions (KRAT(1)) and take action (KRAT(2)) by going out to help them, talking to them and so on, bringing back these experiences to the more 'academic' contexts in which GIG, EMP and PHIL may be further developed, and then going back to the 'real-life' context again by, say, asking some of them to tea, or inviting them to help in the school, or whatever.

It is already clear – and this is what we shall be concerned with in what follows in this part – that in order to do this we have to have 'social arrangements' in the school (an organizational structure) which make it possible, for the classroom or 'academic' context is plainly insufficient for some of the methods we will want to deploy. This leads on to our next point.

MAKING THE SOCIAL CONTEXT FIT THE METHOD

Having a clear picture of *what* we want the pupils to learn is more than half the battle, and having a clear idea of what methods, in general, will be effective is most of the other half. From this most of our practical decisions about what changes to make in the social and organizational arrangements of the school will follow.

I stress this point because it is very easy to regard social contexts as *in themselves* 'educational', or on other grounds desirable. Much of our thinking here tends to be dominated by tradition, fashion or administrative convenience. It is one or other of these three tempters, rather than any serious reflection on our own part, which is probably responsible for most of the social features and arrangements of schools. It is (or is not) traditional for pupils to wear uniform: fashion changes and the school caps come off. 'Houses' in a school may exist because they have always existed in that school, or because it is administratively convenient to divide pupils up in this way, or because it is fashionable to do so. 'Morning assembly' may be retained because it is legally required, but because nobody is clear what the pupils are supposed to learn from it, or what other benefits are to be derived, we do not know what form to give it.

Similarly, it is in terms of current fashion or personal predilection, rather than in terms of moral education, that we incline to think when we enter arenas entitled 'sixth form colleges', 'the integrated day', 'team teaching', 'tutor groups', 'comprehensivization', 'the prefect system' and so forth. Often we are moved by what is popular with the pupils – sometimes rightly, but not necessarily. Thus we sometimes fall in with a particular picture of 'the teenager of today' which, whether true or false, is judged not by any ideal of the 'morally educated person' but rather in the light of what we tend to regard as iron sociological laws: 'the teenager of today' necessarily 'rebels against authority', 'has his own life-style', 'must be treated as an adult', 'can't be expected to exercise prefectorial authority' and so on.

Here too the old, false dichotomy between 'authoritarian' and 'permissive' outlooks lulls us into unreason. We find ourselves taking sides in an irrational dialectic between 'old-fashioned' or 'progressive' methods: the more 'conservative' or 'right-wing' of us will want to stick to certain traditions and styles; the more 'liberal' or 'left-wing' will be carried away by the images of 'participation', 'freedom' and many others. We find ourselves fighting battles which rapidly become political rather than educational. All this is extremely tedious, but it is also extremely widespread, particularly in current educational literature, and it needs to be resisted.

All that we have to do (but it is a lot) is to be clear in our own minds that whatever social arrangements we make *have point*, and that this point derives from a clearly stated educational task. The crucial thing is the *logical* derivation of one from the other. For instance, it is useless to argue on general grounds about whether pupils should be encouraged to talk in class, or whether we should have desks in rows or chairs in a circle: there is absolutely no point in defending or attacking these arrangements as 'good for participation', 'bad for discipline', 'democratic', etc. The question is, what are we trying to *do* in making these arrangements? Well, if what we are trying to do is to teach discussion skills – to give pupils practice in the role of discussing and arguing as equals, listening to each other, making relevant replies and so on – then it will more or less follow logically that they must be encouraged to talk, and that putting the chairs in a circle is a good idea. On the other hand, if what we are trying to do is to give the pupils some information, as quickly and efficiently as possible, then they should not be encouraged to talk, and the arrangement of desks in rows in front of the teacher is probably a sensible one.

This example is deliberately naive, but apply this now to 'social arrangements' in a fuller sense. We can see that 'discussion as equals' entails certain contexts and rules, but what lies behind such important arrangements as the house system, the tutor group, the desire (or refusal) to set and stream, the merits (demerits) of coeducation and a 'charismatic' headmaster, school outings, organized games and so forth? We cannot just accept them as *given*, but what are the basic educational points from which they are supposed to flow?

In the case of highly functional institutions, such as an army or a sailing-ship, the point of social arrangements is usually fairly obvious: they are required by the function of the institution. In order to fight well, or keep the ship off the rocks, large numbers of (non-disputable) rules and requirements are needed. But part, at least, of the function of the school is educational, and this makes clarity much more difficult. If we are setting out to produce good stormtroopers, or good monks, or good army officers, it would be easier; but this is training or indoctrination, not education. We are trying to produce good *people*. And unless we stick very closely to the moral components, taking our methods from what we guess to be relevant to their development, we shall not get very far.

I now want to give a brief outline of two methods which are (1) clearly required by what we have said earlier, with, perhaps, the addition of a little common sense, and (2) largely lacking in schools today.

Chapter 9

A Non-Academic Base for Moral Education

What is wrong with the social set-up of schools as we have it? When asked this, teachers are apt to say such things as (I quote here from informal tape-recordings): 'It doesn't give you a chance to really know your pupils', 'The examination system doesn't give us time to treat our pupils as people', 'We keep having the parents complain', 'You have to change classes all the time, everybody runs around like mad things', 'It's a nine-to-four academic factory, not a school at all', 'The headmaster is just an administrator, the boys hardly know who he is'. All these comments are to the point. Can we generalize them in such a way that we can use the generalizations to determine practical changes?

Some of the comments point to practical pressures (e.g. of examinations) which could in principle be removed, or handled by other methods: these we shall deal with later. Apart from these, the burden of the complaints is simple: it is that the social arrangements of the school *do not give scope for personal relationships*. More precisely, for of course it is not being said that pupils cannot make friends at school, they do not give scope for the kinds of relationship required for moral education, perhaps particularly for interaction between staff and pupils. There is no *social base* for this: that is, no *place* and no *contexts of activity* which would naturally generate this interaction. Of course we are here overstating the case: most schools have *some* sort of 'social base', even if it is only morning assembly or the playground. But the lack is felt.

With what can we associate this lack of 'social base'? There are a number of points, at once vague and obvious, which seem to be required in any serious attempt to 'morally educate' pupils. They include:

1. The pupil's need for a secure framework in terms of a group identity.
2. His need for a 'personal identity' in terms of feeling confident, successful, useful and wanted.
3. The importance of close personal contact with adults.
4. The importance of parent figures and of a firm and clearly defined authority.
5. The need to channel and institutionalize aggression.
6. The importance of co-operation and participation.

And so forth. Nobody, we imagine, will want to say 'no' to any of these: they are boringly truistic. Yet it should strike us that, not only in schools but also in institutions of higher education, we simply *do not cater* for these truisms. It is not clear that we even try very hard to do so; at least, individuals may try, but there is not much sign of collective effort.

What could we conceivably use as a 'model' situation which *does* take care of these obvious needs? Some readers will at once think of the traditional pattern of the 'public' independent boarding schools, and this model is indeed relevant. But the key points lie deeper. We shall use the model of a very old social institution: the family. By this we shall understand a family of reasonable size: say, of four or five children and two parents. The relevance of this model does not, of course, derive from any suggestion that schools should *be* families or that the teacher should replace the parent. It is rather that in the family it appears that certain kinds of need are catered for, certain kinds of learning situation naturally set up, and certain elements of the 'social base' we are looking for naturally exist.

Consider this in the light of our truisms listed above. In a satisfactory family, the child immediately has a 'group identity' (1), and by being born into it, looked after by his parents, etc. he feels 'wanted' – to which parents will naturally add as much confidence and feeling of success as they can (2). He is *eo ipso* in close personal contact with adults (3), and authority is clearly defined by the parents (4). Not all families solve their children's aggression problems (5), but there is a built-in necessity for a good deal of co-operation which will mitigate them to some extent, at least until adolescence, and the child cannot help but 'participate' (6).

What is it that holds families together, and what is it that provides the 'social base' for the immense amount of learning that the child does in the family? How is it that he learns to talk and argue, to behave cleanly, to control his impulses, to master all the many facts and skills that he learns outside school? We do not have to be expert social psychologists to give a general answer to this question. First, the family lives in one place, and has forms of sharing which bind it together. Not only are the members of the family an economic unit, but they share food, drink, holidays, outings and in general all the aspects of life which fall outside the area of work. (Though even some forms of work – and this is important – may be shared, such as housework which the child helps with, minor jobs in which he helps his father, mother or elder brothers, and so on.) Secondly, the child has a strong *emotional* relationship with his parents and siblings. From father and mother will come approval and disapproval, love, anger and all the other emotions, and the child will reflect them back to the same sources. He will learn in order to please, or be like, father or brother, to help mother, to be rewarded by sister, even to commend himself to aunt or grandparent. These people *count* with him; they are all he has.

All this too is obvious enough, and it ought to be equally obvious that too few educational institutions, particularly from the secondary school onward, have made any serious attempt to introduce these factors into their social systems. It has been assumed (tacitly) that the school exists only, or chiefly, to impart information, and that parents or 'society' will do the rest. Clearly this assumption is insane, but it needs to be seen why this is so, for it is emphatically *not* just a matter of schools having to 'fill the gap' which has been created by 'bad homes', or the difficulties of bringing up children in an urban and industrialized society. The whole picture painted in terms of parents doing all the moral education, and the school being required only to pass on knowledge and culture, is a false one; and it would be false even if the 'nuclear' or otherwise unsatisfactory families of today were to be replaced by 'better' families (an unlikely event in itself).

There are two points here. First, there *is* no other way whereby the child can learn, or will want to learn, except the way in which he learns in the family: that is, with a secure 'social base', close contact with adults and so forth. This is a necessary model simply because it is the *child's* model, and the only one he has. To expect efficient learning without a base at all, or on some quite different base, is just silly. (Yet this is what we seem to expect by putting children behind desks from nine to four, and trying to persuade them to learn things.) Secondly, the picture is insane because it implies a sharp break between two different situations: (1) the situation in which the child or teenager is in his own family, under parental authority and protection, and (2) the situation in which he is expected to be responsible for himself, which involves financial independence and perhaps the additional role of husband/wife and father/mother. The implication is that the child can move from the one to the other, from (1) to (2), without difficulty or training. No room is left for any intermediary community between (1) and (2).

It is worth pointing to some of the more obvious symptoms of our failure to cater for these simple truths. Perhaps the most obvious is the existence of teenage or sub-teenage groups and gangs which are not under any kind of educational control, and whose emotional investment is anywhere but in the school or college. With this go many symptoms of the 'youth culture': some upsetting, like drug taking; others less so, like fashions in clothes and music. Again, teachers do not need to be told of the resistance, the 'uphill' nature of the task of teaching many pupils. They simply do not want to learn, and one has the horrid suspicion that new curricular methods alone (team teaching, 'progressive' methods, visual aids, 'real-life' projects and so on) will not do the trick: the teacher may work himself into the ground trying to amuse and educate the pupils, but the motivation is just not there. They don't care.

And, one might add, why should they? If, as is sometimes the case, we take little personal interest in them, they will take little in us. Apart from such interest, where is their motivation to come from? Not, or not much, from the intrinsic fascination of a still largely academic curriculum. Not even from the more 'interesting' and 'real-life' subjects, for in fact the pupil's position is still intensely artificial and *un*real. Disguise it how we may, the school as we have it is an institution for learning, not for amusement or for having a good time, and why should they learn if they have no emotional investment in the place? A little, perhaps, in order to get on – to get better jobs, a place at university, a chance for higher standards of living. But to expect healthy children and adolescents to spend most of their time sitting down and learning school subjects, however delightfully presented, *without* very strong emotional incentive seems grotesquely naive. No doubt they will for the most part go through the motions, but not much more than that.

DECENTRALIZATION IN THE 'HOUSE'

In what follows I shall simply suggest, without benefit of lengthy psychological argument, what seems to be required if the school is to have social arrangements effective for moral education. The most important, and also the most obvious, need is one which the family model seems to imply. If schools are to operate in any serious respect like the family, and to generate the conditions of learning and the 'social base' which the family so well deploys, it is clear that there must be some decentralization. We shall speak of this in terms of the 'house', in the hope that the word will be familiar, but not tendentious, in this context.

The answer to the question 'What makes a house?' will be in many respects similar to the question 'What makes a family?' and there will be parallels to other questions and answers, such as 'What makes a good housemaster (mother/father)?' or 'good prefect (elder brother/sister)?' Obviously enough, simply to *call* one group of pupils 'X House' because their names come in the first half of the alphabet, and another group 'Y House' because their names come in the last half, is unsatisfactory. What do we need to add? Will it help if they parade as houses for an occasional fire practice? Not much, we might think. Very well, then, what will? I suggest the following:

1. Numbers

Numbers in a house must not be too large, but how small we can make them will depend on staffing. Much over 80 is too large; much under 30 impractical, for most schools. For our purpose we need a community where all the members can know each other pretty well, and be known pretty well by the houseparents. Numbers near the upper end of the scale can be handled, if other arrangements are satisfactory (particularly topographical arrangements: see below).

2. Composition

Remember the family. We need all ages within the secondary school age-range, and both sexes. A house composed 'horizontally', i.e. of pupils of the same age or the same academic attain-

ment, is not a family-type house at all, but a vaguely institutionalized peer group or club. It is particularly important, again like the
family, that the *older* pupils should play a full part.

3.   Houseparents

In charge of the house there will naturally be both a housemaster
and a housemistress, representing father and mother. We need not
add that they will be chosen, and trained, for 'parental' or pastoral
ability rather than for academic qualifications. Most of their time
and energy will be devoted to the house. Their prestige and power
in the school must be high.

4.   Locale and topography

Families have homes. One thing that makes a home is shared space;
another is individuality. It must be possible for members of the
house to engage in normal (non-academic) activities together, in
shared space; it must also be possible for them to make it, and feel it
as, *their* home/house, which implies both responsibility for it and
independence from outside interference. It must also be 'home-
like' in other ways. The topography, furniture, etc. must generate
security, 'cosiness', individuality, relaxation. There must be enough
privacy and enough opportunity for sharing.

5.   Shared rituals

Families keep together by sharing certain rituals and other activities. In particular, they eat together, drink together, look after their
own homes and (sometimes) pray together or engage in some
common ceremonial or conventional activity. Houses must do the
same. Some things that families do (e.g. sleep together) may be
impractical for many houses; other things are simple and quite
practical. I stress here what we may call the 'internal' binding forces
in the home/house; they may be less obvious than its external
enterprises and activities, but they are likely to be even more
important.

We do not need professional psychologists to tell us, though they have done so vociferously, that unless a child feels loved, valued and wanted he is unlikely to develop well as a person: in particular, from our point of view, he is unlikely to be able to 'afford' the concern and motivation required to make 'other-considering' moral decisions and act on them. This can be put in various terms: 'a sense of identity', 'security', 'self-acceptance', 'self-esteem'.

One of the essential preconditions that the 'social base' of the house will try to generate, then, is this 'self-esteem' for all of its members. How can this be achieved? I suggest three general methods.

1. Multiple criteria of success

We can approach this negatively by observing that, in a system where only certain performances are rewarded, only those capable of such performances are likely to acquire much self-esteem: if we reward those who do well at work and games, those who are bad at both will have even less self-esteem than they had before. We need, then, to adjust the 'desired performances' and their 'rewards' to the capabilities of the members of the house, and *not* vice versa. In particular we need to arrange things so that everyone can shine at something, however stupid, clumsy or otherwise incompetent he may be.

To take an example, suppose (if this is not too unfashionable for modern ears) that we arrange to have an inter-house cup or prize. We allow houses to tot up points for various activities – winning the football matches, passing examinations or whatever. Now we select activities for which it is not only the component performers – the star athletes or scholars – who can score the points in their house. We add the possibility for scoring points for music, or mending motorbikes, or mackerel fishing. We so organize it that the performance of the 2nd or 3rd house football team counts for as much as the performance of the 1st team. We stop only when we are reasonably assured that everyone can contribute *something*.

'Success' depends on the 'rewards' given, in this context. Of course these can be of any form, from material rewards to the mere approbation of the housemaster, via the prestige traditionally attached by the house to certain activities. Simple institutionalized forms, like the house competition mentioned above, are only useful ways of attaching prestige and rewards to new performances.

2.   Co-operative activities (external and internal)

The pupil will naturally want to shine at something: if possible, to do something better than anyone else. We must not try (vainly) to abolish this by any doctrinaire view about the merits of 'co-operation against competition'. But of course it will be true that, however hard we juggle our rewards, there will be some pupils who are to be classified as failures in terms of individual performance. There are two other ways in which the house can do something about this.

The first is by external co-operative activities: that is, activities which depend on collective effort to achieve some external goal. Organized games are the classic example; others are building something, putting on a play or a concert, running a farm or a business. We do not need to say any more about these; they are standard practice, even if not incorporated into a proper house system.

The second requires more consideration. By 'internal' co-operative activities I mean activities which have no external goal (to win the game, make the business pay), but are overtly devoted to co-operation and mutual assistance: for example, getting older pupils to help the younger with their work and other things; having sessions in which the object is to encourage or help unhappy members, 'misfits' or those who are generally a nuisance in the house; allowing the pupils to make and administer their own rules and discipline. (Unfashionable institutions such as 'fagging' may take on a more favourable appearance in this light; the various ways in which some members of the house can be *of use* to others are all valuable here.)

3.   Opportunities to 'patronize'

Characteristically in schools pupils are on the receiving end. They are *done things to* or *at*: they are always in a subordinate role. This does not encourage self-esteem. The pupil must, sometimes, be in a position to feel superior: to patronize, protect, teach, command and control.

This can be achieved by various methods: for example, making sure all members have *dependants*, whether in the form of younger children, animals or individuals outside the house or school whom they can protect and help (infants, backward children, old people, etc.); making sure that each member is allowed to cash in on his possession of particular skills or talents, by teaching them to others (including older members and adults) and thereby temporarily assuming an 'authority' role; in real-life or simulation situations, actually giving the junior members powers, responsibilities and authority (they run the house for a week, for example, or control the house finances, or conduct the rituals, or organize its activities).

4. Physical warmth

To some extent it is true that self-esteem arises because of successful performance, because of taking part in co-operative activities and because of being able to 'patronize': these we have tried to take care of in (1), (2) and (3) above respectively. But this will not be enough. Again, it requires no professional psychologist to tell us that the confidence that goes with 'feeling wanted' or 'being loved' has a great deal to do with simple physical experiences.

Very important for the young child, we are told both by psychologists and by ordinary mothers and fathers, are the straightforward physical expressions of love – cuddling, touching and other forms of bodily contact: the warmth and communication of shared unsophisticated physical activity. To suppose that the child will have totally outgrown the need for this when he reaches secondary school age is just silly. Indeed it is apparent, from the kind of quasi-sexual communal 'clinging' that is characteristic of many adolescents, that they have not grown out of it even in the late teens – perhaps because they have not had enough of it earlier.

Some will think of sex in this context, but I am not talking about the specifically sexual, whatever that is. I have in mind the natural physical contexts, recreative and reassuring for all people, of, say, engaging in a sort of mass free-for-all in the swimming pool, some forms of dancing, some co-operative gymnastic activities. These go together with the encouragement of overt person-to-person physical expression. The importance of this is, of course, *felt* (more or less consciously) even in the most 'stiff upper lip' schools: its repression is part of a tradition we have to get rid of. This does not mean that there may not be natural or inevitable desires for physical privacy among pupils of all ages which have to be respected; but to advocate the expression of sympathy, comradeship, etc. by overt physical means is not to advocate force or interference. The complexities of our existing tradition are such that, besides encouraging social or institutional forms, we shall probably need open discussions and other more 'direct' methods as well.

5. Collective responsibility

We have here quite a different way in which the decentralized house described above can operate. On the one hand, it must give its members confidence and self-esteem, but on the other it must not attempt to shield them from the world as it is. Indeed, it must bring them face to face with the laws of that world, both natural and social, in as crisp a manner as possible. This is perhaps an area where changes in school practice are most of all required.

I can best illustrate the main point here by an example, and I shall take one of the toughest examples from the point of view of the practising teacher: the example of drug taking. It will be well known to teachers who have any considerable experience in this area that very little can be achieved by just *talking* to the children and teenagers who take drugs, and not much more by doing our best to ensure that they do not get their hands on drugs. We can point out to them the consequences, admonish them, threaten them with the law, and so forth – a large number will just not care. So what do we do? Well, one thing we do is to send them for special psychiatric attention, or put them in specially organized communities for the cure of drug addicts, or support and sustain them in various ways. And of course this is not totally silly because no doubt drug-takers have psychological problems which need attention. But there is an important sense in which it is artificial.

Why, we might begin by asking, should people not take drugs? One obvious reason is that it reduces their ability to perform their obligations to other people. The practicability of taking drugs in a society constantly threatened by external enemies, for instance, would be minimal: if you are an ancient Roman surrounded by barbarians, both the task itself and the other ancient Romans would make sure that you are able to stand to arms whenever required, rather than lying in a stupor. Questions about the 'personal morality' or 'ideal' of drug taking (as contrasted with our wicked materialist society, for instance) just would not arise. It is our misfortune – or rather, our fault – that we have a society in which drug-takers can get away with it.

If this *is* at least *one* good reason for not taking drugs, then the educator has to instantiate this reason in a social context, and a purely academic context is unlikely to be sufficient. (Pupils in drugged stupors are sometimes difficult to distinguish from pupils in ordinary stupors.) The question therefore becomes: under what sort of conditions will it become obvious to the members of the house that drug taking is just plain *inconsistent* with what the world requires? Showing that drug taking is inconsistent with working hard, or being good at football, is not crisp enough: we have to do more. Very well, we put the house into situations where, if people take drugs, they get savaged by their peers because they have not pulled their weight in gathering food, or they get left behind in a stupor on the cold mountainside, or they are given no food because they have failed to wash up, or, if absolutely necessary, they run the risk of being eaten by wolves.

I have deliberately overstated this, to make the point. The point is that both school and society are, from the child's viewpoint, so artificial and remote from the underlying realities of life that the lessons need to be driven home in as simple and strong a fashion as possible. This, of course, is the attraction of what we may call the 'Outward Bound' school of thought: on mountains or in sailing-ships the necessities of the situation just *are there*, and it requires a very advanced addict, or a very severe degree of 'maladjustment', to avoid them.

To understand, in anything like a full sense, these 'underlying realities' is no easy task for the child. Basic economic facts, like the necessity to produce food and warmth; basic social facts, like the necessity to preserve some degree of reputation and credit with one's neighbours; basic political facts, like the necessity to have some kind of rules, discipline and sanctions – all these are not made clear to children in the way that they would be clear if the child lived in a smaller, simpler social group. We just assume that children will somehow pick these truths up, and then we are surprised when, as adolescents, they show a virtually complete ignorance of them.

Hence the importance of what I have called 'collective responsi-bility' and 'pay-off'. The former is a matter of the house operating as a group; if not, the 'pay-off' – the good or bad result – must be immediate and obvious even to the dullest. Given even a small number of such experiences, it is to be hoped that the point will sink in, and can be generalized. Here 'life' has, if you like, taught the child; the educator's job is to contrive the experiences and encourage the child to generalize from them. Imagine, for instance, how much could be learned from a 'Lord of the Flies' situation, carefully monitored, video-taped and discussed afterwards: more, one might guess, than from merely reading the book or seeing the film.

The crux here consists in *putting the members of the house on the spot*: that is, in giving *them* the responsibility and the consequent 'pay-off'. They run a business or look after their house finances incompetently: very well, they go broke. They fail to organize food for themselves: very well, they go hungry. They fail to have adequate rules about stealing, or punctuality, or telling the truth: very well, there will be chaos. Of course the houseparents will have to control this method and keep it within limits, but I am much more scared that they will not use it strongly enough.

Amongst other things, it is only by bringing them up against the laws of nature in this way that the 'we–they' feeling is avoidable. In an artificial situation, the standard peer-group rules about 'not sneaking' and the barrier between 'we', the pupils, and 'they', the authorities, is inevitably raised. There is a kind of alienation, perhaps a 'cold war', between teachers and pupils which is as anti-educational as it is boring. In a 'real' situation (think of the sailing-ship again) there is just no scope for the cold war: no time, and not much incentive.

In this chapter I have demarcated the general moves that need to be made in respect of social arrangements: (1) the establishment of an effectively organized and decentralized house – the creation of a social group to work *with*; (2) the task of that group in creating a feeling of security and love for all its members; (3) its task in facing the world we live in and coping with it.

These points, again, are not new, but they need to be institutionalized in our schools. I suggest an approach which is as much unlike our usual acceptance of school systems as 'given' as can be imagined, but which is more likely to stimulate creative thinking. Suppose you are a head teacher with 20 other teachers: you are landed on a desert island with about 650 children and told to educate them, with the help of various buildings and bits of equipment which a mother country kindly supplies you with. What do you do?

Whatever you do, I bet that (even if you disagree with the specific points made so far) what you do *not* do is to put them in one collective lump called 'a school' and teach them subjects from 9 to 1 and again from 2 to 5 – not even if the school steamer ships them to their parents on neighbouring islands every evening and back again in the morning. What you probably begin by doing is to split them up into manageable groups (houses), which will be able to come to terms with life on the island. You will need to get the groups behind you to make and keep rules (not having the benefit of a police force), and you will no doubt rely on the older members for much of this, and for helping with the groups in general. And so on. At some stage, when you have established an effective 'social base', you will turn your attention towards what the groups can profitably *learn*. Much of the learning, at least in the sphere of moral education, you will find to have taken place already, and to have been firmly appropriated by the pupils; but you will, of course, want to add learning of the various forms of thought and endeavour which, we like to suppose, are at least sometimes incorporated in various 'school subjects'. What you do about this is an open question. But at least you will have got your priorities right.

Chapter 10

Direct Teaching of Moral Thinking

Finally, I want to outline and defend a 'practical method' which is, surprisingly enough, hardly ever used (at least in any clear and well-developed form): that is, the direct teaching and explanation to pupils of moral methodology. By 'methodology' I mean, of course, as the reader will by now be well aware, *not* the direct inculcation of particular moral values and beliefs, but explaining the logical basis of rational moral decision-making. In other words, we are to show the pupil 'how to do' morality: how to make up his mind on moral questions, what bits of equipment he needs for moral thought and action. That means, in effect, giving him understanding and practice in using the moral components described earlier in this book.

Putting these components or qualities before pupils may be called a 'direct' method of moral education because we are here directly and openly *telling* pupils what it means for a person to be morally educated, and inviting them to make use of the components to settle moral questions. We may hope that this will itself help to develop the components in our pupils, but we are not here concerned to develop them in any indirect or covert way. We are, in effect, presenting them with morality as a coherent *subject*, analogous to, though in certain respects different from, other subjects which they learn at school.

By contrast, we may make all sorts of arrangements for the curricular content and social context of our school – having a house system, teaching the pupils to appreciate literature, impromptu acting, role playing, voluntary service – which we hope will develop our pupils' qualities or skills, but here we are, in a sense, using *indirect* methods. To take an analogy: we may, indirectly, help our children to play football better by giving them special exercises, making them sprint, breathe deeply, etc., but we can also help them directly and overtly by teaching them to play football as such – teaching them the rules, how to win, and how to settle particular tactical problems: what we might call the 'methodology' of football.

Before considering why this method is controversial, I shall claim some important advantages for it.

1.   It is *honest*. If we suppose that we are in a position to educate pupils morally at all, then we thereby claim to have some idea about the aims of moral education, about the qualities required by people for settling moral problems reasonably, and about how those qualities should be deployed. That is, we claim some knowledge of morality as a subject, and of the methodology appropriate to it. If we do not claim this, we have no right to be in business at all. But if we do, then it is dishonest and stupid to conceal it from our pupils. It would be as if we were scared of laying before our pupils the subjects of science, history and mathematics *as* subjects, together with the methods of procedure appropriate to each, and tried only to give them the necessary skills and techniques by some indirect means.

The point is not that it is always right to tell pupils the truth, though it nearly always is. The point is that, if we do not approach our pupils directly in this matter, we are not treating them as rational creatures at all. Moral education will be merely one more case of educators *doing things to* pupils, without telling them what the point and purpose of these are, and hence – inevitably – without enlisting their co-operation as co-equal, if more ignorant, human beings. The pupils will again be on the *receiving end* of a vast and heterogeneous number of practices whose purposes are known only to the educators. The psychological effects of this would repay research, but we can see a priori that they are not likely to be beneficial. At best, the pupils will be uncertain about what they are supposed to be trying to *do*: they will be confronted by no clear aims and objectives. At worst, the uncertainty may for some pupils turn into an intense anxiety, almost a mild paranoia; the teachers' objectives in moral education, because not spelled out to the pupils, become regarded as sinister, untrustworthy, 'authoritarian', 'indoctrinatory' and so forth.

It seems to me, therefore, extremely important to make it absolutely clear to pupils what we, as educators, are trying to do in moral education, and how to tackle morality as a subject. This would remain true, I think, even if our objectives were partisan – to produce good Communists, or good Catholics, or to force certain other specific moral beliefs and practices on to our pupils. But it is particularly relevant if our objectives consist, as they do, rather in helping people to think and act more reasonably for themselves. We need to get it across to the pupils that we are not out to force them into any kind of mould.

2.   It is *professional*. By this I mean that we ought to, and now can, get well beyond the stage of merely 'discussing moral problems', 'arousing concern', 'stimulating interests', 'being open-ended' and so forth. A lot of (no doubt useful) work has been done along these lines, but so many educators nowadays are scared of being thought 'authoritarian' that they give their pupils no clear idea that there are *right and wrong answers* to moral problems, that there is a coherent *methodology* for settling them. This inevitably creates, or re-inforces, a feeling very common today, not only amongst the young: the feeling that is sometimes expressed in such words as 'It's all relative really, isn't it?', 'It's just a matter of how you feel', 'Different people have their own views' and 'It's a matter of taste'. Just as in science or other subjects it is one thing to encourage and help pupils to find out the answers, and the reasons behind the answers, for themselves, but quite another to imply that there *are* no answers, so in morality the 'open-endedness' or 'child-centredness' of the discussion must not be allowed to obscure the fact that we discuss in order to find the truth – and hence that there is truth to find.

This can only be done by a direct approach, and it is better to err on the side of naivety rather than on the side of vagueness. Of course there are all sorts of philosophical problems about morality, just as there are problems in the philosophy of science and the philosophy of history. But there is nevertheless a coherent methodology which has as much right to be called reasonable, and to be learned by our children, as the methodologies of science, history and any other established subject. There will always be plenty of opportunity for discussion of more complex and sophisticated problems; what is important is that the children should be presented with this methodology in as professional a way as possible.

3.   It *gives the children something to hang on to*. I avoid here the use

of words like 'ideal', 'creed', 'faith', etc. precisely because we are not out to give them any *specific* set of moral or metaphysical beliefs. What we are trying to give them is something far more important, for which 'methodology' is as good a word as I can think of. We are trying to show them *how*, as rational creatures, they can identify and solve moral problems, just as, again, in science we show them *how* to answer questions about the nature of the physical world. It would be comparatively easy, and comparatively worthless, merely to *give* them our own answers (which may be wrong) in either case. But at the same time, we are giving them something: namely, a methodology. This is something which they can and must hang on to.

'Can', although it is difficult, and children (like adults) often prefer quick second-hand answers; 'must' because it is just as bad to give them nothing as to give them something second-hand. All the 'open-ended' discussions in the world do not amount to a methodology: they may do nothing more than dress up the pupil's vagueness and relativism in fashionable clothes. In the course of such discussions (and also in the course of other supposedly 'morally educative' activities, such as voluntary service, or going to chapel, or playing games, or whatever), any pupil with any guts is going to say to himself – and, I hope, to the teacher – something like 'Yes, this is all very interesting, but how do you tell what is *right*?' He will say this in all areas where the teachers do not put a clear methodology before him: in the area of morality and, even more notoriously, in the area of religion. And if there are not many pupils with 'guts', in this sense, then there certainly ought to be.

Much has been said about the 'moral vacuum' left by the anti-authoritarian trend of the last few decades (and earlier), and of course it is right to point to the anxiety, the neurosis, the alienation, the drifting, the sense of being lost, that our pupils will have unless they are given something to hang on to. But it is also important, for the general future of education, that morality as a coherent subject is not allowed to perish by default. This is something which could well happen to religion: because people are not clear, or agreed, about a methodology appropriate for settling questions in the religious area, we may easily relapse into a form of education where the *truth*, if any, or *merit* of religious beliefs is simply not tackled at all, or is tackled only by those pupils who choose to tackle it. If this did happen to religion, and/or to morality, it would be a major disaster. We should have given up the whole idea of *education* in these fields because we should have given up the whole idea of what is true or false, right or wrong, appropriate or inappropriate, and this could have far worse long-term consequences than anything which happens to the pupils immediately under our care. We have to give them something to hang on to, and we have to hang on to it ourselves.

Why, then, should this 'direct method' be a matter of controversy? There are a number of rather vague notions which seem to tell against it, which I shall deal with in turn.

1.   It is sometimes thought that, since morality (unlike science, history and some other subjects) is concerned with behaviour and action, not just thinking, classroom periods are inappropriate; that an 'academic' approach to a 'practical' subject is mistaken. But nobody wants to say that pupils do not need *other* methods of moral education – of course they do; or that these should not be 'practical' – of course they should. Nobody disputes that these other methods – what is done by way of curricular arrangements, the social life and structure of the school, personal contact with a certain type of teacher, and so on – may well do very much more to develop the moral components than can be done by the use of the direct method in the classroom. But this does not show the direct method to be unimportant. It is a disputable question how much 'theory' as opposed to 'practice' we need in morality: how much morality is like, say, learning to swim, where 'theory' is not very helpful, or how much it is like more strictly 'academic' subjects such as history or mathematics. But *some* 'theory' is necessary. Morality is not *just* a matter of practice and habit. So the importance for moral education of the general life of the school, of pupil–teacher relations, or of any other indirect method, must not be allowed to count against the importance of a direct approach.

2.   Some people have the idea that to teach this methodology would be appropriate only for older or very intelligent children. Perhaps they think that to discuss morality as a subject would necessarily involve a prolonged study of the more profound moral philosophers, and react against the (unnecessary) picture of explaining Aristotle and Kant to the fifth form. This is a curious prejudice: we may not explain Rutherford and Einstein to the fifth form either, but this does not tempt us to say that science is only

suitable for clever children or sixth formers. Or they may think that morality as a subject requires a kind of very difficult 'abstract reasoning' which is beyond the grasp of the average pupil. But this is not so, and it is fairly clear from the results of research that some, at least, of the types of reasoning required are well within the grasp of quite young children. If we consider the moral components one by one, we shall not think it too rash to say, on general or a priori grounds, that the vast majority of children, even within the primary school age-range, will be capable of understanding each individually, and of understanding how they all relate to one's eventual moral behaviour.

This prejudice may be only one instance of a more general bewitchment with the notion of certain studies as necessarily very 'high-powered' or 'academic'. What we call 'philosophy', 'psychology' or 'sociology' may be among these. A phrase like 'moral philosophy' is apt to put many people off: surely, they think, this is something which can only be done by Oxford dons? But if these titles stand for basic forms of thought – thought about language and concepts, about the minds and feelings of individual human beings, and about human society – it is in the highest degree unlikely that even young or stupid people could have absolutely *no* chance of learning them. In fact, of course, everybody does think, more or less competently, in these areas: everybody has some (however badly informed) views and beliefs which could be fairly described as philosophical, psychological and sociological; even if they did not, it would not be beyond the wit of man to teach them, so long as we were not frightened by the grandness of the mere *words*.

3. Another sort of objection is somewhat more nebulous, but seems to consist in regarding morality as somehow too 'pure', or 'spiritual', or 'spontaneous', to be taught. Thus the idea of having *examinations* in moral thinking seems to some intolerable, and the idea of teaching pupils 'the right answers', which they then repeat to us, seems to degrade the whole concept of morality and moral virtue. However, this is just a muddle. Of course we shall not catch very much of our pupils' 'inner lives' in this particular net, and only an idiot would suppose that, in examining a pupil's grasp of the methodology of morality, we are thereby examining him as a virtuous *person* – qualifying or disqualifying him for the Kingdom of Heaven. Further, it should be unnecessary to add that we do not teach 'the right answers', but a methodology for the pupil's own use

– just as with any other subject. And a lot of this can in fact be examined or assessed. Only someone with a very curious outlook, who felt that moral decisions should not be rational at all, could sustain this objection.

4. Finally, there are various arguments which may be described as 'political' in a wide sense of the word. It may be thought unwise to put 'morality' or 'moral education' on the school timetable for various reasons, e.g. (a) the title will put students off, (b) it will be taken as a substitute for religious education, (c) it will suggest that this is *all* the school needs to do about moral education (see (1) above), (d) it will be unacceptable to parents, or adherents of particular creeds, or some other group of people, (e) who is to teach these periods? – and so forth. Of course all these points are important. Students must not be put off, the purpose of the teaching must be explained, various groups must be placated, teachers must be trained. But none of these points has very much to do with the question of whether, as a piece of *education*, such teaching would be valuable to our pupils. If so, and if we have a fairly clear idea of what it should consist of, then we must do it, and naturally the *title* does not much matter. I should be inclined to call it something like 'Moral Thinking', since that seems the simplest and most honest phrase to represent the content of the periods, but others may prefer other titles.

These objections, then, seem ill founded. Moreover, there is one necessity which it is very hard to see how anything except direct teaching can meet. This necessity is something that is logically required by the concept of a morally educated person. It is that such a person must not merely act or feel in a certain *way*, but must do so for certain *reasons*. For instance, it is not sufficient that a person should give money to the poor, or refrain from stealing, or feel affection for his wife, for he might do all these for inadequate, or even disreputable, reasons – he wants to ingratiate himself with somebody, or is frightened of getting caught, or is romantically obsessed. He must act and feel *for the right reasons*. He cannot do this unless and until he knows what the right reasons are, and has convinced himself that they *are* right, and he cannot get to know this unless somebody teaches it to him.

This is a simple point, but it has wide ramifications. For example, to develop our pupils' regard and concern for other people as equals means far more than merely enabling them to 'get on with' pupils of a different social class, or 'freeing them from prejudice' against Negroes, Jews or foreigners. This in itself goes no way towards giving them the *right reasons* for treating certain types of creature as equals. We may in some sense persuade them, indirectly, that skin colour or accent or status should not matter, or merely accustom them to these differences, but this may simply result in their developing other kinds of 'class distinction' (perhaps against adults, or fat boys, or ignorant people – the list is endless), unless we teach them what *does* matter, what the real reasons are in virtue of which people have equal importance. These are not to do with their being (in the biological sense) people, human beings, two-legged inhabitants of this planet, which would exclude intelligent Martians; they rest on the fact that certain creatures have wills, desires, purposes and intentions, make free choices and use language. It is because of this that there are good reasons, which we must make plain to the pupil, for counting them as equals, and the pupil must learn to act from these reasons, not from other reasons.

I do not see how any pupil is likely to learn this, or to learn it as quickly and fully as we should wish, unless he is directly taught it: that is, unless the reasons are overtly pointed out to him. If they are not, he is much more likely to fall back on some mode of moral thinking which is not such hard work, but also not so rational. He will have to be taken step by step through the reasoning which necessitates each of the components, and how each of them must operate, consciously or unconsciously, as the background of any moral action. I am not saying that this understanding necessarily involves any very high intellectual ability, but it does involve direct teaching. If we can make such teaching effective, and by the use of other methods make it transferable to real-life situations, then we may save much time that we now spend on particular instances, such as 'class distinction' or 'race prejudice'. If we can establish in the pupils' minds (and hearts) the *general principle*, together with its reasons, which lies behind such cases, we shall have armed him effectively to deal with the particular instances on his own; whereas if we do not, we shall do no more than constantly plug new gaps, and mend the tears in a garment which will only tear again somewhere else because it is not properly made in the first place.

Some of the aims of this direct teaching I have already mentioned *en passant* above:

1. To make our pupils understand that moral thinking, like scientific and other kinds of thinking, is a serious subject of study in its own right, and can result in right or wrong answers to moral questions – that there is a rational methodology – and thereby to provide them with the right reasons for moral action and feeling.
2. To give them, as it were, a psychological resource when confronted with moral situations in everyday life: neither selling them a partisan 'faith' nor leaving them in a vacuum, but initiating them into a technique which they can use for themselves in coping with real-life problems.

To these we can add somewhat different but closely connected aims:

3. To induce, by constant practice, the actual *habit* or using this methodology, so that there is a better chance of their doing so in everyday life.
4. To wean them away from false methodologies (reliance on the peer group, on authority or 'anti-authorities', on false ego-ideals, and so on).
5. By clarifying the logic of the moral components, both individually and in their collective operation, to give them insight into which *particular* components are lacking, both in themselves and in other people, in particular cases.
6. Hence, by making them aware of these deficiencies, to give them at least the chance of developing the components for themselves, and of welcoming any other studies or activities that would encourage such development.

We can claim on a priori grounds that the direct method would at least be likely to achieve these aims to some degree. This is, of course, *not* to make empirical claims about the degree of 'transferability': that is, about how much effect this direct teaching will have on the pupil's actual behaviour and feeling – or even on his moral thinking – outside the classroom. Nevertheless, although we badly need research in this area, this is not a good reason for disqualifying the direct method. First, it is unlikely that this teaching would have *no* effect outside the classroom; secondly, only a fool would fail to back it up by other methods, including those mentioned in this book, which would encourage transferability; and thirdly, to have taught pupils how they ought to operate in the moral area is to have achieved something, even if they rarely do so – we do not normally object to teaching our pupils the truth merely on the grounds that they may not often make use of it.

In considering methods, one distinction needs to be made absolutely clear from the start. As the reader will have grasped already, we shall be teaching the pupils how they *ought* to think in the moral area. This is not to teach them about what they and others *do* think: it may be useful to bring in such facts by way of example, but this is not the purpose of the exercise. To use a parallel, when we teach scientific methods we are trying to show the pupil how he ought to think as a scientist, what procedures he ought to follow in order to answer scientific questions. To tell him about how most (ignorant) people actually *do* think or have thought – about those who think the earth is flat, or who believe in astrology, or who tried to settle questions of cosmology by reference to the scriptures – may be of incidental use, perhaps in pointing the contrast between these false methods and the properly scientific one. But our aim is not to give him such factual knowledge; our aim is to teach him to think as a good scientist ought to think.

This does not make the factual studies – the psychology, sociology, history, etc. of morals – unimportant. But it does mean that we must distinguish them sharply from what we might rather grandly call the 'normative' study of moral thinking: that is, the study of how one *ought* to think in the moral area. Here too there is a parallel with religion. It is one thing to study beliefs and practices of different religions and creeds as an end in itself – the sociology of religion, or 'comparative religion' – but it is quite another to study the principles by which one ought to assess or evaluate the *truth* or *worth* of such beliefs, which necessarily involves having a clear idea of how a rational person should make up his mind in the religious area.

In talking of the 'direct method', or of classroom periods labelled perhaps 'Moral Thinking', I am concerned only with the 'normative' study. It must be clearly understood that this, and not factual knowledge for its own sake, is the central aim. It would, I am sure, be highly profitable for pupils to learn something of the psychology, sociology and history of morals, both for its own sake and because it would provide useful material and examples for the normative study with which we are concerned. But this is a logically different kind of enterprise, and must be kept distinct – at least in the mind of the teacher, and I should guess also in our actual classroom periods.

It will be difficult enough for the pupils to grasp the idea that they are supposed to be learning about how they ought to think – how it is rational to think – without confusing them by telling them, in the same classroom during the same period, about how people actually do think, unless it is quite clear to the pupils that this is merely being offered for the sake of example.

I do not want to enter a debate about details of teaching methods, which can only be resolved by experimentation and research. But the teacher of 'moral thinking' must, at least, not allow himself to be carried away by fashionable talk of 'integration', 'breaking down the subject barriers' and so forth. One of the chief points behind the whole of this 'direct method' is to put 'moral thinking' clearly and firmly on the map as a subject; to make it easily identifiable to the pupils, so that they do not confuse it with other types of study; to make quite sure that they are learning something (rather than merely being stimulated, or having their interest and concern aroused), and that they are learning *this* rather than something else. If we do not ensure this, there is little point in the operation at all. And, subject to research findings proving the contrary, I should argue strongly that we need to keep these periods uncontaminated by other subjects.

This is by no means to say that highly effective methods might not be devised which could be called 'integrated' or 'interdisciplinary'. For instance, we could arrange that, in history or English lessons, or better still in lessons about psychology or sociology, the teachers dealt with material which was in some way relevant, if only as illustration, to the purpose of the 'moral thinking' periods. Or, if we want to be still more 'interdisciplinary', we could take a topic like 'sex' and devote some time to the biology of sex, some time to the psychology, some time to the sociology, or history, or whatever, and also some time to it in the 'moral thinking' periods, where our question would be 'How *ought* we to feel about sex, or to make decisions in the sexual area?' All this may be very desirable, so long as the distinctions between the disciplines are clearly preserved in the minds of the children. But since, to date, they are not even clear in the minds of most teachers, I should question whether most existing integrated or interdisciplinary courses of this kind were anything more than a (possibly stimulating) muddle. There are certainly no solid grounds, based on research, for adopting them, but of course every teacher must decide this individually.

We must also remember what was said about the chief aim of the direct method: to explain the proper *reasons* to the pupil, so that he has some chance of appropriating them for himself. This means that, whatever specific content we give to the 'moral thinking' periods, we must select it with this objective in mind. The pupil must, sooner or later, be able to *understand*, *state* and *apply* the right reasons to relevant cases. This means that, at some stage, the medium of teaching and learning must be *words*. For the notion of having or understanding a reason is bound up with the notion of *saying*, or being in principle able to say, certain things to oneself and to other people: things of the form 'PQR are the case, therefore I should do X' ('So-and-so is a creature with desires and feelings like myself, therefore I should count his wants as of equal importance to my own').

All this may seem very 'abstract' and 'philosophical', but it is not. I am simply pointing to the very important differences between a person who acts for no reason at all, or for the wrong reason, and a person who acts for the right reason. The former may, accidentally, do 'the right thing' out of habit, or impulse, or fear, or conditioning; only the latter will count as being 'morally educated' – and the test will be whether he is in principle able to show us that it was for *this* reason that he acted. He would have to *use* the right reason in his thinking and behaviour. Many of us are like the former person: we use the wrong reasons, or no reason at all, or we think we are using the right reason when really some other reason influences us. Perhaps the really 'morally educated' person – the person who has a genuine concern for others and uses that concern (and it only) in his actions towards others – is pretty rare. But this makes it all the more important to turn our pupils into this sort of person, in so far as we can. And we can only make sure that we are doing so by checking on what they *say*, and thereby on what is really going on inside their heads.

The relevance of this to the specific content is obvious. Of course we shall not teach them simply by *telling* them what the right reasons are and getting them to repeat the reasons. Probably we should then get only parrotted answers. We must show them the existence and proper application of such reasons in various contexts and examples, and the more 'real' the contexts and examples are, the better. As far as possible, we must bring the contexts close to real-life decisions, and we must be open to the use of any method which will do the job. We may think here not just of using modern trendy examples, but also of such methods as acting, role playing, simulation situations, the use of films, tape-recordings, video-tape and so on. Perhaps it will be desirable to take the children out of the classroom and introduce them to situations in the outside world, or in the actual running of the school, or in their own homes. A competent and imaginative teacher, particularly if he follows the 'progressive' fashion, will not need me to tell him about such methods. But – and it is a big 'but' – these methods must be geared to getting the pupil to understand, *in language*, the reasons we have been talking about, and this is a far cry from merely 'stimulating interest' or 'arousing concern'.

It is possible to approach the methodology of morality by various routes, and I do not want to suggest that the methodology which follows is the *only* possible, or the only valuable, approach. Much might be gained, for instance, by making and examining a list of the moral virtues (truthfulness, courage, etc.), and developing classroom periods on these lines. Nevertheless, I think there are very strong arguments for using a methodology based on the 'moral components' mentioned briefly earlier. They have, at least, the merits of clarity, simplicity and coherence. It is essential that the teacher should avoid vague, global terms like 'sensitivity', 'maturity', 'awareness', 'an adult attitude' and so forth; these sound well, but mean nothing specific enough to form a basis for clear instruction.

At the same time, the teacher must be aware that a number of very *different* things are required by the morally educated person. Indeed the attraction, and equally the danger, of the vague global approach (in terms of 'maturity', etc.) is that it saves us the hard work of sorting out these different things. But from this there is no escape, either for ourselves or our pupils: we, and they, must be prepared to work at it. The 'technical terms' – PHIL, EMP and so on – are not merely jargon or unnecessary obscurity; they are required as clearly defined titles for these logically different factors. The distinctions have to be made somehow: if they are not, the teaching and learning will simply not get done. I make no apology, then, for using this terminology and method of approach.

The teacher will find that much profit may be gained by considering cases of moral misdoing, in order to detect which particular component is missing and hence is responsible for the error. (Of course there may be more than one missing.) In the misdemeanours of villains in western films, in our everyday misdeeds, in the faults of our friends, just what is it in each case that is lacking? Some cases, like that of the person who gives his aunt arsenic thinking it to be aspirin powder, are easy enough (lack of GIG(1)); others, like the case of Hamlet, are more difficult. It seems best to move from clear-cut illustrations to the more complex ones, and it is certainly mistaken to concentrate exclusively on moral *problems*, whether in our personal lives or, worse, in the public arena. For most moral situations are not *problematical* at all: there is usually not much doubt about the right answer. What we need is a series of straight-forward cases in our own everyday lives. If a person devotes most of his attention to complex and public-arena cases, it may well be a sign that he does not want to face the more common cases that arise in his ordinary life. I would not recommend the discussion of difficult political or social issues, or of questions of foreign policy; we have to remember that our objective is to clarify the concepts and the methodology, not to conduct vague, if 'concerned', discussions about the welfare state or international relations.

The teacher will inevitably have to deal with wrong (unreasonable, inappropriate) ways of thinking about morality because these are very common among pupils – and adults. Indeed, his practical teaching might perhaps begin with a consideration of the various ways in which people make up their minds: that is, the *types of reason* which they seem to use. From this he might go on to show the correctness of one way (the 'moral components', based on PHIL or concern for people's interests) and the temptations of other ways.

There is a good deal of research material the teacher can use here, but the 'wrong ways' can be fairly simply categorized under three main headings:

1. *'Other-obeying'*. This is the person who refers the question of what he ought to do to some *outside authority* (what God or his parents or the gang-leader says, what the Bible or Mao Tse-tung says, 'the code of the West', etc.).
2. *'Self-obeying'*. This is the person who refers the question to some inner feeling or picture of his own: for instance, to his feelings of guilt or shame, or taboo feelings, or his 'ego-ideal' ('what nice girls/tough guys/English gentlemen/teenagers, etc. do').
3. *'Self-considering'*. This is the person who refers the question to his own advantage or benefit: whether he will be rewarded or punished, gain or lose, improve or diminish his own position.

Following on from this, it will be useful to point out that very often, when people give 'reasons' for their actions – 'Because God

202 A New Introduction to Moral Education

says so', 'I just wouldn't feel right inside', 'It's just wrong', etc. –
they may not really be giving reasons in the sense of *justifications* at
all. They are, perhaps, not trying to show that their choice is right or
justified; they are just explaining it, or saying how they feel.
Anyone who is really concerned with *justification* will be more or
less bound to use another 'mode of thinking', the 'other-considering' mode: this is the mode set out in full with our 'moral components'. Justification must be based on the wants and interests of
human beings, considered equally. The trouble is often not that
people reason incompetently or irrelevantly about morals, but that
they do not really try to reason or justify at all.

This in turn might be connected with the kinds of compulsion,
'raw' feeling and fantasy to which we are all subject, and which are
responsible for these pseudo-reasons. To A, certain things are just
taboo; B somehow feels he must behave as his peer group behaves;
C feels guilty or ashamed if he does not cut a certain kind of figure;
D feels compelled to follow some authority; E feels compelled to
rebel against the authority; F just says, 'What's in it for me?'; and so
on. A brief consideration of some area where *reasoning*, in terms of
others' interests, is in fact extremely rare – say, the sexual area, or
the area of religious prejudice – will show pupils clearly how easy it
is for us to abandon reason altogether, and simply to echo our inner
compulsions and fantasies.

It will not have escaped the intelligent and critical teacher that the
vagueness about moral education to which I have referred is a sign
that we have, so far, failed our pupils miserably in certain areas. All
we seem able to do is either to retain a lukewarm authoritarianism,
or else to talk at them in a 'progressive' but hopelessly incompetent
and febrile way, in the hope that it will do some good. We can and
must do better. In order to do better, we have to put this methodology before them *clearly*. I have throughout tried to stress clarity,
and whilst of course teachers should be imaginative, lively, stimulating and so forth, I would place more stress on terms like 'coherent', 'workmanlike', 'down-to-earth' and 'clearly articulated'. The
vague, the metaphysical, the woolly, the high-sounding and the
waffly must be avoided at all costs, however 'inspiring' or 'stimulating'. We need the clarity of the old authoritarian without his irration-
ality. Of course it is easy for a research worker to say 'This should be
done', leaving the teacher to fill in the details and do all the work for
himself. But I am confident that all those teachers who see the point
of this kind of teaching will be well able to make a good job of it.

Practical Postscript

I have tried in this book, as in other writings about moral education over the last twenty-odd years, to demonstrate the nature of the subject and the kind of demands – psychological, intellectual and pragmatic – that it makes upon us. However, I am not naive enough to suppose that the subject will now take off and fly with raised and steady wings, like Dante's doves (*Inferno*, V.82); it has shown little sign of doing so in the past few decades, and the various kinds of opposition to it remain as strong as ever.

What can we do about this? Well, individuals can try to clarify the subject and practise it, in schools and elsewhere, as best they can, and I have said something in this book about the lines of enquiry and practice that seem most promising. But there is a limit to what individuals can do, and governments and other agencies with money at their disposal can do a great deal more. What they should do – and I owe it to such agencies at least to make this clear – is to establish centres for the research and practice of moral education which are (1) permanent, (2) properly funded, (3) interdisciplinary (including empirical workers under some general philosophical direction), and above all (4) *not partisan* or in any sense 'political': that is, based not on some specific moral, religious, 'social', political or other set of values, but only on the educational values that I have described earlier in this book. Such centres would at least keep the right sort of flag flying, and the work that would flow from them ought to have the kind of rational authority that the subject above all needs, both in terms of pure research and in terms of practical development.

Alas, the reasons why no government or official agency, or

indeed any independent organization that I know of, has done this are, in the main, that they suffer from one or the other of the two central errors I have mentioned. Either (1) they are partisan, and want to base moral education on Christian, or Islamic, or socialist, or some other set of partisan views; or else (2) they are wishy-washy, and want only to establish some sort of forum for discussion, sets of materials, workshops and the like not based on any proper methodology (perhaps for fear of offending particular interest groups), and hence not likely to lead to any very clear results.

It is to be hoped that this depressing state of affairs will not continue indefinitely. Some individuals, governments and societies in the world today seem so firmly wedded to partisan beliefs that one can expect little encouragement, but it is possible, perhaps in liberal and comparatively rich countries, that there are individuals or institutions with enough money, and enough understanding of what is needed, to get things properly moving. This is not, of course, to discredit the work either of scholars in the area or of those many practising teachers in schools who do their best. But the matter requires institutional not just individual effort, and we may legitimately, if not too boldly, hope that centres of the required kind may be financed in the future, by those who understand the needs of the subject. I shall be content if what I have written has clarified what these needs actually are.

What can we do as individuals in the meanwhile, apart as I have said from trying to clarify and practise the subject as best we can? There are perhaps two points worth making.

1. I have tried to show throughout the book that the chief obstacles to moral education are to do not with lack of money, intelligence, will-power or passion, but rather with the very deep-rooted fantasies and prejudices that human beings have not yet grown out of, and that the chief hope for the future is that the disciplines of analytic philosophy and psychology will be more widely and effectively practised, since they alone can help us to grow out of them. Any person seriously concerned with the advancement of moral education should attempt to promote these disciplines with all his might: at home, at school, in institutions of teacher education, and in all contexts where any sort of education is supposed to be going on. It is easy to plunge into a more activist approach – to form working parties, run up research projects, mess around with the curriculum, produce 'materials', kits, packs and

other potentially useful pieces of technology, and make various administrative arrangements in schools and elsewhere. Of course these are not to be condemned, but the fact is that, unless and until they are based on a proper and fantasy-free understanding, they are virtually useless and will disappear when the fashion for them changes. Time spent on the basic disciplines is not only time well spent, but the most *practical* way of spending any time and resources we have. A great deal has been 'going on', as one might say, in moral education all over the place, but nearly all of it has not done much more than satisfy an unconscious need for *busyness*, in order to persuade ourselves that we are not inert and uncaring. We have to go much deeper than that if we are to get anywhere.

2.   Clearly these enemies of moral education will not disappear either through more frenzied activity or overnight. They are very powerful and very profound. Think how long it took the human race to establish science as a respectable and productive form of thought, now only a few centuries old; the obstacles to the establishment of moral education are at least as powerful as the obstacles to science. So we need patience. It is naive to suppose that things can be changed quickly: the deficiencies of government mentioned above only reflect the general fantasies and misunderstandings of almost all individuals and societies. We simply have to learn to tolerate the slowness of progress. On the other hand, we may reasonably be sustained by some faith in the future: in some quarters, at least, the tools for doing the job are in existence, if we will only use them; and it may be that, if conditions are favourable, we can make progress more quickly than we might fear.

References and Further Reading

There is an enormous volume of literature directly or indirectly relevant to moral education, and there is a greater danger of the reader getting lost than of being short of material. Consequently I have listed here only (1) the works to which I have referred in the main text and (2) a small selection of other works which seem to me most useful and relevant to this particular book. From these the reader may easily pick up references to any other works that may be needed.

Aristotle, *Nicomachean Ethics* (translation). London: Penguin.

Badcock, C. R. (1983) *Madness and Modernity*. Oxford: Blackwell.

Fowler, H. W. (1965) *Modern English Usage*. Oxford: OUP.

Hamlyn, D. (1978) *Experiences and the Growth of Understanding*. London: Routledge & Kegan Paul.

Hare, R. M. (1981) *Moral Thinking*. Oxford: OUP.

Hirst, P. H. and Peters, R. S. (1970) *The Logic of Education*. London: Routledge & Kegan Paul.

Loukes, H. *et al.* (1983) *Education: An Introduction*. Oxford: Martin Robertson.

Murdoch, I. (1970) *The Sovereignty of Good*. London: Routledge & Kegan Paul.

Peters, R. S. (1966) *Ethics and Education*. London: Allen & Unwin.

Plato, *Republic* (translation). London: Penguin.

Rawls, J. (1972) *A Theory of Justice*. Oxford: OUP.

Strawson, P. F. (1974) *Freedom and Resentment*. London: Methuen.

Wallace, D. and Walker, A. D. M. (1970) *The Definition of Morality*. London: Methuen.

Warnock, G. J. (1967) *Contemporary Moral Philosophy*. London: Macmillan.

Warnock, G. J. (1971) *The Object of Morality*. London: Methuen.

Wilson, J. *et al.* (1967) *Introduction to Moral Education*. London: Penguin.

Wilson, J. (1971) *Education in Religion and the Emotions*. London: Heinemann.

Wilson, J. (1972) *Philosophy and Educational Research*. Slough, UK: NFER.

Wilson, J. (1975) *Educational Theory and the Preparation of Teachers*. Slough, UK: NFER.

Wilson, J. (1977) *Philosophy and Practical Education*. London: Routledge & Kegan Paul.

Wilson, J. (1979) *Preface to the Philosophy of Education*. London: Routledge & Kegan Paul.

Wilson, J. (1986) *What Philosophy Can Do*. London: Macmillan.

Wilson, J. (1987) *A Preface to Morality*. London: Macmillan.

Wilson, J. and Cowell, B. (1990) *Children and Discipline*. London: Cassell.

Index